FOOTHOLD ON ANTARCTICA

By the same author

An Alien in Antarctica, The McDonald & Woodward Publishing company, 1997

Forty Years on Ice, The Book Guild, 1998

FOOTHOLD ON ANTARCTICA

The First International Expedition
(1949–1952)
Through the Eyes of its Youngest Member

Charles Swithinbank

Charles Swithinbank
3 Dec 2011

The Book Guild Ltd

Sussex, England

The Book Guild Ltd.
25 High Street,
Lewes, Sussex

First published 1999
© Charles Swithinbank 1999

Set in Times
Typesetting by
Acorn Bookwork, Salisbury, Wiltshire
Printed in Great Britain by
Thanet Press Ltd, Margate, Kent

A catalogue record for this book is
available from the British Library

ISBN 1 85776 406 4

CONTENTS

Maps

PREFACE

Fifty years ago, few men in a generation were offered a place on an Antarctic expedition. Fewer still jumped at the opportunity. It was in 1948 that I first learned of the planned 'Norwegian–British–Swedish Antarctic Expedition 1949–52'. The three-year time-span hinted that it would be like the classic expeditions of old in which men would not see a blade of grass, a new face, an armchair, a tomato, a woman or a child for two and a half years. But with three languages, five nationalities and no possibility of escape, could we make it work *and* keep peace between us?

Apart from the devastating loss of three of our number in an accident, the expedition went broadly according to plan. Another accident took the sight of a man's eye. All of us took risks but I was lucky and had the time of my life.

The nature of Antarctic exploration has been transformed since the nineteen forties. At that time, half the coastline of Antarctica was unoccupied. Today, 18 nations maintain a total of 35 permanent stations. We used sledge dogs – today there is not one dog in the whole of Antarctica. We had to handle accidents, however serious. Today, casualties are often flown out.

The Norwegian-British-Swedish expedition helped to end the series of competing national expeditions that characterized the first half of the 20th century. Instead, it led to an era of international cooperation and collaboration that continues to this day.

A narrative of our adventures was published in ten languages.[*] But it was the *official* account, and now – 50 years on – I have tried to add another dimension.

---

[*]John Giaever, *The White Desert. The Official Account of the Norwegian–British–Swedish Antarctic Expedition* (London, Chatto and Windus, 1954)

ACKNOWLEDGEMENT

I am particularly grateful to all those who read and commented on the whole or parts of the manuscript: Geoffrey Hattersley-Smith, Bob Headland, Gwyn Roberts, Gordon Robin, Fred Roots, Mary Swithinbank and Bob Wells.

I thank Peter Melleby, Nils Roer, Nils Jørgen Schumacher and Walborg Snarby for biographical data; Gordon Robin for his diary of the seismic journey; Dick Laws for identifying whales; Hans Oerter and Jens-Ove Näslund for topographic data.

Random House UK Ltd have kindly allowed me to include extracts from John Giaever's *The White Desert*.

For photographs and permission to use them I thank Norsk Polar-institutt (pp. 57, 72, 145, 155, 165, 206), Stig Hallgren (pp. 76, 79, 88, 92, 99, 101, 102, 103, 107, 109, 116, 179, 184, 185, 188, 190, 191, 193), Anna Schytt and the heirs to Valter Schytt's estate (pp. 13, 14, 17, 31, 67, 68, 77, 83, 84, 89, 98, 111, 115, 117, 163, 178, 186, 195, 220, 221), and the US Geological Survey (Map 8 on p. 153).

As always, my wife Mary Swithinbank encouraged me to write the book and kept a happy home while I did so.

Charles Swithinbank
Cambridge
December 1998

1

CONCEPTION

By 1949, Norway had been a maritime power for centuries but her overseas possessions were in the Arctic, not the Antarctic. The Svalbard archipelago north of mainland Norway, much of it covered with ice, was in earlier years a paradise for hunters of whales, walrus, seals, polar bears, reindeer and Arctic foxes. There are coal beds, and miners had been shipping coal overseas for a hundred years.

At the other end of the world, Norway dominated the southern whale fishery but had never made territorial claims on any part of mainland Antarctica. However, Norwegian whalers had played a major part in charting the Atlantic sector of the coastline and they felt that it was theirs.

Then, unexpectedly, the German Government despatched a secret expedition to the area in 1938 with the intention of claiming sovereignty. Luckily, the news reached Norway through intelligence sources before the claim was made – but only just before. On 14 January 1939, as the catapult ship MS *Schwabenland* approached the coast, the territory of Dronning Maud Land was formally constituted by decree of King Haakon VII. It was defined as the land between longitudes 20° west and 45° east of Greenwich, though no northern or southern limits were specified. The Queen of Norway (Dronning Maud), after whom it was named, was the youngest daughter of Britain's King Edward VII and Queen Alexandra. In the convoluted ways of European royalty, Alexandra herself was the daughter of King Christian IX of Denmark and Haakon was one of his grandsons.

Questions of sovereignty in the Antarctic became irrelevant for Norwegians on 9 April 1940, when German forces invaded Norway, and they remained a very low priority for five long years until the end of the war in Europe in May 1945.

Although most Europeans were preoccupied with warfare, a narrative of the German Antarctic Expedition of 1938–39 was

1

published in Leipzig in 1942 and came into the hands of Professor Hans Ahlmann of Stockholm University.[1]*

Ahlmann was a geographer who had spent half a lifetime studying glaciers in Scandinavia, Greenland, Svalbard and Iceland[2]. He saw in the German aerial photographs areas of ice-free land, suggesting that the ice sheet had been more extensive in the past and might now be retreating. Ahlmann knew that most glaciers in the Northern Hemisphere had receded during the first half of the twentieth century but it was not known whether this was a global phenomenon, perhaps in response to changing climate. Glaciers are highly sensitive to the nuances of climate, so Ahlmann conceived the idea of an expedition to address this question. A party of scientists would study the area photographed by the Germans.

Ahlmann's wife was Norwegian and he had influential contacts in Norway who were quick to espouse his idea after the war ended on 14 August 1945. Thus it was that barely 11 months after the surrender of German forces in Norway, the Norwegian Government decided to mount an exploratory expedition to Dronning Maud Land. However, at first they were split on the question of international collaboration. The Norwegian and Swedish foreign ministries were both in favour, aware no doubt that neither could afford to go it alone. Then Ahlmann wrote to the Royal Geographical Society in London to propose a tripartite expedition.

The British response was positive, although the UK was already running its own permanent Antarctic expedition, the Falkland Islands Dependencies Survey (FIDS). Shortly afterwards, Norwegian, British and Swedish national committees were formed, each to be part of an international committee under the chairmanship of Professor Harald Sverdrup, Director of Norsk Polarinstitutt (the Norwegian polar institute). Sverdup was a distinguished oceanographer and had been a member of Roald Amundsen's *Maud* expedition through the Northeast Passage in 1918–20.

The joint committee spent the next two years planning the expedition and raising sufficient funds. In the end, all three governments contributed, though the Norwegians shouldered most of the costs. The scientific objectives were to be not only in glaciology but also in meteorology, geology and mapping.

The original plan was that 14 men should spend two years living on the ice sheet – without a break. As it turned out, one man joined the expedition when we landed in Antarctica and two were added in 1951.

---

* Superscript numbers refer to end notes.

2

I came into the story in November 1948 when I heard about the expedition and applied for a post. I was a third-year undergraduate reading geography at Oxford and had long harboured ambitions to join a polar expedition. The vacancy was for an assistant glaciologist to work under an experienced Swedish glaciologist. Although the post was quite widely advertised, the British committee considered a short-list of only three. Few people, I suppose, relished the idea of two and a half years of isolation with a small group of people, none of whom were known to them, with no women, no mail and no possibility of escape – however difficult the conditions turned out to be.

The selection procedure was unorthodox. The British committee was led by the Director of the Scott Polar Research Institute in Cambridge (SPRI) and the Director of the Royal Geographical Society in London (RGS), though other members came from a variety of institutions. Instead of being summoned to a sombre interview board on the far side of an oak table, I was introduced to the Reverend Launcelot Fleming, then Director of SPRI, who was both a geologist and a cleric by training, and had worked in the Antarctic as a member of the British Graham Land Expedition of 1934–37[3].

Launcelot quickly put me at ease by making it more of a discussion than an interview. Learning that my sport was rowing, he suggested that we take out a pair-oared boat on the Cam. It did not take me long to discover that he was an accomplished oarsman. Aware that one of the vital qualities of an expedition man is that he accepts his share of the hard work, I saw that I was being put to the test. A boat powered by unequal oarsmen soon veers towards the river bank. What better trial of a man's willingness to share the load? As it turned out, we did not hit the bank – so I had surmounted the first hurdle.

The next hurdle was that another person being considered for the post of assistant glaciologist was Gordon Robin, an Australian physicist working at the University of Birmingham. Like me, he had served in the navy but, unlike me, he had already wintered in the Antarctic as a member of FIDS. Although I had been on two summer expeditions, one to Iceland and another to the Gambia, there was no doubt that he was the better qualified.

The British committee was reluctant to make a choice. Luckily for me, the problem was solved in January 1949 by appointing both of us, Gordon to occupy an extra post as physicist. His principal responsibility would be to undertake seismic ice-depth sounding, whereas I would fill the assistant glaciologist post. There were to be two other members of the British contingent: Fred Roots, a Canadian, as chief geologist; and Alan Reece, a Londoner, as assistant geologist.

To be a member of a major Antarctic expedition at the tender age of 22 was, until that time, beyond my wildest dreams. Soon the chief glaciologist, Valter Schytt, came to Oxford to meet his new assistant. A powerfully built Swede who towered above my own far-from-minuscule 185 centimetres, he was Ahlmann's protégé and destined to become Sweden's leading glaciologist. After a day of discussions, he spent the night in a small hotel. His room was equipped with a gas heater; gas was procured by putting shillings in a slot. Running it continuously to compensate for inadequate bedclothes, he kept the heater going until he ran out of shillings, after which the room cooled to the temperature of the frost outside. Years later, after we had spent two years in the Antarctic, he confessed that his night in Oxford was the coldest he had ever endured.

I myself was rapidly immersed in training. Although I had a long-standing interest in the study of ice and had read a paper on my researches in Iceland to a meeting of the British Glaciological Society,[4] I knew that an honours degree in geography would not be the best foundation on which to build. On the advice of Dr Max Perutz, an Austrian who had made significant contributions to the study of glaciers and was later to win a Nobel prize for chemistry, I took an intensive course in crystallography. Then in March I was sent for two weeks of practical experience with Valter Schytt to a camp high up on the Kebnekajse massif in Swedish Lapland.

Valter's field station could only be reached on skis from the Lapp village of Nikkaluokta, half a day's bus and sledge journey from the iron-mining town of Kiruna. In my childhood I had enjoyed skiing holidays in France and Switzerland but had no experience of cross-country skiing. Skiing towards the field station through an Arctic blizzard at a temperature of –15°C, I failed to keep up with Valter, so he asked an ancient Lapp to stay with me. Despite the blizzard and with no language in common, that man taught me things about skiing that proved invaluable on many later expeditions.

During the following three weeks Valter showed me how to determine the rate of movement of glaciers, to drill into them, to dig pits to study snow structure, and to measure snow temperatures. It was an intensive learning experience.

Valter was born in Stockholm and had graduated from the Geographical Institute in Stockholm University, where he decided to specialize in glaciology. It was not long before I formed the impression that he did not find me easy, perhaps because I was cheeky and opinionated ('insolent' and 'priggish' – as one colleague wrote later). From my point of view, Valter himself seemed parochial. Confined to Sweden throughout the war, he had never really rubbed shoulders with foreigners. It was as though he believed that every aspect of life in

4

Map 1 Where it all began

5

Sweden was superior to life elsewhere. I learned later that he had some doubt as to whether the two of us would make an effective team. As it turned out, we did, and in due course our relationship became one of mutual respect and friendship which lasted to the end of his life.

On my return from Sweden, Alan Reece and I were despatched to an army camp for an intensive course in driving and maintaining 'weasels'. The expedition had acquired from the British Army three M29C weasels – amphibious tracked vehicles designed for landing on enemy shores and traversing snow-covered terrain.[5] Apart from dogs, these were to be our principal means of transport for inland journeys. Although a Swedish mechanic was to be our main defence against breakdown, he could not be with every field party because he would also be responsible for the diesel generators at the base.

Later in the summer, Professor Ahlmann, Gordon Robin, Valter Schytt and I went to Kebnekajse to attempt seismic soundings on Storglaciären, one of a number of glaciers close to Valter's field station. Carl Gustav Rossby, at the time Professor of Meteorology in the University of Stockholm, had arranged for a portable seismograph to be lent for the occasion. Trials by R. Tegholm indicated that it was possible to measure the depth of ice by detonating small charges of dynamite on the surface and timing the reflection from the glacier bed.

On returning home, the British committee confirmed my appointment as assistant glaciologist, offering the princely salary of £450 per annum. This meant that we were to be the highest-paid polar expedition in British history. I gladly accepted the salary without revealing that I would have been willing to go south without pay. Although by this time I had graduated from Oxford and was in debt, I needed very little money to survive.

In October I was required to undergo a medical examination by a retired RAF medic, Wing Commander Roland Winfield.[6] He asked if I had any skeletons in the cupboard. I knew that I was reported to have had rheumatic fever in Burma as a boy. I also knew how seriously that would be taken, so I lied to him. I must have lied convincingly because he asked no further questions. On learning that my sport was rowing, he felt that there was no point in prolonging the examination, so picked up a pen and wrote:

At the request of the Director I have carried out a comprehensive physical and psychological examination of Mr C.W.M. Swithinbank to assess his fitness for the Norwegian – British – Swedish Antarctic Expedition. As a result of my examination I certify that in my opinion his physical condition and psychological state fit him for exposure to conditions which may impose upon him stresses which will call for the highest degree of physical and mental endurance.

Now I was over the last hurdle. However, in order to ensure that none of us should profit from writing about the expedition to the possible detriment of the expedition's own publications, each of us had to sign a draconian contract, one clause of which read:

All results and collections of the expedition shall be the property of the International Committee. This applies to any form of collections, records, official diaries, maps, charts, etc. The ownership and copyright of photographic material and other materials for illustrations shall belong to the International Committee, even if privately owned still or motion picture cameras are used.

The international team finally selected comprised:

John Giæver (49), Norwegian, leader of the wintering party[7]
Valter Schytt (30), Swedish, chief glaciologist, second in command
Gordon Robin (27), Australian, geophysicist and third in command
Nils Jørgen Schumacher (30), Norwegian, chief meteorologist
Gösta Liljequist (35), Swedish, assistant meteorologist
Fred Roots (26), Canadian, chief geologist
Alan Reece (27), British, assistant geologist
Charles Swithinbank (22), British, assistant glaciologist
Nils Roer (34), Norwegian, topographic surveyor
Ove Wilson (28), Swedish, medical officer
Bertil Ekström (29), Swedish, mechanical engineer
Egil Rogstad (41), Norwegian, radio operator
Peter Melleby (33), Norwegian, in charge of dogs
Schølberg Nilsen (46), Norwegian, cook

Giæver, Liljequist, and Roer were married, the rest unmarried. Not many wives would be happy to see their husband disappear for two and a half years, knowing that in the event of any emergency at home, there would be no way in which he could help them before the end of the expedition.

The national committees agreed to share the responsibility for gathering the many thousand items of stores and equipment needed to keep us housed, fed, clothed and secure for two years. The British were to procure clothing, electrical equipment, diesel generators, radios, sledging rations, weasels, dogs, dog sledges, tents and alpine equipment. Norway was responsible for fuels, some provisions, more dogs and dog sledges, dog food, skiing equipment, leather garments, sleeping bags, and heavy sledges for towing behind weasels. Sweden would look after the bulk of the provisioning, wooden huts, kitchen equipment, tools, bedding, medical supplies and more.

There were uncompromising views on the merits of some items. Whereas the Norwegians favoured fur clothing, some on the British side felt that furs were fit only for Eskimos. The Norwegians wanted dog sledges made from hickory, whereas others were dead set on making them from laminated woods. As John Giæver put it later:

> Nobody must think that the current conception of John Bull as a phlegmatic and extremely diplomatic gentleman applies to absolutely every Englishman. For it does not.[8]

For the most part, differing views were accommodated by buying what members from each country preferred.

The expedition ship *Norsel*, a 600-ton[9] ocean-going tug converted into a sealer powered by a German U-boat diesel engine, was in Flensburg, Germany. However, Sverdrup had approached the owners of a whaling factory ship to ask if five members of the expedition could hitch-hike to the Antarctic together with the expedition's three weasels, Valter's two-tonne ice-drilling machine, and all of the sledge dogs. *Norsel* was considered too small to accommodate them for a long sea voyage. Moreover, in the tropics the dogs would have had no shelter from the overhead sun, which might lead to fatal overheating.

The British committee arranged for a small Royal Air Force detachment to take two Auster VI aircraft on the ship for reconnaissance purposes. This flying group consisted of:

> Squadron Leader Brian Walford
> Flight Lieutenant Hugh Tudor
> Sergeant Peter Weston
> Corporal William Gilbey
> Corporal Leslie Quar

My colleagues and I became aware that newspapers were showing great interest in the expedition's plans. Press contracts were negotiated with *The Times* in London, *Aftenposten* in Oslo, and *Svenska Dagbladet* in Stockholm. They in turn sold stories to newspapers around the world. *The Times of Malta* found the scientific objectives esoteric and tried to bring these closer to home by claiming that we hoped 'to find a reason for the drought in Central Africa'.[10] The *Natal Mercury* wrote under the headline '10-year Luftwaffe secret out:

Precious metals may be discovered and traces of long-dead civilization are not ruled out'.[11] The *Daily Herald* interviewed the British members and headlined: 'Young Britain shows its mettle. Danger? they just laugh'.[12] None was quite so bizarre as the *New York Herald Tribune* report of ' . . . Bedouin encampments, date palms and camels at the South Pole'.[13] Simply bringing the newspapers down to earth would keep us busy.

2

OCEAN FACTORY

On 24 October 1949 I was one of five members of the expedition to board the whaling factory ship *Thorshøvdi* in the port of Sandefjord in Norway. With me were Bertil Ekström, Peter Melleby, Schølberg Nilsen and Alan Reece.

Thorshøvdi belonged to A/S Thor Dahl of Sandefjord. The company was headed by Lars Christensen, whose father, Christian Christensen, played a major part in establishing the Norwegian whaling industry in the Antarctic. Lars financed a series of expeditions which, before the war, made studies of the distribution of whales and also flew over parts of the coastline of Dronning Maud Land. No doubt this explained his willingness to help by carrying us to the seaward edge of the Antarctic pack ice, where we could meet and transfer to *Norsel*.

Thorshøvdi was built in København in 1948 and at 24,000 tons (gross) dwarfed the whale-catchers beside her. She sported twin funnels above the stern whale slipway, each decorated with a laughing whale in the form of a C (for Christensen). Half a century on, it seems grotesque to think of whales laughing at their imminent demise, but in 1949 it was unremarkable. Greenpeace was still a generation away.

Very few of the factory ship's crew had arrived on board, so we went ashore for meals. I ventured into a shop to buy some chocolate but was sternly reminded that it was rationed. The assistant relented when I related that in May 1945, while serving in the cruiser HMS *Berwick* immediately after the German surrender, our crew of more than 600 had given up their entire week's chocolate ration to the children of Trondheim, many of whom had never seen chocolate, let alone tasted it.

On *Thorshøvdi* we were preoccupied with getting the dogs fed, watered and settled. Of the 62 for which we were responsible, 28 were bought from Jakobshavn and Christianshåb in Greenland at a cost £3 15s each. 12 were bought in Longyearbyen, Spitsbergen, at a cost of £7 10s each; 22 came from FIDS as a gift to the expedition. The dogs from Spitsbergen had originated from Canada in 1945; those from the

Antarctic had been bred from dogs originally brought from Labrador in 1945 and 1946. The Spitsbergen dogs were larger than the others – several weighed well over 50 kilos. Those from West Greenland and the Antarctic were smaller, averaging 40–50 kilos.

Sledge dogs are mongrels. Although not descended from wolves, there is little doubt that, intentionally or unintentionally, wolf strains have sometimes joined what was primarily a dog stock.[1] A number of our dogs, though smaller than wolves, had some of the colouring of wolves. Like wolves, sledge dogs are pack animals, and as such, they generally work well in teams and enjoy each other's company.

However, our three groups had never met before coming on board. Some fought with gusto at the slightest provocation – even dirty looks could precipitate a battle. The whole pack was to live in the open on the fo'c'sle, each dog chained separately to the deck rail. Their 2-metre chains were positioned so that they could rub noses with a neighbour on either side but could not become entangled.

They ranged widely in temperament from sociable animals bent on licking people all over to cowering creatures who made clear that they were not to be touched. Peter explained that while some Greenland Eskimos smother their dogs with kindness, others handle them roughly. The buyer of sledge dogs soon learns that the seller has an interest in parting with his worst dogs.

It would take time for us to make friends with the dogs. Of the five of us, Alan and Peter were the only ones who had ever driven dogs, so they took charge of animal welfare while I served as understudy. Dogfood was not a problem; with a large crew coming aboard, kitchen scraps would be plentiful. We also had a supply of Norwegian stockfish – sun-dried cod that we immersed in barrels of water for a few hours before throwing half a fish to each dog.

During the first night in Sandefjord, the air temperature dropped to –9°C, so the dogs at least felt comfortable. I wrote last-minute letters and went shopping. On the morning of departure, there was many a tearful family on the jetty who would not see husbands or fathers for the next six months.

Thorshøvdi steamed into Oslofjord and I felt the world I knew fading into the mist. We learned that the ship was to pass through the Pentland Firth and that a couple weeks later we would call at Curaçao, a tiny Netherlands colony in the Lesser Antilles. This substantial diversion from a straight line between Europe and the whaling grounds was justified, in spite of the cost, because Curaçao sold the cheapest bunker fuel in the Atlantic. Two women were taking passage to Curaçao, but I never saw them because they were confined to their cabins by seasickness.

11

As the days passed, I began getting to know my colleagues. Alan Reece was a Londoner and, like me, had only just graduated from university. Trained as a geologist at Imperial College, London, he had earlier notched up some quite unusual experiences. While a sub-lieutenant in the Royal Navy, he had been trained as a meteorological observer. In 1944 he was transferred to FIDS, where he spent two winters at different stations in Graham Land. However, his real passion was dog sledging, and he had been able to escape from base duties to join survey parties working in the area of James Ross Island. It was probably for this reason that he, with Melleby, had been assigned to look after the dogs on *Thorshøvdi*.

Peter Melleby, a wiry man of medium build, smoked a pipe and bore an expression of perpetual calm. Although he had more cold-weather experience than the rest of us put together, he never pushed it on others. Ask advice, and it would be forthcoming, but he was not offended if his advice was not taken. He had worked from 1939 to 1941 as a coal miner in Svalbard before escaping to Scotland, where he joined the Norwegian Army and served as ski instructor to the British army of occupation in Iceland. Then, in a secret operation in May 1942, he sailed from Scotland with two small ships and a 60-man task force to establish a weather station in Spitsbergen. While in Grønfjorden, both ships were sunk by German bombers, with the loss of 17 lives. The survivors landed at Barentsburg, at the time an unoccupied Russian coal-mining settlement.

There were German detachments operating their own weather stations, so there followed a protracted cat and mouse game, first to detect and then to neutralize the enemy stations. In September 1943 the Norwegian detachment was attacked by German marines landed from the battleships *Tirpitz* and *Scharnhorst* with an escort of destroyers. In the face of a superior force, most of the Norwegians surrendered. Peter and one of his colleagues retreated up a glacier while the enemy soldiers shot at them with rifles. The glacier front was steep, and Peter's companion lost his footing and slid down to the bottom, where he was taken prisoner at gunpoint. Peter got away and returned to Britain.

After a year's training as a radio operator and meteorological observer, he was once again despatched to Spitsbergen, remaining there until the end of the war.

In an Oslo street he came face to face with the man who slid down the glacier into the arms of the Germans. The poor fellow had spent years as a prisoner of war.

Afterwards, Peter had been a fox and wolf trapper in north-east Greenland, travelling between trap lines by dog team. Thus his sledging experience had been partly in Spitsbergen and partly in Greenland.

12

Alan Reece

Peter Melleby

13

Schølberg Nilsen was from Vesterålen in Norway and was older than the rest of us. Like Peter, he had substantial experience of Arctic hunting and winter travel. However, in his own eyes he was the humblest member of our party, and felt ill at ease with a tablecloth in front of him.

Bertil Ekström – who liked to be addressed by his nickname Knalle – was short and wiry. Although Swedish, he had served as a volunteer armoured-car mechanic during the Finnish winter war of 1939–40, when Finland's armed forces were desperately outnumbered by Russian invaders. He had learned to repair vehicles under fire when most mechanics simply fled. I realized that this background would be priceless if we ever had difficulty with the weasels.

All told, there were nearly 400 men on board – the crew under the command of Captain Thorvald Hansen, the whalers led by a disagreeable gunner called Andreason, who was said to be very rich because of the accuracy of his shots. Gunners command the catcher boats and fire the harpoons.

My colleagues and I found some confusion about where we, as

Bertil (Knalle) Ekström

14

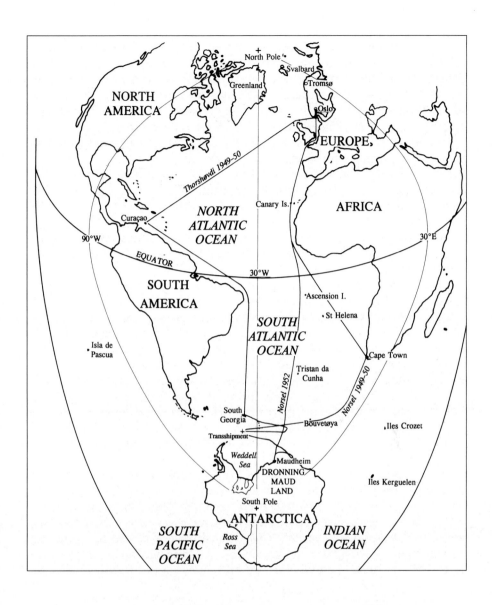

Map 2 Routes to and from Antarctica

15

passengers, should eat. At first we were consigned to the crew's mess, on second thoughts to the officers' mess, and finally segregated, with three of us in the captain's saloon while the rest ate below. However, we felt that class distinctions were inappropriate on an Antarctic expedition, so negotiated with the chief steward for all five of us to be given places in the officers' mess. Alan and I were the only ones who felt at home on the messdeck, at home with the officers and at home with the captain, because our years of naval service had included all three. My diary notes: 'The food is very rich for one used to English rations.' We enjoyed unlimited quantities of meat, bacon, eggs, cheese, butter, sugar and tea – all of which were still rationed in England.[2]

Seated opposite me in the officers' mess was an American engineer who was on board to supervise the installation of a machine for dehydrating whale meat. Until 1949, the pelagic (offshore) whaling industry had used only the oil, not the lean meat of the whale. After the meat and blubber were rendered in pressure cookers to extract the oil, the protein was simply pumped over the side, much to the delight of fish and seabirds. Foreseeing, I suppose, the death knell of the industry because of rampant overfishing, whalers were just beginning to think about using the meat. Although fresh whale meat is consid- ered a delicacy in some countries and I myself had enjoyed many a braised whale steak in Lyons teashops in London, the ship would be dealing with many thousands of tonnes of it. Dehydration was the only practical way to keep it. Moreover, we hitch-hikers might benefit from the experiment because our dogs needed dehydrated food for use in the field.

The ship herself seemed colossal. We lived aft but meals were in the forward superstructure, so we had a healthy walk over the upper deck each way. Aft of the superstructure was the forward flensing deck, where whales are flensed (butchered).[3] It seemed the size of a football pitch and, beyond that, another vast flensing deck connected with the forward part through a bridging gantry. At the stern, leading onto the after flensing deck, was the slipway up which whales were winched. It was unfenced and slippery, so I kept well clear. Beneath, stretched over the full length of the flensing decks, was the factory, with rows of giant pressure cookers, separating tanks and centrifuges for refining the oil. It was an eerily quiet and shadowy place, but we knew that it would spring to life when the first whales came up the slipway.

An electrician showed me over the engine room, with its massive, spotlessly clean diesel engines supervised by a single engineer. Next the generator room, where diesel generating sets with a total output of more than two megawatts – enough for a small town – stood ready to supply the factory and all the ship's domestic services. Now, with the factory silent, most of the generators too were silent. One electrician in a soundproofed room controlled the whole system. Next door was the boiler room, looking quite big enough to drive a steamship this size but really intended only for supplying steam to the blubber and whale-meat cookers.

Shortly after *Thorshøvdi* began to heave on an Atlantic swell, Peter found that three dogs were suffering from a foot disease manifested by raw areas between the toes. To avoid cross-infection, he isolated them on the after main deck. However, by the end of October, only six days into the voyage, four more dogs had foot trouble. Telegrams flew back and forth between Alan Reece and veterinary surgeons in England, but there was no firm diagnosis. The ship's doctor provided penicillin, but the infections only got worse.

Meanwhile, the whalers began laying a new deck on top of the permanent deck planks, gradually depleting great stacks of sawn timber that had been with us from Sandefjord. The planks, soon to be blood-soaked and splintered by nailed boots and whalebones, were to

The author

17

Laying the temporary deck on *Thorshøvdi*. The dogs (left), most of them in cages, lie prostrate in the heat.

be ripped up and heaved over the side on the homeward voyage at the end of the season. Only in this way could the population of Sandefjord be spared the acrid scent of putrefaction throughout the following summer.

Ekström and Nilsen began the tedious job of strengthening the tracks of the weasels. This was done with strips of reinforced rubber belting, drilled and then bolted onto each track lug. The French explorer Paul-Emile Victor had used weasels in Greenland, only to find that flexing of the tracks over rough sastrugi[*] was damaging these after a few hundred kilometres. We needed to keep them going for thousands of kilometres. All the spare tracks had to be strengthened too, and this was to keep the pair busy throughout the voyage.

Another task was sewing dog harnesses. Although the Norwegians preferred factory-made leather collars (scaled down from the carthorse variety), Alan came with a strong preference for everything to which he had been accustomed as a dog driver with FIDS. The FIDS

---

[*] Sastrugi are sharp, irregular ridges formed on a snow surface by wind erosion and deposition. The ridges are generally parallel with the direction of the prevailing wind.

method was to use 50-millimetre lamp wick, which has the advantage of remaining soft and pliable in low temperatures. Each harness had to be made to measure from 2 metres of lamp wick, after which we wove the name of the dog into the crosspiece.

Peter Melleby was fluent in English but Ekström and Nilsen spoke none. Because Scandinavian was the language of the majority and we were to live together for two and a half years, I set out to learn Norwegian, mostly by ear but also with the help of an elementary grammar book. It struck me that possibly in a moment of crisis, rapid communication could make the difference between life and death. I was determined neither to let the side down nor to put myself at risk. It was not long before I concluded that Norwegian is probably the easiest to learn of all European languages, though Swedish follows close behind. While in English we conjugate the verb *to be*: I am, you are, he is, Norwegians in effect say: I am, you am, he am, we am, and so on. Similarly with the other tenses.

The chief difficulty was that many of the crew wanted to learn English. They held a two-hour 'English by film' session once a week, and Alan and I were invited to help. Our job was to read the film script out loud afterwards, asking them to repeat each sentence, and stopping for clarification of difficult words. The 40 or so who attended were keen and attentive students, and at the end of the lesson they applauded and asked us to come back the following week.

This we did for several weeks. In one class I was teaching them the use of the word *worry*, so asked if they were worried about anything. They solemnly intoned 'No'. However, the factory manager, who spoke perfect English and had just dropped in to listen, added 'Bloody liars!'

Liquor was discouraged on board because some Norwegians, like Russians, tend to over-imbibe. However, one day the chief steward gave Peter a bottle of brandy, so we took it to our cabin and drank and conversed late into the night.

Radio reports revealed that a veritable battle fleet of factory ships was on its way south. Steaming somewhere on the Atlantic were the Norwegian factories *Antarctic, Kosmos-3, Kosmos-4, Norhval, Pelagos, Sir James Clark Ross, Suderøy, Thorshammer* and *Thorshavet*. In addition, there were three British factory ships, two Japanese, one South African, one Dutch, and one from the USSR. A total of 216 small catcher boats, ranging in size from 500 to 800 tons (gross) were spaced out across the ocean, also heading for the fray.

Approaching the tropics, we put many of the dogs in wire cages and moved them into the shade of the midships gantry. The occupants of each cage were selected on grounds of compatibility, and the captain arranged for a large awning to provide shade for those not under the gantry. We supplied drinking water in buckets, and the warmer the weather, the more we had to keep the buckets topped up.

One of the dogs showed symptoms of distemper, a highly contagious virus; this confused Peter and the ship's doctor because all of them had been inoculated. In discussions with the captain it was decided that if there was no improvement, this poor animal must walk the plank.

Peter and Alan decided that four of the five dogs with bad paws should also be put down. Their claws had fallen out, leaving them effectively without traction, and they were in considerable pain. A crewman volunteered to use the back end of an axe and the bodies went over the side.

While trying to suppress any emotional involvement with the dogs as individuals, I was not yet hardened to summary executions. I never got used to thinking only in terms of the pack as a whole.

Films were shown daily on the flensing deck after nightfall. Our group was given deckchairs on the officers' deck, representing the dress circle. Before one of the films, the doctor made a speech about the prevalence of venereal disease in Curaçao, explaining that none of their brothels was subject to medical inspection. We were exhorted not to stray from the straight and narrow path of righteousness. I never found out how many did.

At 0700[4] on 12 November we steamed into Caracas Bay past low forested sandstone hills to a berth beside dozens of giant fuel tanks with SHELL painted in big letters on each one. This being a bunkering station, the hills around were dotted with bungalows for staff, together with a convent, a pumping station, and an old Spanish fort. Palm trees, bananas and cacti were growing on all sides. A few miles to the west we could see Willemstad, the capital of the colony, with its cluster of roofs of many colours. Far away to the south I could make out a mountain range on mainland Venezuela.

I volunteered to stay on board to watch over the dogs while the others went ashore. Some dogs were in real trouble if any of us allowed the sun to get to them even for a moment. Their respiration rates rose above 180 and they leapt around in the cages, only worsening their distress. No doubt we humans would feel the same in this climate if, like the dogs, we were dressed in fur coats. The poor dogs wore them all the time.

When Alan returned from Willemstad I went there for a couple of hours. The shops were loaded with what, to my eyes, was a dazzling variety of American goods. There were many items such as refrigerators and washing machines that we had not seen in shops in England since 1939. It was truly a wealthy place, with lavishly – even gaudily – dressed, smiling people of every imaginable race and skin colour.

In the streets I found myself continually greeting *Thorshøvdi* folk loaded with parcels. For just a few hours we had flooded the place with Norwegians – and one Swede. A deckhand accosted me and said: 'Please tek Sveeden home!' And then came Knalle, blind drunk but delighted to see me. He fell into my arms and I bundled him into a taxi. Nilsen appeared at the same time and collapsed into the back seat. I thought how bad it would look if I had to report to Norway that we had left them behind in Curaçao.

Back on board, I struggled up the gangway, supporting my limp colleagues. This was not without hazard because sharks frequented the oily pool below, waiting perhaps for scraps of food or falling sailors. Once on board, I observed many bottles of liquor surreptitiously unwrapped – the sailors were not to be beaten by the ship's rules.

Thorshøvdi, meanwhile, had taken on 7,000 tonnes of bunker fuel. The same tanks that held diesel fuel would later be used for whale oil. A foul white slimy substance had been sprayed all over the tanks before the ship left Sandefjord. From now on, as fuel oil was consumed during the voyage, the empty tanks would be washed down with fresh water and subsequently filled with whale oil. The whale oil would of course be contaminated by the residue, but after sufficient dilution the mixture could be brought within government limits for impurities. By this means the capacity of a modern factory ship had been more or less doubled, reducing the number of tankers that came south in the course of the season to relieve the factory ships of their burden. All in all, three-quarters of the total volume of the ship consisted of oil tanks.

The explanation of tank-sharing did nothing to dispel my lingering suspicion that margarine, which in those days contained whale oil, must also contain substances that we would rather not know about.

On leaving Curaçao we were bound for the island of South Georgia, a British possession at 54°S latitude in the South Atlantic.

As the ship steamed east along the coast of Venezuela, our group was told to eat in the captain's saloon. The two women passengers had left the ship in Curaçao, so there was more space in high places. By now, even Nilsen had adjusted to opulent eating and was enjoying it as much as the rest of us. However, it took some days for Knalle Ekström to appear on the scene – he had made friends with people working through a plentiful supply of liquor. The captain accosted him one day, saying: 'Have you not started taking food again yet?' They both laughed. Evidently the skipper knew a good deal about what went on behind the scenes. I suppose he reckoned that the liquor would be gone before *Thorshøvdi* reached the whaling grounds.

3

SOUTH LATITUDE

A radio message reported that *Norsel* had left Oslo according to plan on 17 November after being inspected by King Haakon and Crown Prince Olav. That day was also my twenty-third birthday, but I did not tell anyone. Two days later we overtook another factory ship, *Antarctic*, the oldest of the Norwegian fleet. Smaller than *Thorshøvdi*, she had no stern slipway, so whales had to be flensed in the water before being winched aboard in pieces.

On 21 November, the equator was celebrated when King Neptune appeared on a chariot hauled by huskies. It was all good fun, but my mind was on other things. New cases of the paw disease were appearing almost daily. We found one dog with a bleeding foot wound infested with fly larvae; he had to be put down. We tried a gun, but after four shots to the head, the animal still took a minute to die, so we reverted to the axe. Now there were 18 sick dogs and we began to wonder whether any would ever again step ashore. The ship's doctor was doing his best, syringing their wounds and putting in DDT powder. No vet in England could offer a diagnosis or suggest anything better.

A week later, having left Norway with 62 dogs, we had lost 15. We were devastated with grief, not least because the losses would seriously curtail our first season's inland travels. A telegram from Sverdrup said: 'Bitches – keep us daily informed.' He knew that if we were losing bitches, our problems could be insuperable.

At this point we decided to move all the sick dogs back to the fo'c'sle, where they would be isolated from the others, though windswept and blinded by sea-spray. Every day one of us hosed down the deck under each dog to maintain some semblance of hygiene, and all the cages of the healthy animals were scrubbed with a powerful disinfectant. Soon we were asked to move even the fit dogs to the fo'c'sle because the mate, Mandus Hansen, wanted to prepare the flensing decks for action. A telegram from Sverdrup said: 'Kill all sick dogs.' My diary reports: 'We had half expected it but it was not a welcome command.' We held off killing a number on the grounds that only we were in a position to define 'sick'.

With the onset of cooler nights, the evening film shows moved indoors, ours to the officers' mess, the rest to the messdeck below. In working hours, Alan and I began to assemble plywood boxes that had come aboard in pieces in Sandefjord so as to take up less cargo space. These were for the dog food that we planned to make by mixing whale-meat powder with enough oil to hold it together. Nobody had ever tried this but our instructions from John Giæver were to make 5 tonnes.

On 1 December the factory under the flensing decks came alive to test everything. Steam was fed into the cookers, driving out the putrid smell of last year's whales. It was a sickly stench that was soon to pervade every compartment of the ship. However, when I finally got used to it, I concluded that rotting whale was one of the less obnoxious of the vile smells of this world.

Perhaps it was the smell that brought seabirds. A dozen or more albatrosses followed the ship, most of them giant wandering albatrosses with a wingspan of up to 3 metres. Effortless in flight, they seldom flap their wings, relying on a kind of dynamic soaring, skimming millimetres over the waves, so close that I could see the reflection of their wing-tip feathers coincide with the feathers themselves, yet there was never a splash. At intervals they climbed, turned, stalled, and dived back to the waves. As we drew nearer to South Georgia, some of the smaller royal, black-browed, grey-headed and sooty albatrosses joined the flock. Transfixed by the elegance of their soaring, we watched the spectacle for hours, often anticipating mid-air collisions, but their reactions were so fast that even near misses were rare.

On 3 December we crossed the Antarctic Convergence in latitude 50°S. This is where cold waters from the Antarctic meet warmer and more saline waters from temperate regions. The sea temperature dropped several degrees and so did the air temperature; we found ourselves donning not just one but often two thick sweaters.

Thorshøvdi ploughed relentlessly on through swell and storm, pitching and rolling, with salt spray blinding the dogs on the fo'c'sle, a picture of misery that broke our hearts. They stood all the time because the wet deck was too cold to lie on, and they howled pitifully every time the spray cut into their sides. The watchkeeping officers could see it all from the bridge, and the captain promised to slow the ship if we began 'shipping it green' over the bow.

Fine sunset tonight – cold hard clouds, driving snow falling from some, the sky vicious and alive, the sun outlining one cloud with incredible brilliance. It is one of the things which can take my breath away, make life doubly worth living, and make me long to see more.[1]

Outside the next morning, the mountains of South Georgia loomed ahead – snow-covered peaks that soar to nearly 3,000 metres, black rock outcrops, great snowfields and winding glaciers plunging to the sea. I broke off box-making to photograph the scene – to my eyes more stunning than anything I had seen before.

During the forenoon I saw the first iceberg, way off to starboard, twin-peaked, distinctly blue, and about the size of a large house. This, I knew, was tiny compared with the flat-topped, tabular icebergs that we would soon see.

At noon we entered Cumberland Bay, an 8-kilometre wide break in the rugged coastline, offering shelter and a good anchorage in King Edward Cove. Although South Georgia was a dependency of the Falkland Islands, Norwegians far outnumbered the British administrators. Grytviken, one of three shore whaling stations on the island, had been operating since 1904 – manned by Norwegians but owned by Compañia Argentina de Pesca of Buenos Aires. The Argentine company leased the station site from the Falkland Islands Dependencies government.

Thorshøvdi and the government outpost at King Edward Point, Cumberland Bay, South Georgia

25

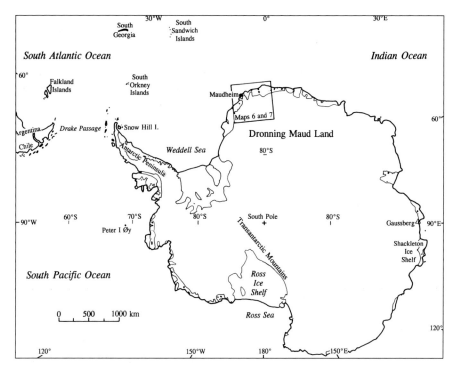

Map 3 Antarctica. Inset shows area covered by Maps 6 and 7

I could see why Norwegians would feel at home here. Surrounded by mountains, the place was reminiscent of the many small fjord-side settlements of northern Norway. Catcher boats scuttled to and fro, some hauling in whale carcasses to the slipway, others queuing to come alongside *Thorshøvdi* for supplies.

Alan and I hitched a ride in a motor boat to a group of small wooden houses on a gravel spit some way from the whaling station. This was the seat of government. The British population was about a dozen, comprising a magistrate, a policeman, a customs officer, a meteorologist and two radio operators each with wife and child. We were entertained to tea in the radio station. The families claimed to love their isolated life in these surroundings, half a world away from the bustle of Britain.

From here we walked round the cove to the whaling station. A sperm whale and a fin whale were on the slipway, men peeling back the blubber from the flesh with vicious-looking knives shaped like hockey sticks. Strips were then dragged away by winches up a steep wooden ramp, where they were guided into giant pressure cookers below. It was a sight and a smell that we would get used to.

Beyond the factory was a small hydroelectric power station and a little fenced cemetery. Most of the graves were Norwegian, but the place was dominated by a granite headstone over a well-kept grave with an inscription reading:

To the dear Memory of

ERNEST HENRY SHACKLETON

EXPLORER

Born 15th Feb. 1874
Entered Life Eternal
5th Jan. 1922

Shackleton had died here in King Edward Cove aboard the small steamship *Quest*, while heading south as leader of his fourth Antarctic expedition.

Close by the graveyard, elephant seals basked on the foreshore and – incongruous in this setting – cattle chewed tussock grass while wandering amongst the seals. Alan said that not only cattle but also pigs, goats, sheep and reindeer had been introduced to the island from time to time to provide fresh meat for the whalers. Even some horses were kept as working animals. A few gentoo penguins (*Pygoscelis papua*) added to the scene. Perhaps surprisingly, all the animals we saw seemed to be living in peace with each other.

The following day we sought and received two tonnes of dehydrated whale-meat powder from the station to augment the supply that *Thorshøvdi* expected to provide us with, and also sufficient whale meat to keep the dogs happy until *Thorshøvdi* began whaling. This had to be fin whale meat, because the oil of the sperm whale was known to be toxic. Although the station was taking filter-feeding baleen whales (blue and fin)[*] as well as toothed whales (sperm), the International Commission on Whaling had decreed that factory ships could only fish for baleen whales from 22 December onwards. This meant that for two and a half weeks, *Thorshøvdi* could only take the less valuable sperm whales. An old catcher, *Polar V*, came alongside flying the red ensign. I hailed

---

[*] *Baleen*, commonly known as whalebone, occurs as a series of flexible, horny plates in the palate on the roof of the mouth. It is used to separate krill from sea water.

27

Shackleton's grave at Grytviken, Cumberland Bay, South Georgia

the skipper, asking how it came about that a British vessel was taking supplies from a Norwegian factory ship. He explained that *Polar V* was registered in Jersey, owned by Norwegians, and was on charter to *Thorshøvdi*'s owners – there was not a single British subject on board. It was a telling measure of the dominant position of Norway in the whaling industry.

That evening we weighed anchor and steamed out to sea escorted by 13 catchers – *Enern, Falk, Fyrern, Gribb, Nebb, Niern, Odd XII, Polar V, Syvern, Thorarinn, Thorbrinn, Thorfinn* and *Thorgaut*. One, I learned, had lost a man overboard in an Atlantic storm. He was replaced by one of the factory hands.

We were the mother ship – everything that the catchers asked for was available and freely given. Whaling is a team effort, so if any of

Nebb, one of *Thorshøvdi's* whale catchers, in Cumberland Bay, South Georgia

the catchers were not well supplied, there would be fewer whales harvested.

Our escort now formed up in two lines, one on each side of *Thorshøvdi* as though in battle array. We were the flagship of the fleet and, as darkness fell and their lights came on, I felt proud to be at the centre of a great enterprise. Every one of the catchers had powerful engines and could chase whales at high speed. The newest, *Odd XII*, had a 1,700-horsepower diesel engine. *Thorshøvdi*, with 50 times the tonnage of the catcher, had only 4 times the power.

One day Alan and I were entertained by one of the ship's chemists. He had a degree in chemistry from the University of Durham and was, by chance, related to Professor Harald Sverdrup. He said there were also two inspectors on board, both independent of the whalers and employed by the Norwegian Government to ensure that the ship worked within the rules of the International Commission on Whaling.[2] Their job was to monitor the species, the numbers and the size of the carcasses as they were hauled onto the flensing deck. In order to protect the stocks, the catchers' gunners were supposed to judge the size of the beast before despatching their harpoons. Depending on the

29

species, we should only take whales with an overall length greater than:

Blue (*Balaenoptera musculus*)	21.3 metres
Fin (*Balaenoptera physalus*)	16.8 metres
Sei (*Balaenoptera borealis*)	12.2 metres
Humpback (*Megaptera novaeangliae*)	10.7 metres
Sperm (*Physeter macrocephalus*)	10.7 metres

To me it seemed impossible to judge the length of a whale from the heaving gun-platform of a catcher, and I was interested to see how the inspectors recorded any 'mistakes'. Not wishing to cause offence, however, I never probed too deeply, nor did I wield a tape measure.

Since whale meat was brought on board during our short stay at Grytviken, the dogs had been fed on it in preference to kitchen scraps. We tried making dog food according to John Giæver's recipe, using whale-meat powder, maize meal and whale oil. Try as we might, we could not get the mixture to hold together – it was just a sticky powder. It took 35 per cent of whale oil to make it like putty, which was too much fat for a balanced diet. We fed the mixture to Knoll, one of the Spitsbergen dogs, but it was hard for him to muster enough saliva to swallow it.

At this stage of the voyage, our dogs numbered 44 out of the 62 that came aboard in Sandefjord; 18 had succumbed to the unknown disease. Our only chance of completing the planned inland travel depended on a vigorous breeding programme as soon as we stepped ashore.

Our evenings were spent reading, writing or partying. At one party we were working on a bottle of cognac when Mr Holden, the factory manager, dropped in to see the cabin occupant. More than anyone, he needed to keep a sober workforce, so there was an embarrassed silence as he surveyed the scene. The silence was broken when one brave soul said: 'Come and join us!' Holden smiled, sat down and joined the party. This gesture did much to explain the easy relations that we found between managers and the crew.

None of the whalers could understand why we, the expedition five, would want to be shut away from civilization for two years in the Antarctic. Some said they would consider it for a vast sum of money but not otherwise.

On returning to my cabin I saw that we were stopped at the edge of the pack ice and close to several tabular icebergs of varying shapes and sizes, one of them perhaps 5 kilometres long and 15 metres high. Evidently the captain did not want to work through pack ice in darkness.

Thorshøvdi with a tabular iceberg behind

In the morning we steamed through strips of pack ice with some quite heavy floes. When the ship struck a big floe, shock waves raced through the structure before *Thorshøvdi*'s heavy bow plating edged the ice aside. Several of us newcomers to the Antarctic leant over the side to watch the spectacle, marvelling at our seemingly unstoppable progress through floes, each of which must have weighed several hundred tonnes.

Knowing that whaling was about to begin, an air of excitement pervaded the ship. The flensing decks were cleared for action, steam winches were kept turning, derricks were rigged, and razor-sharp flensing knives were stacked beneath the forward superstructure. Whereas sickles are ground on the inside of the blade, flensing knives are ground on the outside, making them a real danger to anyone touched by the weapon.

The catchers were some way off when one of them made the first kill. Early on 10 December, just off one of the South Sandwich Islands, every department of the ship came alive. I looked out to see a sleek black sperm whale being dragged up the stern slipway, mouth open, its lower jaw studded with a vicious array of big teeth.

The catchers were soon bringing in fleets of whales, sometimes three at a time, towed tail first by a wire strop threaded around a tail fluke. The corpses were rapidly secured on lines astern, while a man on the catcher's harpoon gun-platform heaved a line to *Thorshøvdi* to take on fresh bread and whatever else they had requested. A provisional reward, I thought, for their good work. Then the catcher raced away.

Up to seven whales could be secured astern, waiting their turn for the slipway. If more were brought in, the catchers would come alongside, using one or two whales as fenders. This seemed to work even in a rough sea or an ocean swell.

Flensing began by manoeuvring a whale into position in the gaping mouth of the slipway. There a giant scissor-like steel claw was lowered onto the whale's tail, and as a deck winch began to haul, the scissors tightened. Even when hauling a 100-tonne blue, I was told, the claw was totally secure.

As the whale reached the flensing deck, I could see the harpoon hanging loosely, blood spurting from the wound and pouring from the animal's mouth. Three or four men leapt onto the carcass while it was still moving, cutting longitudinal strips of blubber, threading a giant wooden toggle through one end of each strip before securing it to a cable leading to a deck winch. From then on it was like peeling a banana, one strip at a time. Each strip was winched to the side of the

Sperm whale on the flensing deck of *Thorshøvdi*

deck, men nonchalantly standing on it as it slithered. Then it was cut into pieces and heaved into one of six gaping manholes, to fall into a cooker in the factory below. As soon as one side of the whale had been stripped, a grappling iron attached to another winch turned the carcass over, whereupon the men leapt on it to finish the job.

Once the blubber was dealt with, the rest of the whale was hauled through the midships gantry onto the forward flensing deck. This was the meat and bone deck. Men leapt onto the flesh, carving it into rough strips. Each piece was then, like the blubber, winched towards a manhole and consigned to the cookers. At intervals, a cloud of steam enveloped everyone as a cooker was discharged. Men walked around in the fog, holding their knives in front of them and coming danger-ously close to their colleagues. The casual way in which men swung these giant razor blades seemed to me the stuff of nightmares.

A derrick pulled the jaw apart. Sperm whales have teeth in the lower jaw that fit into sockets in the upper jaw, which itself has only vestigial teeth. By far the most frightening appliances on deck were the bone saws. They had straight blades nearly 2.5 metres long, steam pistons thrusting the blade back and forth at high speed, slicing through vertebrae, jaws and ribs with the greatest of ease. The pieces were then dragged to separate cookers to be rendered eventually to bonemeal.

The deck was covered with blood, slime and fat. My abiding terror was the thought of someone slipping on the deck and having his leg sawn off before the operator had time to stop the blade. Another hazard was the rate at which blubber and flesh slid headlong into the cookers once gravity took charge. A moment's hesitation could lead to disaster. Accidents of various kinds were not uncommon and, in the fleet as a whole, lives were normally lost before the end of the season. Whaling was a well-paid job and the risks were part of it.

From start to finish, the whole process of dismemberment, from slipway to cookers, sometimes took as little as 35 minutes. Long before one whale was finished, another was on deck being peeled. Only the stomach and entrails were pushed overboard – to the constant delight of flocks of circling seabirds and sometimes killer whales (*Orcinus orca*).

If there was a moment to spare between whales, men swept the layer of blood and slime from the deck into the cookers. I wondered if I could ever again eat margarine. The only occasions when the flensing crew evinced any emotion other than grim determination was when one of their number slipped and fell into the blood and guts on deck. Peels of laughter erupted among those who witnessed the incident. If there was any sympathy, it was lost in the mirth.

After passing four of the South Sandwich Islands, *Thorshøvdi* turned east and headed for Bouvetøya, an isolated volcanic island in the Southern Ocean. The catchers spread out in line abreast according to a pre-determined plan, each one so far from the next that it was below their horizon. This was a search sweep across a vast area. Now we were looking for the mighty baleen whales, the blue and the fin. However, we still could not kill them until the legal starting date of 22 December. The purpose of the sweep was to find where in this vast ocean there were concentrations of baleen whales. As soon as the season began, our catchers would then systematically return to the best areas. It was a bold and costly strategy, costly because we were leaving the best areas for sperm whales. However, in the long run it paid off because baleen whale oil was more valuable.

Odd XII went ahead of us as far as the Greenwich meridian but on 17 December, in position 58°S and 10°W, *Thorshøvdi* turned to head west because, at the start of the baleen season, the best fishing areas were closer to South Georgia. I thought it odd to be 'fishing' for whales, which are mammals, but that was the term used – in Norwegian as well as in English.

We were often in pack ice. It was well known – thanks in part to the British 'Discovery Expeditions' – that whales tended to concentrate at or near the ice edge. On some days we were in a sea of icebergs, 50 or more visible at once. Most were flat-topped ice-shelf bergs, of all sizes from 100 metres or so to many kilometres long. Fog was common and because we ploughed on regardless, I thought of *Titanic*. As Alan put it: 'If there is a crash and we start going down by the bows, we shall know that radar does not see icebergs.'

On 21 December we were back in sight of the South Sandwich Islands. Sperm whaling stopped at midnight. The scoreboard for the 11 days in which we were taking them was 159. Immediately after midnight, baleen whales started coming up the slipway. Many were two or three times the size of the sperm whales that we had been catching. Unlike sperm whales, baleen whales have no teeth. They live not on cuttlefish and squid like sperm whales, but on krill, crustacea less than half the size of an average shrimp. Gulping open-mouthed as it swims through a krill swarm, the whale closes its mouth and expels the water through the plates of baleen before swallowing the krill.

4

THE NINE-HOUR HOLIDAY

At breakfast the captain said that he had already had a piece of meat put aside for us. The piece we found at the side of the flensing deck must have weighed between 1 and 2 tonnes, though we had no way of telling. The foreman handed us flensing knives. The meat smelled more fishy than sperm-meat, 'just as whale steaks smell when we see them in a butcher's shop at home'.

We had to carry the meat, chunk by chunk, onto the fo'c'sle, where we were invariably greeted with a concert of delighted howls from the dogs. In the following days, our only official contact with the flensing crew was when one of us approached the foreman to ask for another half tonne of fillet steak.

Flensing a fin whale on *Thorshøvdi*

Some of the meat was very fresh but, when it was not, the dogs did not seem to mind eating putrefying meat – I suppose it had more flavour. When we first tried giving them 1 kilo per dog per day, they swallowed the whole piece in seconds without chewing. So we upped the ration to 3 kilos. Never in their lives had they been offered as much fresh meat as they could eat. The greedy ones were soon identified by the heaps of vomit beside them. Teeth were bared in anger if a neighbour so much as glanced in their direction. Most were so protective of their new-found wealth that they used hunks of meat as pillows to sleep on. However, over the next few days they gradually came to understand that, for the time being at least, an unlimited supply of best steak had become everyday fare.

The factory manager was now able to supply fresh dehydrated whale meat powder to make dog food. We could specify the amount of residual water in the product. More water would make digestion easier but would necessarily add weight. Weight, of course, would be critical on any long sledge journeys, so we faced a dilemma because a high water content would limit our range. However, on the understanding that thirsty dogs would simply eat more snow, we opted for a tinder-dry 3 per cent water content. Mixing 25 per cent whale oil, 10 per cent maize meal and 65 per cent meat powder, we made a sort of oily dumpling that would, we hoped, satisfy the dogs. Over the next few days we made and packed 90 boxes of this concoction, each one containing sixty plastic bags of a dog's daily ration of 0.5 kilo. In addition, we filled six sacks with protein concentrate for human consumption.

Whereas most of the catchers' activities were out of sight, one day we saw a chase nearby. Although the catcher was going at full speed, the whale stayed just ahead. We could see the gunner, his harpoon gun silhouetted against the sea, waving directions to the helmsman on the bridge. Twice the whale reversed course. Twisting and turning to follow it, the catcher heeled steeply as she tried to keep up but, as long as I watched, there was no kill. Some whales still manage to outwit their tormentors.

Flensing the baleen whales was similar to the sperm whales but, surprisingly, took very little longer. The baleen itself, almost priceless as a support for ladies' corsets in the eighteenth century, was now worthless and was put over the side with the entrails.

On the best day for the whalers – the worst day for the whales – more than 2,000 tonnes of dead whale were cut to pieces inside 24 hours. One blue whale I saw measured 26.5 metres. Sometimes catchers had to queue to transfer their catches. Meanwhile the pod of warm, waiting corpses astern was putrefying. I asked the senior chemist if there was any problem in marketing putrefied whale oil. He answered that it was mixed in the factory with fresher oil, so keeping the level of putrefaction products just below the government's upper limit. This struck me as a cynical ploy – but it was legal.

I found one of the government inspectors with a couple of fin whale's testicles. From the look of them, each must have weighed about 10 kilos. Collecting them was part of his research into breeding cycles. He was also collecting baleen for later analysis of the age of the

Baleen in the mouth of a fin whale

37

whale. The annual growth cycle leaves a succession of light and dark bands in the baleen which, like tree rings, can be counted.

A foetus emerged as one blue whale was dissected – murdered in its mother's womb, 'as sad a sight for the whalers as it is for a human being, for it means one less whale next year'. My slur on the humanity of whalers was unintended.

Christmas celebrations were on 24 December, as is customary in Scandinavia. Whaling stopped for nine hours to allow the flensing and factory crews to relax – the only holiday they were to have during the whole season. They would have been given even less time if there was a big queue of whales off the stern. Bloody clothes were temporarily discarded, showers taken, and every man dressed in his best. Collar and tie looked out of place under young beards and fresh, suntanned faces.

The captain's saloon was decorated and there was a Christmas tree. A small Norwegian flag and a Christensen house flag stood on each table. A surfeit of bottles made clear that, whatever the ship's rules, Scandinavian feasting habits were not to be denied. We were assigned places at table, each with our name, and beside each place was a parcel. Telegrams from home gave pleasure to many. All the parcels were identical and, on opening them, we found a pewter dish embossed with the company flag and a classic whaling scene: catcher boat on an angry sea, the gunner at his platform, the harpoon finding its target, and the whale writhing. At the time it seemed just a natural part of life's rich pageant.

My neighbour at table was a shy, friendly and handsome man of about 35. As the war had played a big part in the lives of most Norwegians, I began by asking if he had been involved. Yes, he said. On discovering the tribulations of life under the Nazis, he had sailed from Göteborg in Sweden in an attempt to run the gauntlet to England under cover of darkness. Intercepted by the German Navy off the coast of Denmark, he spent three years 'as a guest of the Third Reich'.

I put the same question to Larsen, the senior chemist. He had spent 18 months in a concentration camp for 'thinking the wrong way', as he put it. However, being fluent in German, he was given a privileged position and allowed access to camp records. Often he was given a set of clothes and told to list the contents of the pockets – the owner had just been shot. He remembered the winter's snow being red with the blood of Jews. To test whether his thinking had been 'cured', as his hosts put it, he was asked if he thought Jews were human beings. He replied that if you looked at it in a biological way, they were. The Gestapo recorded that Mr Larsen was 'not yet cured'.

In Norway's war there was none of the mass slaughter of battles

38

elsewhere. Those who fought in occupied countries fought alone. I turned to young Sverdrup, on the other side of the table, asking how he had spent the war. He was so young that I could not imagine that he had done any more than I had, but I was wrong. He had been a radio operator sending messages to England from a secret transmitter. When the Gestapo finally tracked him down and he heard their approaching motorcycles, he escaped from the back of the house. A few seconds later and his fate would have been to be lined up against a wall in Oslo's Akershus Fortress – and shot.

Each man's story was different. Though modestly – sometimes humorously – told, in all of them were acts of courage, endurance, and self-sacrifice played out against a background of simple, unbreakable patriotism. Some of their tales were so harrowing that it almost seemed that to die in battle would be an easier way out.

When finally we retired to bed after six hours of feasting, talking and singing, the flensing deck was bathed in floodlights and whale carcasses were once again on the move. At home, I realized, Christmas was just beginning.

The next few days found us catching more whales than any other ship in the Antarctic. There were as many as five whales on deck at once, each one stretched out over its full 20–25 metres. The queue

Whales in the queue for flensing

astern was full of whales bulging like balloons with the gases of putre-faction, half their bulk out of the water. Catchers were circling the ship, each one towing two, three or four whales. The factory cookers were becoming a bottleneck because they could not do their job fast enough – there was a minimum cooking time for each load. For one period the catchers were even told to stop catching, because it was illegal to flense whales which had been dead for more than 33 hours. At other times the flensing crew sacrificed half their lunch hour to hasten the whales on their way to the cookers. Rotting whale meat was no longer red but a shade of light green, and the stench was awful. 'The scene on deck is repulsive', I wrote.

Some days later, the captain invited us for drinks in his cabin to celebrate the New Year and the glut of whales. The factory had processed 13,000 barrels of oil in the last seven days, against an average week's haul of 4,000. The atmosphere was festive, with the captain and mate chirping and grinning like children. This was Hansen's first factory command. He was probably the youngest skipper afloat and his whole future depended on the size of the catch.

John Giæver asked us by radio to bring 20 tonnes of whale meat with us when we transferred to *Norsel*, 2 tonnes of it for human consumption and the rest for the dogs. Whale meat goes off fast if left in large chunks, so we had to cut it into pieces weighing 10-20 kg and hang each one separately on the deck rails to dry. In that position, salt drying out of sea spray would help to preserve them. For days on end we arranged with the deck foreman to set aside a tonne or more to be cut up. By the time the work was finished, our clothes were as bloody and stinking as the whalers'. It was a miracle that we were still allowed in the captain's saloon. The explanation must be that if everyone stinks, nobody notices.

By this time we were looking forward to the rendezvous with *Norsel*. However, there was a problem – *Thorshøvdi*'s position was a well-kept secret. This was because the weekly catch of each factory ship had to be reported to the Bureau for Whaling Statistics in Oslo. Anyone reporting good catches would act as a magnet to other factory ships. The purpose of reporting was to tally the numbers of each species taken, so that the fishery could be closed on reaching an agreed total. This was a sensible device designed to protect the stocks from overfishing. The agreed total for this season was 16,000 'blue whale units'. One blue whale unit was decreed to be equal to 1 blue whale, 2 fin whales, 2½ humpback or 6 sei whales.[1]

How was *Norsel* to find us if she did not know where to look? Weather reports might give an indication. Most of the factory ships sent weather reports to Cape Town so that meteorologists could make

40

forecasts. Positions were in code and only the South Africans had the key, but ocean weather charts and forecasts were broadcast.

Norsel had left Cape Town on 28 December. From earlier discussions, they expected to find *Thorshøvdi* roughly in the longitude of Cape Town (18°E), so headed due south. However, the meteorologists in *Norsel* noticed that the weather *Thorshøvdi* was reporting was not what the weather charts indicated for longitudes east of Greenwich.

It came as a bombshell when, on 2 January 1950, they learned that we were hove to in the Scotia Sea between South Georgia and the South Orkney Islands. At this latitude, their position and ours were nearly 5,000 kilometres apart, equivalent to 12 days' steaming. This was a most unwelcome delay in our transfer and the expedition's progress.

Norsel now sent us her position daily and it was evident that she was struggling through storms. When she eventually found us in a fog on 12 January, there was a sea running and we were amongst icebergs. The icebergs made it impossible for them to distinguish between *Thorshøvdi* and many other radar targets in the vicinity. Impossible, that is, until they found themselves downwind of us. The smell struck them like a sledge-hammer. Then all they had to do was to head upwind until our great bulk loomed out of the fog.

The rough sea made trans-shipment impossible for two days, but one thing could not wait – the mail for *Thorshøvdi* from Cape Town. A catcher drew alongside *Norsel* and transferred the mail sacks on a heaving line. Shortly thereafter, 400 men were eagerly opening letters from home, though some were disappointed.

Captain Guttorm Jakobsen of the *Norsel* and the expedition leader Captain John Giæver, anxious not to add to the already serious delay in our timetable, suggested heading for calmer water in the lee of an iceberg. Behind the iceberg the ocean swell was still heavy but Captain Hansen raised a loudspeaker and yelled, 'Come along, *Norsel*, come along! We're making an attempt.' The moment for which we had waited for months had arrived.

A catcher towed a couple of whales to *Norsel* and secured them alongside, one forward, one aft. Many of *Thorshøvdi*'s crew lined the rails as *Norsel* gingerly warped alongside; we could see how overloaded she was. Only small patches of deck space showed between bunches of fuel drums lashed to the rails. An enormous crate sat by the after cargo hatch and on top of it was one of the RAF Austers. The second Auster, without its wings, was inside the crate.

Rather than shouting from the deck below, Captain Jakobsen climbed up his mast to the crow's-nest to discuss the cargo transfer eye to eye with Captain Hansen. We wondered how the crew could transfer weasels, each weighing 2 tonnes, to the deck of a rolling,

Norsel alongside *Thorshøvdi* using whales as fenders. One aircraft sits on top of a crate containing the second aircraft

heaving ship below, without killing or injuring men waiting on the fo'c'sle to receive them. There were anxious faces and then anxious moments as we realized that, because of the great disparity in size, *Thorshøvdi*'s sedate pitching was out of phase with *Norsel*'s faster bobbing motion.

The first thing to go across was the crated ice-drilling machine, all 2 tonnes of it. Ten men stood on the opposite side of the fo'c'sle, hauling on a line to slow the swinging crate towards its allotted spot. With consummate skill, the crane driver lowered away fast at the exact moment when *Norsel* was falling into a trough. The crate was then levered into place with crowbars. Next came the weasels, one on the hatch cover and two beside it. Then the spare weasel tracks, and after that, the crates of dog food that we had made. By this time there was no space that was not buried beneath cargo. Finally the dogs were transferred a few at a time in a cage and then let loose on top of everything else. There they were to stay, urinating and defecating at random, until we reached our destination. There was no other way.

The focus then moved aft to load the whale meat. There was no deck space there either, so the meat was hurled, chunk by chunk, on to a pile of cargo sledges sitting on the after hatch cover. From there it

The ice drilling machine is swung aboard *Norsel* from *Thorshøvdi*

43

was spread out on top of everything else. One of the whalers, keen to get the job done quickly, missed his target and hit the tail of the Auster. The RAF crew were mightily upset but decided that the damage could probably be repaired.

Jakobsen and Giæver were invited aboard *Thorshøvdi* for lunch with Captain Hansen. The pair of them were hoisted in a large wicker basket hanging precariously from a derrick. An hour later, it was our turn to ride the basket, lowered two at a time onto the heaving deck of *Norsel*.

I sensed what the whalers were thinking. Anyone who would voluntarily sacrifice the security of a factory ship for an overloaded coracle about to cross some of the stormiest seas on earth must be unbalanced. As we cast off and moved away, there was many a sceptical face looking down on us; but they smiled and waved. Thus did Norway's largest whaling factory and Norway's largest sealer part company.

John Giæver was tall, handsome, and had a commanding presence. He kept a ready smile and I liked him at once. John told me that he had grown up in Tromsø and, after training as a journalist, served on the local newspaper. Tromsø was full of the comings and goings of sealers, trappers and fishermen, and John succumbed to the lure of adventure. As a trapper in north-east Greenland, he lived through four polar winters before becoming a sealer. Then from 1935 until the war, he worked for the government department that oversaw Norwegian Arctic research. In 1940 he led an expedition to Greenland to recover the trappers marooned by the war, but decided not to return to occupied Norway. After a period in London he joined the exiled Royal Norwegian Air Force and was made head of a training camp in Canada known as Little Norway. After the German surrender he helped to reinstate the civil administration in Finnmark, while organizing supplies of food from Sweden. After staying in the air force until 1948, he had returned to the newly constituted Norsk Polarinstitutt in Oslo.

Isolated though we were, the expedition's press contracts required John to transmit progress reports almost daily. As I later discovered, half the world knew what we were doing – certainly readers of *La Prensa* (Buenos Aires), the *New York Times, Times of Malta, Egyptian Gazette, Calcutta Statesman, Bulawayo Chronicle, West Australian, Toronto Globe, Johannesburg Star* and *New Zealand Herald*, in addition to countless newspapers in our home countries.

Below decks in *Norsel* we were soon preoccupied with joyful reunions with colleagues whom we had not seen for three months, and with introductions to the rest. Many of them sported beards, which

John Giæver

gave me a moment's hesitation before recognizing some. There were three strangers, belonging neither to the crew nor to the wintering party. One was Phillip Law, Officer in Charge of the Australian National Antarctic Research Expeditions. He came as an observer to learn about problems of working in Antarctica. Australia had maintained stations on Heard Island and Macquarie Island but now hoped to extend their work to the mainland. Short and wiry, Phil had a pointed beard and was known on board as Saint Paul the Apostle.

The second observer was Joseph King, head of the Synoptic and Forecasting Branch of the South African Weather Bureau. A genial man with a roundish face, he seemed like the archetypal Afrikaner. The third stranger was Tom Stobart, film photographer from the British Crown Film Unit, here to make a record of the first stage of the expedition. Clearly an enthusiast, he was disappointed to find no great eagerness for helping him to produce a blockbuster.

Several members of the expedition I had not met before. Nils Jørgen Schumacher, the 30-year-old Norwegian chief meteorologist, had short hair and big round eyes. He looked faintly Russian, and was

45

referred to as the Russian spy. Ove Wilson, the doctor, was 'a small pale-faced little boy of 26'. Perhaps his diary in its turn portrayed me as a child of 23 – I shall never know. Ove had served his stint in the Swedish Army, spoke fluent English and radiated self-assurance. Whether or not he was competent, on the other hand, none of us knew at that stage. Evidently he was sensitive to the people around him and certainly more imaginative than the rest of us. He delighted in pedantic argument and found in me a soulmate.

Captain Jakobsen, Guttorm to us, wore battledress and seemed to be intentionally inconspicuous. Small in stature, he was 39 years old and had been at sea since the age of 15. I was told that by the time war broke out in 1939, he had years of experience on the sealing grounds and had acquired both master's and radio operator's licences. During the war he was injured when the freighter *Vito* was bombed and sunk. Later he was master of a tanker and, four years on, survived the sinking of *Herøyfjord*, sister ship of *Norsel*, while she was carrying 25,000 sealskins on a homeward voyage from Newfoundland. Typically, he frowned with the distant look of a sailor, but this was only because he chose not to wear sunglasses. He took his meals in the crew's mess. On the bridge he worked as navigator, watchkeeping officer and radio operator. I soon realized that he was liked by all on board.

The chief engineer was Guttorm's brother, Torgils Jakobsen. Both were partners in Brødrene Jakobsen of Tromsø, *Norsel*'s owners. The family atmosphere was enhanced even further by the fact that John Giæver had been at school in Tromsø with Guttorm. In their youth, both had encountered Roald Amundsen, Tromsø's most famous son.

Norsel seemed to us a very small ship. Only 46 metres long, 9 metres wide, and overloaded, she seemed unstable. We newcomers were allotted cabins aft. In rough weather this meant a traverse in seaboots along an open deck to reach the shelter of the forward super-structure. Freeboard on the well deck was only 0.3 metres, so that in high seas, when *Norsel* was shipping it green, we just had to judge the right moment and run – on penalty of being washed overboard.

Conditions on board, to put it mildly, were crowded, but everyone seemed to behave in a cheerful and tolerant manner. There was a comfortable saloon for the expedition members, and surprisingly, a cupboard full of gin, whisky, wine, brandy and aquavit. We could help ourselves to whatever we fancied. As my diary put it, 'There are plenty of compensations for moving to this small ship.'

The food, however, was not one of them. The cooks had to prepare meals within the confines of a tiny overheated galley, feeding all the crew and expedition members without fail whatever the weather. One memorable staple of our diet was pork pickled in brine. It came from small wooden barrels and was served in the form of amorphous chunks, more fat than meat and with tufts of skin and hair still attached. The cabbage and potatoes had evidently suffered in the tropics but good fresh bread was baked daily. Another staple was *labskaus*, a sort of hash of slightly spoiled meat and potato mixed into a warm sludge. Then there was *klippfisk*, rehydrated cod served as a *bacalao*. However, nobody was expecting gourmet food, and meals always ended, as in all of Scandinavia, with each of us thanking the cook for the food: '*Takk for maten.*'

5

ORDEAL BY ICE

In describing our progress southwards across the Weddell Sea, Giæver wrote:

> Norsel set out on her maiden voyage like a lively young filly, buoyant and gay, fresh in her coat of gleaming white. Now she is more piteously overladen than a donkey of Arabia and she lumbers along with the heavy motions of a sow. For that matter, she is just as dirty and smells worse. May the weather-gods of the Antarctic have mercy upon us![1]

Sir Miles Clifford, Governor of the Falkland Islands, had kindly offered 13 new dogs if we could come to South Georgia to receive them. The expedition sorely needed more to make up for the casualties on *Thorshøvdi*. Giæver, however, was acutely concerned for the seaworthiness of our overloaded ship, so opted instead to head south-east, straight for the shelter of pack ice. We could breed dogs ashore, he argued, but if the ship capsized, neither dogs nor men would ever breed again. He had a point.

We were soon ploughing through strips of pack ice. Adélie penguins (*Pygoscelis adeliae*) offered an endless source of entertainment, racing along just beneath the waves before porpoising clear of the water. Then seals appeared on ice floes, arousing the killer instincts of our crew, most of whom were professional sealers.

I went up on the bridge at sunset, to find the captain crouched behind the sights of a rifle, the muzzle pointing to an ice floe. On the floe, now sliding down the starboard side of the ship, was a sleeping crabeater seal. Guttorm fired. The seal heaved, quivered, and fell. Guttorm fired again and blood spurted over the clean white snow. A seaman leapt onto the ice, attached a line to the seal, and jumped back aboard. Eager hands hoisted the animal on board; it was 2 metres long and must have weighed about 150 kilos. A couple of seamen skinned it with consummate ease in the space of two minutes, after which Alan Reece and Tom Stobart fumbled around in its steaming innards to extricate the delicacies. They went to the galley to prepare a midnight feast of liver and kidneys.

The dogs dealt with the rest of the seal. One sailor told me that, during the Newfoundland sealing season, the long cold hours he spent on ice floes were relieved by the constant availability of hot drinks: he would stab a seal's artery and drink from the fountain of blood. Later he demonstrated before wiping his mouth with snow.

No mercy was shown because we needed the meat to feed the dogs – it seemed that anything that moved was shot. One day a gigantic blue whale surfaced beside the ship and a seaman shot it. He could not have killed it, but that one callous act of unthinking brutality has haunted me for half a century. By now I could tolerate killing, though not pointless killing.

On crossing the Antarctic Circle on 20 January, all newcomers had to undergo an initiation ceremony. A ghostly, bearded figure appeared, veiled in white and wearing flying boots. Bearing some resemblance to Phil Law, it exhorted us to behave properly in the Antarctic. A minute later it reappeared without the veil but instead with a double dog chain, then beckoned to the captain and John Giæver. They were led away like dogs and followed at intervals by the next hapless pair. When my turn came, I was made to stand on a box with the skin of an emperor penguin (*Aptenodytes forsteri*) draped over it. I knelt as Gordon Robin directed me to recite an oath printed on a card that he held. As long as I stayed in 'the icy realm', I had to foreswear the company of women and several other 'iniquities' of civilization. At my side stood Alan, dressed like a pirate, holding the bitch Sally. Now Sally's paw, dipped in fresh warm seal's blood, was pushed into my hand to seal the oath. This was followed by a more congenial rite – a swig of *brennevin*. When crew members knelt before the officials, their oath was seen to be written – conveniently – in Norwegian.

Giæver had to curb some overzealous sailors from shooting at penguins for the fun of it. A former sealer himself, it was not that he was squeamish about killing but simply that in terms of dog food, penguins were not worth stopping for. Seals were. However, he did allow some emperors to be slain for the pot. That evening the cook, Selmer Øvergård, served breast of penguin with bacon slices. While somewhat fishy in taste, it was dark, dense and satisfying. Others preferred braised whale steak with onions. The leftovers became next day's whaleburgers.

Fred Roots and Hugh Tudor prepared a midnight feast of seal's heart, tongue and liver – and for good measure – emperor penguin's liver, kidney, heart and testicles.

The following day we entered heavy, continuous pack ice. Guttorm climbed to the crow's-nest and from there conned the ship by remote control. It was an eerie sensation to stand in a deserted wheelhouse while the bow twisted and turned to avoid the heaviest chunks. *Norsel* seemed to plough on inexorably, crashing headlong into floes, rising up on them, splitting them, and wriggling through the gap. Her rapid response to the helm meant that she could find the weak points and push floes apart. Her slim width at the waterline meant that she could slip through gaps which would bring a beamier ship to a standstill. Surrounded by whiteness solid enough to stand on, we noted how fast the ice closed in behind the ship. Our track was marked only by a meandering line of broken ice floes. Most of the time we made about 4 knots, but at intervals we were brought to a standstill. After motoring astern for a length or so, we again charged the ice.

Sometimes we came to open areas and made good progress. However, we had problems with slushy ice. Although quite thin, it caused so much friction that *Norsel* was struggling. If the propeller was stopped, it took only five seconds for the ship to stop dead in the water. Although a swell was coming in from the open sea, the slush was so dense that a man could stand on it.

Walking on an ocean swell was not something that I had expected to do in the Antarctic. However, Tom Stobart did put a foot through before deciding that this was not the best platform for filming.

A sailor strode in shirtsleeves over the undulating mass of snow, casually driving a wriggling seal before him. Using a stick to direct it, the scene was reminiscent of a country farmer guiding a solitary cow towards his barn. On reaching the ship, he shot the animal.

Several penguins came to admire the ship, standing a few metres away while chatting to each other and waving their flippers. Some were brought aboard to amuse the crew. The penguins were left to explore the ship and soon became accepted as part of the scene. They wandered along passages and into rooms, looking mystified and perturbed, though by no means cowed, when any man approached them. I found an Adélie inspecting the bathroom facilities and, when I too needed to pay a call, he waved his flippers, bursting with indignation and pecking at me. Fred Roots was writing letters in the saloon, unmoved by three penguins arguing with each other under the table.

On 25 January we entered heavier ice at 69°S, 06°E and were brought to a standstill. We saw and killed three of the quite rare Ross seals. Phil Law prepared grilled seal brains according to an Australian recipe, but there were few takers.

Several of us took skis onto the ice to get some exercise. Egil Rogstad had once had the distinction of competing in national ski-jumping competitions at Oslo's Holmenkollen in the presence of King Haakon. Now he marked a circuitous course with pieces of wood and empty beer bottles, and with a loud hailer announced an international ski race. We were hardly surprised when he won the first race. The second was a relay race with contestants from Norway, Sweden, England, Canada and Australia. Nils Roer won in a very fast time, closely followed by Ove Wilson. I felt proud to represent my country in an international ski race on a 2,000-metre-deep ocean – though my country could never be proud of my performance.

The sky was clear and the sun, reflected from the snow, was so dazzling that for the first time in my life I had to set my camera shutter to one thousandth of a second. It proved to be the first of many such occasions. The air temperature on days like this was hardly below freezing but at night the thermometer dropped to around –7°C, just pleasantly nippy as long as there was not much wind.

The fresh water supply on board was running low, so next morning a working party went over the side and hacked lumps off ice hummocks. It was well known that brine slowly drains out of sea ice, so hummocks often yield faintly salty but still acceptable drinking water. Using a human chain, we passed the blocks to an open tank on

International ski race on the pack ice

51

the after deck in which steam-heated pipes gradually converted the ice to water.

Two sailors went for a walk on the ice and reappeared driving three emperor penguins before them. Laughing heartily at the birds, they hit them over the head and skinned them, evidently with the intention of taking the skins home as gifts. Later, braised breast of penguin steaks appeared on the menu.

The weather was fine at the time but a brilliant ice blink – the white glare reflected on the underside of overcast clouds – warned of unbroken pack ice to the south. *Norsel* was able to move at intervals by opening narrow leads. I imagined our ship as a steamer plying rivers that were too narrow for us. Though aiming for midstream, we sometimes rammed the banks and bounced off. When meanders became too tight, we simply ploughed across the flood plain to the next meander. My daydream ended as we came to the source of one meandering river and stuck fast.

For two whole days we were beset – unable to move. John Giæver felt that we were getting nowhere by trying to press on east of the Greenwich meridian, so he asked Guttorm to retreat to the ice edge and then attempt to penetrate the pack in longitude 5°W. In prepara-

Norsel beset

tion for reconnaissance sorties, the Auster on top of the aircraft crate was mounted on floats. Brian Walford and Hugh Tudor were aching to get into the air, if only to check that everything was functioning.

On 1 February, Brian finally persuaded Giæver to let him have a go. He rushed below crying: 'Hugh, we're airborne!' The aircraft was suspended on a tiny wire from the main derrick. Guttorm worked the derrick because he would not trust anyone else to handle such a delicate load. Manoeuvring the Auster over the ship's side was hair-raising because there was very little clearance on all sides. So close were the floats to the ship's side that Hugh had to stand on one, pushing hard to keep it clear. Once on the water, a dinghy towed the machine away from the ship before embarking Hugh and leaving Brian alone to fly. The engine started easily, and Brian taxied back and forth to make sure that there were no small half-submerged ice blocks on his intended runway. A cheer went up from the bridge as the little plane rose from the water, back in its element for the first time in months.

The flight lasted 73 minutes, tracing the trend of the ice edge but failing to find any good leads southwards. On the basis of this report, Giæver decreed that *Norsel* should steam west along the ice edge before launching another flight in the hope of finding leads going south.

Removing the wheels before fitting floats to one of the Austers.

The next day dawned cloudy but flyable. This time it was Hugh Tudor's turn and he took Guttorm with him, reporting loose pack ice extending as far as he could see southwards. On landing, Hugh not only had to beware of ice on his runway but also whales. As the aircraft was being towed in by the dinghy, with Hugh and Guttorm each standing on one of the floats, two giant shiny black rumps heaved out of the water not 10 metres away. They were fin whales, startling us with a loud 'Poof' as they blew. All on board were afraid that they might come up underneath the plane, with potentially disastrous results, so the machine was lifted out of the water in record time.

Now thoroughly impressed by what the aircraft could do, Giæver quipped that a halo was rapidly forming over the airmen's heads. On the basis of their information, *Norsel* turned south.

Invited to have a go at the wheel, I steered for an hour. We were making about 5 knots south-south-west through some heavy and rafted floes, but there were leads and it was not difficult to push the floes aside. Guttorm seemed impressed with my ship-handling, before Valter whispered in his ear that I had been a watchkeeping officer in the Royal Navy.

By 3 February we were approaching the coast in clear weather. The mate was first to see it from the crow's-nest, and soon afterwards we all saw an unbroken line of cliffs ahead, looking not unlike the white cliffs of Dover. It was an ice front just like the 'barrier of ice' that Captain James Clark Ross had discovered a century ago on the other side of Antarctica. Ross's ships were HMS *Erebus* and HMS *Terror*, the date was 28 January 1841, and he was looking at what we now know as the Ross Ice Shelf.[2]

Norsel was not the first ship to approach the coast of Dronning Maud Land. Lars Christensen, scion of the family celebrated by the big C on *Thorshøvdi*'s funnels, had financed expeditions to these waters on board *Norvegia* before the war. *Norvegia* was a coal-fired converted sealing steamer of only 285 tons – small by any standard but evidently not too small to carry two floatplanes.

On 18 February 1930, Hjalmar Riiser-Larsen and Finn Lützow-Holm flew along the same stretch of coast that now, 20 years later, loomed ahead of us.[3] They described the ice front and also an ice dome rising to about 300 metres above sea level. They named the north-west corner of the dome Kapp (Cape) Norvegia; we could see that too on the starboard bow. Curiously enough, Ross's ships had come within a whisker of discovering this same ice dome on 5 March 1843, but missed seeing land because of 'constant snow and hazy weather'.[4]

Norsel stopped in a pool of water surrounded by pack ice. It was just large enough for the Auster to get airborne, so Giæver asked Brian Walford to search for any possible place where the ship could unload. Brian's response was succinct: 'Righto!' Flying south, he reported heavy hummocked pack ice beneath him, with floes about an acre in size. Reaching the ice front, he asked forgiveness for lapsing into poetic language to describe what he saw. The sun, now in the west, was shining obliquely on the dazzling ice cliffs. Never in his whole life, he said, had he seen anything so transcendingly beautiful. No words could 'capture the greatness and the awfulness' of the scene. Listening in to the radio exchanges, I could tell that he was overcome with emotion.

Most of the ice front was more than 20 metres high, making it impossible to unload hundreds of tonnes of cargo from a small ship. We needed a place where the cliff was no more than 5 metres high and was backed by a slope gentle enough for weasels towing sledges. Throughout the flight, we could see the aircraft through binoculars, a tiny dot in space, poised above the whiteness. Now flying east, Brian reported finding open water right up to the ice front. Putting his wing-

An Auster prepares for take-off. The ice front behind is 20 metres high.

tip level with the cliff top, he reported an altimeter reading of 125 feet (38 metres). 'Unscalable,' he said, 'even by commandos.' Finally turning homeward, he traced a path through leads that *Norsel* might push through.

An air of excitement filled the ship – at last we felt that our hopes and dreams might come to pass. Fred Roots, geologist by training but gourmet chef by inclination, served up whale steaks with chips and onions, and even made a Christmas pudding. We had thought that the ship was out of beer, but now eight hidden cases were discovered; aquavit and liqueurs were washed down with Norwegian ale late into the night.

Meanwhile *Norsel* worked steadily towards the coast. Guttorm was in the crow's-nest, so I climbed the mast and offered him a whale steak. He seemed to be spending most of his day and most of the night there, staring into the distance to plan the best way forward.

On 4 February, Hugh Tudor continued the search for an ice dock. He found three valley-like depressions that offered possible routes to the top. Meanwhile a seaman on the bridge kept watch on the echo sounder. At first he found no bottom at 1,000 metres, then as we came on to the continental shelf it showed 500 metres of water, and finally the seabed shoaled to 55 metres beside a promontory off which there were grounded icebergs. This was in 71°09′S, 11°24′W. By chance, it was the very same promontory that Riiser-Larsen had photographed from the air in 1930.[5] After supper Hugh took John Giæver flying to inspect the three possible landing places, but John judged each of them to be hazardous in one respect or another. On returning, he asked Guttorm to work his way west, round Kapp Norvegia to Selbukta (Seal Bay) in the hope of finding better conditions there.

We soon encountered larger, thicker, and more hummocked floes with greenish and jagged underwater shelves jutting from them. *Norsel* took blows greater than any we had experienced before. Several times there was a resounding crash, the ship heeled over, shuddered, and sheared away from a great cake of ice. From the bridge one could see them coming. Below decks, however, we were thrown against bulkheads without warning as though tossed in a great storm. We were grateful that the outside skin of the ship was both welded and riveted, and that her bow had 50-millimeter thick armour-plating.

A dog named Bosun, terrified by the commotion of ice-breaking, jumped overboard and swam to the nearest ice floe; he was picked up none the worse for it. When we tried to dry him with a sack, he wondered what all the fuss was about.

Early the following morning we were wakened by an explosion. Fred Roots had left a primus stove full of petrol on top of the cold, cast-iron

The ice shelf near Maudheim. The grounded promontory with icebergs in the foreground is the one seen by Riiser-Larsen in 1930. Norselbukta is the farther of the two inlets in the ice front

galley stove. He failed to notice that a crewman had come to light the stove to warm it up for the cook. The vapour exploded when Fred and a seaman were standing nearby. Fred's hair and beard were singed and the seaman's clothes were alight. Both rushed outside and managed to extinguish the flames. On returning inside, they found the varnish on the galley cupboards burning. The pantry door had been blown off its hinges, a dozen other doors were damaged, and the glass fronts of two cupboards in the officers' mess were shattered. Some of those below who tried to leave their cabins found the doors jammed. The chief engineer was furious because pieces of his door were scattered over the deck. Fred was embarrassed and chastened, his hair now shorter, his beard lopsided, and he had minor burns on his cheek. The only good thing to come out of the affair was a general realization that if anything ignited the aircraft fuel on deck, *Norsel* would retire to Davy Jones's locker and our families would never know what happened.

At this stage I felt there was rather too much indecision on the bridge. The question was whether we should try reaching the coast further west, or instead take a closer look at the coast to the east. Brian flew into Selbukta and pronounced it impenetrable by the ship, so we turned east. All of us were now aware that the season was well advanced: we must find a place to land – or risk spending the winter trapped in drifting pack ice.

We would not be the first. A couple of days' steaming from our position, Wilhelm Filchner's *Deutschland* had been beset and forced to spend the winter of 1912 in pack ice,[6] and Sir Ernest Shackleton's *Endurance* spent the winter of 1915 in the same area before being crushed and sunk.[7] Riiser-Larsen himself had specifically warned Giæver: 'Beware of the Weddell Sea!'

On attempting to return to the area where the airmen had reported possible landing places, we spent four days stuck or moving slowly through very rough ice floes, some of them 3 metres thick. It was not the kind of ice for *Norsel* to break; she could only find weak points where floes could be pushed apart. After sighting the ice front, all was obscured by a drifting fog bank.

Guttorm was summoned to the bridge when the officer of the watch realized that the ship was in a perilous position – directly upwind of a couple of icebergs and inexorably drifting towards them. The pack ice, and with it the ship, was being driven by wind and tide, whereas the icebergs were motionless and probably aground. On surveying the situation, Guttorm rang down 'Full ahead', and with considerable difficulty fought clear before we were pushed against ice cliffs taller than the mast. Passing the icebergs, we noted that there was a 'wake' of open water in their lee as if they had been charging through the pack ice. It was hard to comprehend that it was not the icebergs but the pack ice that was moving.

On 10 February Hugh Tudor took off in the Auster, flying very low because the cloud base was barely higher than the ice front. Disappearing from our view, he told us that he had been forced to climb to clear the cliffs. Not long afterwards he reported finding a potential landing place in a bay that was free of pack ice. Returning to the ship, he next took off with John Giæver to seek a second opinion. Excitement rose as John sounded optimistic, and finally Brian Walford took Gordon Robin up for a third opinion. *Norsel* followed and, after ploughing through some heavy pack ice, entered a V-shaped inlet

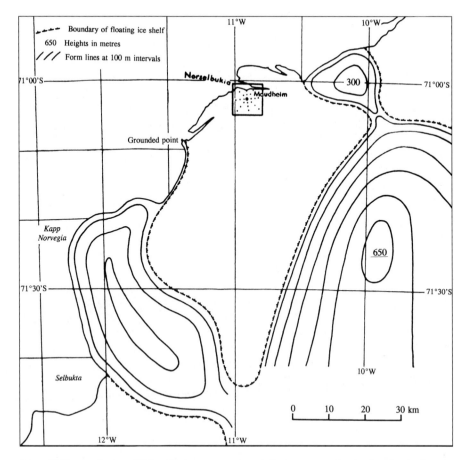

Map 4 The environs of Maudheim—reproduced from a map drawn by the author in 1952. Inset shows the Maudheim stake pattern used in ice deformation and snow accumulation studies

about 3 kilometres in length. Everyone came up on the bridge and we waited and watched – in hope and in silence as the calm water hissed against the bows. On the north side of the inlet there was a point curving upward to a level some metres higher than the rest of the cliff. On the south side there appeared to be a cove just large enough to take the ship. Only inside the cove was the ice cliff low enough to bring the ship alongside – everywhere else it was mast-high. A sounding showed 400 metres depth of water.

Norsel gingerly 'docked', securing the ship with lines attached to 'deadmen' – logs buried in the snow. The lines were kept taut, with no slack allowed for tides, because the ship and the ice front would rise

59

and fall together. The ice dock was barely as long as the ship but it was 3 metres above sea level and ideal for unloading.

We wondered whether the ice shelf might offer a good site for our base. However, one thing gave pause for thought: like it or not, ice shelves are the mothers of icebergs. From time to time, great slabs 'calve' from the ice front and drift away to sea, where sooner or later they melt. As Giæver put it, 'The thought that we might eventually sail into the Weddell Sea on top of an iceberg was not entirely pleasing.'[8]

But at this stage of the season it was too late to pick and choose. Valter Schytt was despatched with a party on skis to reconnoitre the area. We watched them climb the initial slope that appeared to be well within the capacity of weasels towing sledges. The skiers disappeared over a horizon perhaps 300 metres away. After venturing 1 kilometre inland, they reported a valley which might represent a line of weakness along which calving could occur. Beyond this valley, the surface of the ice shelf appeared as a level, featureless and crevasse-free plain.

It was what we had been looking for. Unloading began immediately; first the 43 wretched dogs, who had not been able to stretch their legs for months, and then the weasels, on which we depended for moving hundreds of tonnes of cargo a safe distance inland. By *inland* I mean towards the continent, because it was now evident that the nearest land, or even ice resting on rock, was far away. For two years – if the worst did not happen – we would be living on ice that we had to assume was attached to the continent, while all the time our home would be rising and falling with the tide. I even wondered whether we might, on stormy days, feel an ocean swell under our feet. However, from now on we would have no time for morbid thoughts.

On the first day of unloading I worked with Ekström on getting the weasels working. Sea water had penetrated the gearboxes of two of them and there were electrical problems from corrosion. We finally retired to our bunks at 0300 the next day. From now on, I could see, the concept of working hours was dead – we were to work until cross-eyed, and then start again a few hours later.

6

TERRA INFIRMA

After breakfast on 11 February, Giæver summoned Valter Schytt, Knalle Ekström and me to go with him to reconnoitre for a base site. We took two weasels connected by 20 metres of wire rope, so that if one vehicle lurched into a crevasse, the other could arrest its fall. Knalle drove the lead vehicle, with Valter as passenger, while I drove the second, with Giæver as passenger. It was the first time I had ever contemplated falling into a crevasse with 2 tonnes of steel under me. As it turned out, the trail of the earlier ski party was crevasse-free. After driving nearly 3 kilometres we stopped on a level plain 37 metres above sea level that appeared to continue unbroken towards a distant ice ridge. There the ice must be resting on rock and thus beyond the reach of any possible calving. It was out of the question, however, to attempt to haul several hundred tonnes that far within the time available and with the weasels in their present condition.

After consulting with us, Giæver kicked his heel into the snow and said, 'Let us build here.' It was a defining moment of the expedition: on his choice could our fortunes or our lives depend.

If all went well, we would be the first wintering party on the continent between Snow Hill Island (57°W) in the west and Shackleton Ice Shelf in the east (95°E). Attempts had been made, but there had not been a foothold on almost half the coastline of Antarctica. Snow Hill Island was occupied in 1903[1] and Shackleton Ice Shelf in 1912.[2]

The surveyor Nils Roer in due course reported that our position, based on his astronomical observations, was 71°03'S, 10°56'W.

Back at the ship, unloading was getting into high gear. The dogs were already ashore, but now followed everything on the upper deck: sledges, fuel drums, dog-food boxes, whale meat, spare weasel tracks and the drilling machine. The aircraft were literally put on ice, towed away and fitted with skis. Only then could the ship's hatches be opened to get into the holds.

The dogs were on 2-metre chains fixed at intervals along a length of steel wire. Each end of the wire was secured by metal stakes hammered into the snow. Before being put ashore, the animals had been drinking water from buckets for months and some had forgotten that there was any other way to quench their thirst. Soon desperately thirsty like rabid dogs, they became progressively more frantic. Casting around in their rage for something or someone to bite, sooner or later they gnashed their teeth into the snow. Then one by one, they began to notice that their lips were wet. It was fascinating to watch as it dawned on them – some faster than others – that there was an unlimited supply of fresh water right under their noses. They had seen buckets for the last time.

Guttorm had remained calm throughout our long search for a landing, but he now realized that *Norsel* was pushing her luck. It was late in the season and his thoughts were already turning towards a period of sealing off Newfoundland. By staying with us, he could be sacrificing part of the company's chief source of income, quite apart from the risk of becoming frozen fast in the Weddell Sea.

His crew were thinking along the same lines. The result was a phenomenal pace of unloading the cargo, night and day. At the same time, *we* knew that because the integrity of our ice dock could not be guaranteed, everything had to be moved away from the ship as fast as possible. It would be all too easy to lose some vital supplies – or people – to the sea if a slice of the cliff should fall away. Such thoughts raced through my mind every time I backed my weasel up against the ship.

Up at the base, Nils Roer laid out the site plan, deciding where to build the two living huts, the diesel generator hut, the 'rawin'* hut and the drilling machine hut. Next, encircling the site, bamboo poles were planted to mark where each category of cargo would be unloaded from the weasel sledges. Many months before, much thought had gone into the classification of every case and every item in it so that, when it was needed, we would know in which heap of stores to look for it.

The sections were:

1. Base provisions
2. Sledging provisions
3. Household equipment
4. Kitchen utensils
5. Bedding
6. Clothing
7. Cooking and heating stoves

---

* Radio theodolite used to track radiosonde (meteorological) balloons.

8.   Paints and brushes
9.   Tools
10. Huts
11. Electrical equipment
12. Fuel and lubricants
13. Skis and sledging equipment
14. Hunting equipment
15. Stationery
16. Books and maps
17. Meteorological equipment
18. Glaciological equipment
19. Geological equipment
20. Biological equipment
21. Surveying equipment
22. Other scientific equipment
23. Photographic equipment
24. Radio equipment
25. Medical equipment
26. Weasels
27. Aircraft
28. Dories
29. Miscellaneous
30. Medical research equipment
31. Dogs and dog food
32. Chronometers and watches

Each of the three countries had been allocated 3,000 case numbers, so that the national origin of any box could be seen at a glance. Some sections listed one or two cases, whereas others, for example Section 1, listed more than 500. In principle, it was not difficult for the weasel drivers to unload at the right spot. The problems, we all knew, would begin when the boxes disappeared under snowdrifts during the first blizzard.

Brian Walford generously gave us his aircraft crate; it was dismantled on board and re-erected on base to serve as a garage. Now Knalle would have somewhere – apart from the open air – to overhaul the weasels. They kept failing as a result of their prolonged immersion under waves breaking over the bow of the ship. One of the drawbacks of amphibious vehicles like weasels was that water accumulated in their bilges instead of draining out. Knalle worked long hours every day to bring lifeless machines back into service. We thought of using the dogs to haul cargo but they were no match for weasel loads of 2–3 tonnes.

The base was to be known as Maudheim.[3] In a historical context, it

63

echoed the name of Framheim, Roald Amundsen's base on the Ross Ice Shelf in 1910–12[4]. An agreeable parallel – though not for us a race to the South Pole, or anywhere else, for that matter; our journeys would have no purpose apart from science.

On 13 February the base party was busy laying the foundations of the first living hut when Giæver received a telegram from Sverdrup advising him to move Maudheim 3 kilometres further from the ice front. After some discussion, John decided to ignore it. To me, Sverdrup's advice bore the hallmark of the maddening tendency of distant officials to believe that they know better than men on the spot. Giæver was right to ignore the advice. If we drifted away to sea, none of us would blame him.

There was, however, one pessimist on board. Schølberg Nilsen had not reckoned with living afloat in these circumstances, so he went to John Giæver with his concerns. John concluded that it would not be wise to keep any man against his will – yet what would we do without a cook? With Guttorm's permission, he approached the ship's steward, John Snarby, inviting him to consider taking Nilsen's place. Snarby, young and adventurous, had become a friend to all of us and he was said to know how to cook. Giæver gave him half an hour to think it over. Guttorm generously gave permission for Snarby to sign off if necessary. However, there was one slight problem: Snarby was married and they had a son. All of us were on tenterhooks until, following a brief exchange of telegrams, Mrs Snarby agreed.

Once again we numbered 14; but Giæver was also concerned about the heavy load that would fall on Gordon Robin in terms of the electrical installation on base and on Rogstad in terms of radio operating at unsocial hours.

The air unit's radio mechanic Leslie Quar had often spoken of his wish to join a wintering party. He was a first-rate technician and well liked by everyone. Now he reported for duty. Walford readily agreed and made arrangements with the Air Ministry that the expedition should have Quar on loan from the RAF until 1952. We were all delighted with this accession to the wintering party.[5]

Now we were 15. The food supply could stretch to that.

By the next day, *Norsel*'s after hold had been emptied, the aircraft were flying, all weasels were operating, and the heaps of boxes at Maudheim were growing. Later in the day, however, drifting snow was snaking over the surface and there was a whiteout.

In the absence of sunshine, some people think that their eyes can handle the glare. Whereas most of us wore sunglasses, John Giæver had been supervising both at the ship and at Maudheim without eye protection. By evening he was in great pain from snow blindness. He described it as feeling as if someone was poking pins into his eyeballs. Ove Wilson applied atropine to relieve the pain and prescribed total darkness for at least a week. John was not seen on deck again for a long time, and then only with dark glasses. It was a timely warning for all of us.

On 15 February I was up at 0530 and worked until 2300. The base crew of Valter, Fred Roots and Nils Roer, supported by half a dozen of the ship's crew, finished the external cladding on the first hut, so at last they had a snow-tight shelter.

For me there was one delightful interlude. The weather was fine and warm and some of the construction crew were working in shirtsleeves. Brian Walford invited me to fly with him to get a feel for the surroundings. Maudheim, I noticed, was about halfway between an ice dome to the east and the grounded point that we had found on 4 February and that Riiser-Larsen had photographed in 1930. By analogy with a glacier flowing between fixed margins, we must be on the fastest-moving part of the ice shelf. Sooner or later, the base would go out on an iceberg. However, being some way from grounded ice, we were also clear of areas where crevasses could be expected. Surveying the scene, I noted that our new home appeared as a very tiny dot in a vast wilderness. That was never to change.

Southwards lay a monotonously level plain reaching to a line about 30 kilometres away where the ice surface rose steeply towards an ice ridge perhaps 500 metres above sea level. Nowhere, not even to the farthest horizon, was there any sign of rock showing above the ice; just whiteness in directions east, west and south – and an ocean of pack ice to the north. After flying for 80 minutes, we landed, the skis quietly hissing as we slid to a halt close to where the ship was moored.

In the evening a telegram came from HM King Haakon VII of Norway, agreeing to the name Maudheim; as a matter of courtesy, his approval had been sought.

There was great excitement the following day when Brian Walford flew inland with Peter Weston from Kapp Norvegia to 73°S and discovered nunataks (rock outcrops) that were not on his map. Hugh flew with Leslie Quar over the same area in the afternoon and confirmed the discovery. Normally, the pilot who was not flying would act as air controller. However, this time both aircraft were in the air at the same time, so I was recruited as controller. The pilots' voices came bubbling over the airwaves and all of us shared in their elation. For each of them, it was the high point of their all too brief sojourn in

Antarctica. Walford felt as if he had intruded on a sacred place. Of sighting Maudheim in the distance he wrote:

> . . . a tiny dot appeared like the first signs of cancer on a healthy body. Man had come to stay. I felt ashamed that we in the air had helped to make this intrusion possible and I think I understood for the first time in my life that it was in fact 'the uttermost parts of the earth' untouched and unseen by man that were the purest both in spirit and form and thus the best and most vivid link between ourselves and our Creator.[6]

Later it transpired that the airmen had probably seen what the German expedition of 1938–39 had named Kraulberge. However, the Germans had put the nunataks on their map at a point 80 kilometres from their true position.[7]

Now 450 tonnes had been moved up to Maudheim and Giæver fixed the time of *Norsel*'s departure as the morning of 20 February. Guttorm could have departed immediately but felt a share of the responsibility for our welfare. This meant offering the ship's crew to

Maudheim four days old. One hut is already built and four men are digging foundations for the second

66

help with building and also with a more permanent arrangement of the vast array of stores and equipment.

The biggest of many piles of boxes belonged to Section 1 – base provisions. I learned that we had provisions for three years, slightly less now that a fifteenth man had been added. The 12-month safety factor allowed for the possibility that *Norsel* might fail to get through the pack ice in 1952. That would add an involuntary year to the two years for which we had signed on.

Fuel drums, of which there were hundreds, were sorted into diesel fuel for generators, gasoline for weasels, and kerosine for cooking and space heating. The remaining sections of goods would be arranged in parallel lines between the huts and close to them. The gaps were to be roofed over with tarpaulins to form corridors giving access to the boxes in any weather. With boxes one on top of the other, we could never open a lid, so we planned to hack through the sides with an axe. It was crude, but the boxes served a structural as well as a supply function.

Norsel after unloading, her paint at the waterline stripped by the battle with pack ice

Giæver declared a day of rest on the day before the ship's departure. In practice this meant a busy day of writing letters to parents, wives and sweethearts. The aircraft were hoisted on board and the shore party packed. After an orgy of photography (while joking to hide our apprehension) and much arm-waving back and forth, *Norsel* eased out of her berth and sailed for home at 0930 on 20 February. It was a solemn group of 15 men who watched the ship round the mouth of the cove and disappear from view after three long blasts of the siren.

Now we really were alone. At the same time, I believe, we felt a thrill that, come what may, we depended on each other. Be it injury, death, starvation, or drifting away on an iceberg, nobody beyond ourselves could help. We could report an emergency over the

The wintering party on the day that *Norsel* left us (20 February 1950). L to R: Robin, Quar, Roer, Schumacher, Wilson, Roots, Swithinbank, Rogstad (above), Ekström (below), Reece, Schytt, Liljequist, Snarby, Melleby, Giæver

radio—but that would be the end of the matter as far as the outside world was concerned.

I felt mixed emotions: from now on there would be no letters to open, no letters to write, no telephones, and only brief radio telegrams at monthly intervals. Rogstad's main transmitter put out only 100 watts, so communications would be rationed simply because every word of every message had to be tapped out on a morse key. Exceptionally, there were occasions when voice contact could be made, but they were few and far between. On top of official radio traffic, there was only so much that one could expect from radio operators who had also to transmit meteorological reports every few hours for two years without a break.

Our thoughts quickly turned to all that had to be done before snowdrifts and the winter overwhelmed our new home. No longer a weasel driver, I became a tunneller. This was made difficult by the fact that there were already substantial snowdrifts, so I had to dig trenches to get down to the original snow surface. Half finishing any job could lead to starting all over again the next day because of overnight drifting. It was a race against time.

We were living in tents until the first hut was ready for occupation. A critical moment for the builders was when the frame was finished but the cladding was unfinished. Tonnes of snow could enter the building in a few hours. However, in spite of setbacks, there was rapid progress. After a couple of days we moved into the unfinished first hut.

In spite of chaos and cramped conditions, John Snarby prepared satisfying meals three times a day. At night, some spread their sleeping bags on any unoccupied space on the floor, others on boards laid over the roof joists. I slept on the dining table. The British members began learning some essential words of Scandinavian and vice versa. Morale was high and misunderstandings due to language generally ended with a laugh.

By the third day at Maudheim the radio masts had been erected and the first meteorological report had been sent out. One of the diesel generators was in service and the floor of the second hut was finished. *Norsel* reported that she was struggling through heavy ice. I recorded, 'Fine warm weather with mirage* in forenoon', but the met men (meteorologists) said that day temperatures this week had hovered around –8°C. As long as there was no wind, I only noticed the cold when taking off my gloves to handle a bolt or a screw, which we all had to do many times a day.

---

* Mirage is an optical phenomenon in which distant objects appear uplifted above the horizon. It is caused by abnormal refraction during a surface temperature inversion when air temperature increases with height.

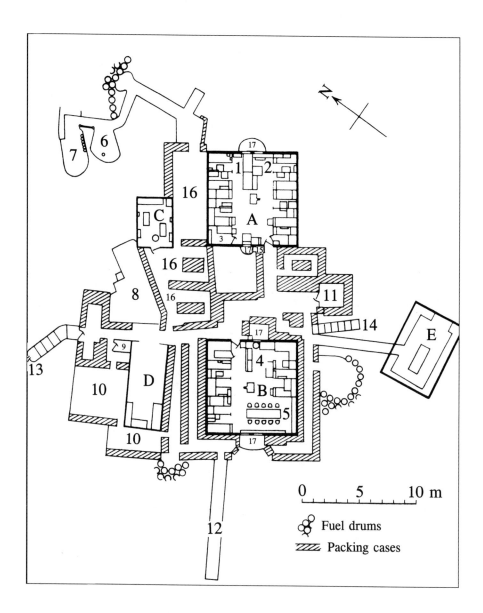

Map 5 General layout of Maudheim. A: Command hut, B: Kitchen/dining hut, C: Diesel generators and shower stall, D: Workshop, E: Drilling machine hut, 1: Meteorological office, 2: Radio office, 3: Darkroom, 4: Kitchen, 5: Dining table, 6: Hydrogen generator cave, 7: Balloon-filling cave, 8: Ramp to workshop, 9: Privy, 10: Garages, 11: Cold lab, 12: Tunnel for dogs, 13: Entrance (1950), 14: Entrance (1951), 15: Blizzard entrance, 16: Storerooms, 17: Window wells. There were hundreds of fuel drums. The rawin hut is beyond the area shown

One task that could not be postponed was making an outside privy, because there were to be no facilities indoors. Giæver, with a wry sense of humour, assigned the task to the glaciologists. After all, he argued, it would involve digging a deep pit, and Valter planned to dig pits to study snow strata. Here was a handy practice pit – with a purpose.

Having chosen a site that could be connected to the tunnel network, Valter dug and dug deeper, while I carted away the snow. His head was so far below the surface that, when he stopped digging, he had difficulty in climbing out. Finally, a seat was fashioned from a box lid and Valter himself inaugurated the contraption. The seat being at the ambient temperature of the snow, nobody sat on it for longer than necessary. The privy came to be known as the 'schytt-house'.

In the true spirit of scientific enquiry, Valter had calculated that his snow pit could contain everything that 15 men could produce in the space of two years. However, we had not allowed for the effect of freezing temperatures. Consequently, instead of the day's additions spreading out in the pit, a stalagmite was formed. After some time its summit rose right up to the seat. The first person to feel something tickling where he least expected it uttered a resounding yell. The glaciologists were summoned to solve the problem. Lassoing the stalagmite with two well-separated wire loops, we broke off the top half of it and lifted it vertically through the seat.

On 27 February a large dome-shaped tabular iceberg approached from the east and was swept by a sea eddy into our bay – now known as Norselbukta (Norsel Bay). As the berg was quite high, it hid the raised point on the far side of the bay. For a moment we thought that the point might have calved and drifted away – an unwelcome change in an ice shelf that we had hoped was stable. However, a quick ski trip to the bay showed that the point – Pynten as we now called it – was intact behind the iceberg. The afternoon tide carried the berg away.

Tunnel-building went on steadily. With admirable forethought, the base provisions had been packed in specially made plywood boxes, most of them 60 x 60 x 30 centimetres but some 60 x 60 x 60 centimetres. The uniform sizes made tunnel-building much easier because we could fashion walls of food boxes stacked neatly like bricks.

By the end of February, both living huts were finished. With the tunnel between them still open, drifting snow threatened to fill it.

Panic in evening to cover main tunnel, so all hands turn to and finish it after dark. To bed with tot of RAF rum. Rog got Bergen direct for first time . . .

71

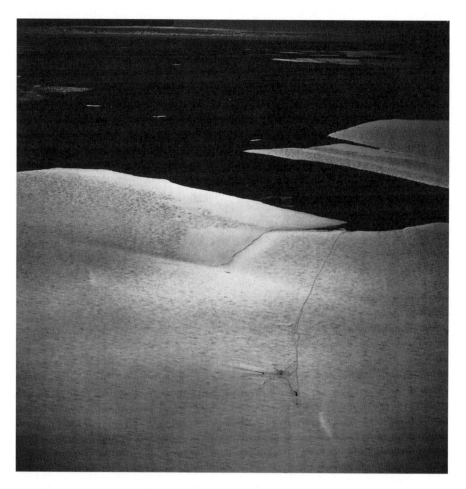

Maudheim from the air. Weasel tracks lead to the 'dock'

This was the first mention in my diary of darkness. Although in this latitude the sun had been setting for a few hours at night since before we arrived, it had never been too dark to work outdoors. Now the days were becoming shorter and the nights longer. We knew that from 21 May the sun would stay below the horizon until 22 July, but with twilight at noon we would still speak of days and nights. Only at the South Pole, where nobody was living, would there be one six-month-long night with never a ray of sunshine.

We were delighted to receive a telegram from King Haakon, wishing us luck, also a telegram from the Norwegian Prime Minister on behalf of his government. Ernest Bevin, the British Foreign Secretary, added his congratulations 'on behalf of His Majesty's Government'. Brian Walford informed us by radio that his 'summer tourists', as he modestly described them, 'had a hellish trip back' in the ship but that the Antarctic part of their work was 'all the greatest of fun'. Indeed, *Norsel* did have a desperate fight on her hands, many times being brought to a halt and frozen in new ice. Fifty kilos of dynamite had been used in attempts to free the hull, one charge unfortunately damaging the rudder. Yet she had reached the ice edge on 26 February and set course for Cape Town.

A telegram from Sverdrup told us that we would have a ship visit next summer. Until then, we had not been expecting to see anyone from outside until two years had elapsed. I do not know what behind-the-scenes machinations brought about this change. However, it did mean that we would be able to ask for things that had not been supplied. I soon had a list.

A few days later I was driving a weasel in a white-out. Unwittingly, I was crossing a long linear snowdrift and, in doing so, very nearly turned the weasel over. Shortly afterwards Alan did the same thing and ended up with the weasel resting on its side. If it had turned right over, he would probably have been killed because there was no roll

Emperor penguins come to greet visitors

73

bar to keep the weight of the machine off the driver. He and I were shaken but hoped that we had learned our lesson.

Whiteout is something that people do not believe in until they have learned about it the hard way. It is caused by multiple reflection between a snow surface and overcast cloud, and the effect is to diffuse the daylight and obliterate all shadows. On a uniformly white surface, shadows provide the only clue to scale and to where the surface lies. Men have been known to march unwittingly over an ice cliff in a whiteout.[8]

Apart from the meteorologists, who were already doing their observations in order to obtain the longest possible run of weather records, the rest of us were still full-time builders. The first task of the transport gang was to finish organizing and bringing in every item that could be brought in. In gaps between outdoor work, I dug and roofed yet more tunnels; when we finally finished the job, there were about 80 metres of tunnels, most of them lined with boxes. Then we chinked holes in the tarpaulins, shovelled away snowdrifts, marshalled stores, glazed the windows and made bookshelves.

7

FEATHERING THE NEST

For permanent quarters, I was assigned to the kitchen and dining hut, as were Reece, Roer, Roots, Schytt and Snarby. The 'command' hut was to house Giæver, Ekström, Liljequist, Melleby, Quar, Robin, Rogstad, Schumacher and Wilson. The arrangement worked well because everyone had to foregather for meals in our hut, so we never felt isolated from the rest.

Partitions separated what were to be our private cabins. Cabin is a rather overblown word to describe our individual cubicles. Each one measured 2 x 1.5 metres and had a sloping roof. As Giæver put it, 'Such a cubicle is smaller and considerably lower than the minimum size cow-stall in an ordinary cow-barn . . . '[1] There was room to stand only at one end, where a curtain separated us from the rest of the hut. The other end (the outer wall of the hut) was only 1 metre high. We slept on narrow Swedish sprung beds with a thin mattress. Each of us was issued with four beautiful warm blankets, generously presented to the expedition by the Hudson's Bay Company. Opposite my bed I made a desk out of a box lid. There was no space for a chair, but the edge of the bed served the purpose. Bookshelves of box wood lined the high end of my cabin. The temperature at floor level was sometimes -5°C, so I kept my boots on during the day. At head height, however, the temperature was comfortable.

Giæver spent most of his time in his cabin but made himself freely available for discussions on anything, or just for yarning. He had plenty to yarn about. John had published two books about his Arctic experiences and in the early months at Maudheim was formulating plans for his third – the official account of our expedition.

On fine days in this period, Gordon Robin and others were busy erecting the rawin hut. One of Gordon's jobs while not busy with field-work was to track the daily balloons launched by the met men. Some 100 metres from the living huts, the rawin hut was to contain a large and cumbersome directional aerial that could pick up the faint signals from a small transmitter, and from these calculate the speed and direc-

Gordon Robin testing a rawin transmitter

tion of winds aloft. For this reason it was the one hut that could not be left to become buried under snowdrifts.[2]

Gordon was a powerhouse of energy and a respected member of our highly cosmopolitan team. Short in stature – his head came up to Valter's shoulder – he had more stamina than most of us. He had graduated from the University of Melbourne in 1940 before joining the Royal Australian Navy. Later he was seconded to the Royal Navy and served in submarines. After the war he went to the University of Birmingham as a graduate student, before joining the Falkland Islands Dependencies Survey. As resident meteorologist, he was officer-in-charge at Signy Island in 1947–48. At Maudheim, Gordon struggled to speak Norwegian but without much success.

The dogs had been spanned out on long wires 100 metres from the huts since the whale meat and dried fish came up from the ice dock. However, we had to secure as many seals as possible to stretch out the food that we had brought ashore. I went with Melleby, Roots, Reece and Wilson on a seal hunt, skikjøring behind Peter's team of five dogs. Norselbukta was now covered with fast ice as far as Pynten, the

Gordon Robin and Nils Roer insulating the rawin hut

upturned point at the entrance. Seals thought the ice was an ideal place for resting – no doubt they had been doing it for centuries. As we approached, they had no inkling of their fate. From a distance of a few metres we took off our gloves, raised the rifle, aimed at the head, and fired. One by one they were picked off, sometimes a dozen or so within a minute, depending on how many were available. The noise alarmed them but they did not know what it meant.

I shot 25 and the doctor shot 13. Having lived through weeks of whale slaughter, I myself was now quite brutalized, and felt no qualms about wiping out as many seals as were needed to feed the dogs during the winter. We left 20 unmolested, not out of compassion but because we did not want them to conclude that this was an inhospitable spot. Their turn would come.

Now the task was to slit the seals down the middle with a sheath knife before gutting them with our bare hands, while the carcass was still warm. Alan showed me how. The one good thing about plunging cold hands into warm blood was that it thawed them fast. Although the dogs would gladly have wolfed down every morsel of the seals, we

77

were afraid of diseases that might linger in the gut. It was only afterwards that I learned from the Norwegians about *spekk-finger*, a
common but potentially dangerous infection transmitted to humans
from the innards that we were handling. We should have used surgical
gloves but in those days nobody did.

On another day we drove a weasel down to the fast ice to recover
the corpses. After knifing through the tail and threading a rope, we
secured each seal behind the weasel before driving home. After a day
or so, the carcasses became frozen and a felling axe or a woodman's
saw could be used to cleave off meal-sized pieces. As each dog was
thrown his iron-hard daily ration, he fought for it like a tiger,
growling through his teeth to show that, at this time, he would not
welcome visitors of any species. After a few minutes, only tiny chips of
meat and bone showed where his portion had been.

The Times of London informed us that there was to be a solar
eclipse on 18 March and asked if we would describe it. Before the
appointed hour, Nils Roer set up his theodolite with a smoked-glass
filter on the lens, and waited. The air temperature was –22°C, which
was not conducive to comfort while standing for hours at the instru-

John Giæver guts seals

78

ment. The moon's shadow, he noted, first touched the sun at 1342 GMT and lasted for 2½ hours. Throughout the period, Liljequist was measuring incoming solar radiation. He reported that at the darkest period, the energy coming from the sun amounted to only 23 per cent of what it would have been without the eclipse.

Valter and I were able to start our scientific work the same day. The first task was to use a hand auger to drill a hole to 10 metres' depth and to suspend in it a string of electrical thermometers to observe the downward penetration of the winter cold wave. However, my own principal task for fine days during the winter was to survey lines of stakes set out in a regular pattern extending 3 kilometres from base through eight cardinal points of the compass. The main purpose was to study the deformation of the ice shelf as it flowed seaward. I was using a Kern DKM–2 theodolite screwed to a tripod. In good hands, the instrument was capable of determining the angle between any two points sighted through the telescope to better than one-millionth of a 360-degree circle. However, with heavy gloves turning delicate tangent screws, my survey fell short of that.

The author surveying in reindeer parka and dogskin gloves. The angles were recorded on a piece of plywood

On many days the wind was too strong for outside work, so it took Valter and me about a month to establish the stake pattern. By measuring the exposed height of each stake at intervals, we would also determine the rate at which snow was being added to the surface of the ice shelf.

Air temperatures were now down to –25°C at night. Up to this time, we had been scarcely bothered by the cold, but now it was time to see what the management had provided for really harsh weather. As far as I could see, I might be spending more time out of doors during the winter than anyone else. John Giæver was a traditionalist, favouring furs made from reindeer, bear, seal, sheep, dog and cat, whereas Reece and Robin favoured wind-proof outer garments made from finely woven cotton. British 'Ventile' cloth was supplied in the form of anoraks and wind-proof trousers, and the same material was used for the pyramid tents that we would take into the field.

Next to our skin we wore a pure wool vest and matching long pants presented to the expedition by Wolsey, the same company that had supplied Scott and Shackleton. Then came a thick wool lumberjack shirt, heavy blanket-cloth trousers and on top of that, lightweight hand-knitted Shetland wool pullovers and/or heavyweight Norwegian sweaters. For long periods standing outside surveying the stake network, I topped all those with dog-skin pants, reindeer-skin leggings and a thick reindeer parka. The parka was the most expensive item, costing £20, because it required most of one reindeer. On my head was a sheepskin cap held tight with the elastic strap of ski goggles.

The choice of polar footwear has always been controversial, different people swearing by what they love best. To avoid acrimony, Giæver had brought almost every known variety, and left it to each man to make his choice. This was wise, because we never did agree on what was best. For skiing, I preferred Norwegian ski boots copied from those worn by Roald Amundsen on his way to the South Pole in 1911. They were made from alternate layers of leather and felt and cost £8 5s a pair. They were soft, flexible and warm, yet firm enough for me to control the skis. Inside the boots – depending on the temperature – I could use dog-skin socks as well as the Wolsey woollen ski socks that we wore every day.

Alan was adamant that ordinary ski boots were too cold for the Antarctic. Mukluks, he said, were essential to keep the feet warm in cold weather. Traditionally, mukluks were made from seal or bearskin, but we also had modern Canadian mukluks made from canvas. Inside the mukluk we could wear wool socks, together with bootees made from blanket cloth, dog skin or sheepskin. Special bindings were needed to hold the mukluks in place on skis. While this combination was warm enough, its softness made lateral control of the skis difficult.

Another choice for outdoor or indoor work was finnesko, the traditional reindeer-skin boots made and worn in Lapland. They have an upturned toe, which Lapps use to hook under their ski strap. Inside the finnesko I used sennegrass (*Carex vesicaria*), a variety of sedge that absorbs foot moisture yet is easy to dry out afterwards. It has the unique advantage that a fistful pushed into the toe of a boot adjusts itself to fill the space between one's toes and the leather. Offering insulation from the cold where it matters most, sennegrass is unrivalled. It has been in use for thousands of years.

I found that keeping hands warm was only a problem after taking off my gloves to handle instruments, tools, nails or screws. Then it could be hell. By the time the pain becomes unbearable and one returns to the gloves, recovery can take an age because hands *and* gloves have cooled during the interval. For manual labour in summer, most of us wore ordinary gardening gloves. For colder conditions, we used thick woollen mittens inside leather outers, and for the very coldest conditions, I used reindeer-skin gloves on top of everything else.

However, wind is the real enemy. Even a light breeze carries away several times more body heat than still air. In a book I found a table of the so-called wind-chill factor, showing the cooling power of moving air. At an air temperature of $-20°$, for example, a 20-knot wind makes the body feel as cold as in still air at $-35°C$.[3] Although bare skin was the most vulnerable, most of the time we wore nothing on our faces. A face mask protects to some extent, but it soon becomes ice-bound with condensation from breathing. From then on, it can only be separated from skin or beard after thawing indoors or in a tent.

A heavy load of clothing invariably made us clumsy. One day Valter was understandably angry when my own clumsiness led to dropping a new pipe wrench down an 8-metre hole in the snow that I had just finished drilling. Retiring to lick my wounds, I spent several hours covertly making a powerful electro-magnet from a piece of steel bar and a coil of wire. Lowering it down the drill hole, I connected a weasel battery and heard a satisfying click as the magnet grabbed the pipe wrench. Valter was mollified – indeed quite impressed – when I handed him the lost tool.

Disappearing tools were an occupational hazard. A spanner inadvertently dropped on soft snow could vanish without trace. After several embarrassing losses, we learned to put a piece of canvas or a box lid under the object we were working on, so that dropped tools would be saved.

Nils Roer

Nils Roer was an indefatigable outdoor worker throughout the construction period. His own professional task would be to make a triangulation network of the mountains inland with a theodolite, but a start on that was still nine months away. Friendly to all, he neverthe-less kept his own counsel and worked as well alone as in a team. Nils was tall, 36 years old and a married man with two children. He had worked with the Norwegian Resistance Movement, though I felt he had the bearing of an army officer. He told me that shortly after the German surrender in 1945, the Norwegian military set out to destroy all war *matériel*. A colleague was led to a room full of theodolites and told to destroy them. Protesting that theodolites were the prized stock-in-trade of surveyors throughout the world, he was told that *these* theodolites were war *matériel*. He obeyed the order but never forgave the army. Not long afterwards, the Geographical Survey of Norway was buying new theodolites.

Fred Roots was an outdoorsman if ever there was one.[4] After graduating from the universities of British Columbia and Princeton, he had worked as a meteorological observer, lumberjack, prospector, surveyor and teacher. He was the only one of the scientific staff who came to us with a Ph.D. For several years he had worked for the Geological Survey of Canada. Fred had begun early on mountain climbing and ski-mountaineering and had served in the Canadian Army Reserve in Combined Operations and Mountain Warfare. He proved to be one of the most universally liked people at Maudheim – always willing to interrupt his own work to help others.

John Giæver and Peter Melleby discussed the make-up of dog teams for the summer journeys, and who should drive and train them. It was

Fred Roots

Digging out the entrance to the tunnel system (April 1950)

clear that the strongest teams should be offered to Roots, Reece and Roer on the grounds that they proposed to make the longest inland journeys. That left the glaciologists with two rather ragtag but – we supposed – adequate teams. Peter, the most self-effacing of men and the only one employed as dog-driver, agreed to take on some of the smaller Greenland dogs, among them those showing signs of earlier mishandling.

At Maudheim, Nils Roer could not wait to see what lay over the horizon. On 3 April, together with Reece, Roots and Melleby, he left to make a reconnaissance inland with two seven-dog teams. It was the expedition's first excursion into the uncharted wilderness of Dronning Maud Land. They were aiming for a col that we could see between the ice dome in the east and the long ridge in the south-east. At –25°C, the weather was cold but sunny. There had been very little time for training the dogs, so their departure was anything but orderly.

I learned that the social hierarchy in sledge dogs is established by a show of fangs, or a feint or nip. Like wolves, however, they have a team instinct, and in victory they are magnanimous. The loser lies on his back, exposing his throat to the winner, who accepts surrender at the very moment when he could have dealt the *coup de grâce*.

It is remarkable how little entrenched enmity there is in the dog or wolf kingdom. Sometimes, confusion about what a driver wanted could precipitate a scuffle, and it was the driver's job to calm his dogs to reduce the risk of injury. Alan generally chose to take a running jump into the middle of the mêlée, hurling obscenities at the perceived aggressor and flailing with whatever he had in hand. The most surprising thing was that, in the midst of their frenzy, his dogs somehow avoided taking a bite out of his leg. John Giæver sometimes helped to sort out dogfights with blows from a piece of dunnage (the short planks used to separate layers of cargo in a ship's hold). I was

Alan Reece heads for a skirmish

85

always amazed that, despite wincing, none of his targets ever suffered a broken skull.

When the two teams did get away, it was at a fast run. The party took a radio, but that night there was no contact. The next day it was –30°C, the day after –33°C, and still no contact. I began to realize that in the field, we would be on our own – nobody would come to our assistance in an emergency because they might never hear of it.

The reconnaissance party arrived home after 11 days, on 5 of which the weather had prevented travel. They had covered 120 kilometres and established that there was a route inland that appeared safe for weasels. They were also well satisfied with the dogs and with their equipment: sledges, tents, sleeping bags and rations. Not, however, with the radio. They had listened for Rogstad every day, but all they heard was Handel's *Messiah* from a broadcast station.

In March, Belle, one of Melleby's bitches, had given birth to two males and three bitches. It was a happy occasion, the first fruit of our plan to replace the animals lost during *Thorshøvdi's* voyage. Not long afterwards, Faith presented us with four pups. Two weeks later, Patches produced seven. At this rate, we would recover our dog strength in time for next summer's travelling. However, the run of luck ended when Moe was found in a blizzard with eight newborn pups beside her, all of them dead. Our intention was always to bring bitches into the shelter of a snow tunnel when close to term, but sometimes the signs were missed – with tragic consequences. However, Curly produced four pups in April, bringing our total strength to 63 – one more than the number we started with. In spite of this, we had no plans to stop breeding, because some might not survive. I was told that it was bad for the development of young sledge dogs to put them in harness too soon, but we had no choice if the fieldwork was to proceed as planned.

Other dogs failed to grow their winter coats. No wonder they were confused – they had come from the Northern Hemisphere, where at this time of year, summer was imminent and they would be moulting. It was quite normal for the dogs to be drifted over in a blizzard; they knew that the snow protected them from the wind. Sometimes not even their black noses were showing above the surface. However, if they spent days in one position under the snow without getting up and shaking, their body warmth melted snow and soaked their fur. When they finally stood up, their damp fur froze. At that point they could no longer shake it off. Having lost some of their insulation, the situation would go from bad to worse. If we saw what was happening, we brought them indoors to thaw.

Truls was dried out, put back outside, and found dead the next day.

Milagtose and Uvak spent a night just outside my cabin in a pool of melt water; but they survived. Nafalik, one of the survivors of the foot disease on *Thorshøvdi*, did live in our hut for some weeks while he was being treated. One day he was found reclining on Alan's bed with his head on the pillow and all four legs in the air. The dog was asleep, and looked very pained when disturbed.

One day I carried Belle's young family indoors for a drink of milk. It was a wonder to behold as her little balls of fur fell about the milk dish, their eyes exploring the unfamiliar surroundings before scampering off to investigate. Most of us were dog lovers, so there was always a temptation to have a house dog as people do at home, but we knew that keeping them outside was the only way to make their coats grow thicker and to train them to live through blizzards without getting iced up.

Separated as most of us were in our daily jobs, meals were happy occasions during which news was passed, progress was compared, and appetites were appeased. John Snarby was proving adept at satisfying 15 hungry men and, considering the limited variety of foods he had to choose from, he produced extraordinarily good meals. The most popular dish was Norwegian fish balls, though meatballs in gravy came close. Both came out of tins. John baked fresh bread twice a week, and we always had unlimited butter, cheese and jam. The butter, supplied in 3-kilo tins, had suffered in crossing the equator and was rancid. In the circumstances, the choice was simple: eat rancid butter – or none at all for the next two years. I came to like the taste.

Seating at the dining table depended only on finding a vacant seat, so nationalities and occupations were randomly mixed. Language was a hotch-potch, with the British members picking up words of Scandinavian and vice versa. When addressing each other, Swedes and Norwegians use their own dialect, so for me it was confusing to decide which language to settle on. Unwittingly, I developed my own dialect, which ignored nuances while being universally understood. Now too busy to study the language in textbooks, I invented words; some of them stuck. Needing a term for a bed, I invented the word *sov-maskin* (sleep-machine). This caused so much mirth among the Norwegians that I never did bother to adopt the proper word *seng*.

I was consumed with admiration for the diligence of the meteorologists. One of them had to venture outside to take observations every three hours – on the hour – regardless of the weather. The only one that they missed was at 0300, when civilized people are generally horizontal. Nils Jørgen Schumacher, the senior of the two, was 31 years old and hailed from Finnmark. He had studied meteorology at Oslo University until the Germans closed the university in 1943. Of

Nils Jørgen Schumacher

medium build, serious but amiable, he loved to tease his colleagues.
Nils Jørgen (who was always addressed as such to distinguish him
from Nils Roer) had black hair and a black beard. At one stage during
the winter he succumbed to John Snarby's suggestion that shaving his
head could save brushing and hair washing. After this he looked like a
Cossack warlord.

Gösta Liljequist celebrated his thirty-sixth birthday in April.
Although senior to Nils Jørgen in terms of age and experience, he
had been appointed as assistant meteorologist for political reasons.
The International Committee had made a decision that each national
committee should appoint a scientist to lead one of the main fields
of research. Thus meteorology fell to Norway, glaciology to Sweden,
and geology to Britain. In practice, our meteorologists studied
different aspects of the subject, so seniority became irrelevant. They
did share the three-hourly observations, because no man could be
expected to handle seven outdoor excursions on every day for two
years.

Gösta was by far the most scholarly of the scientific staff and also
one of the three married men at Maudheim. He was slim, had blue
eyes, a long straight nose and was often clean-shaven. Brought up in

Gösta Liljequist

Kalmar, Gösta had studied oceanography and meteorology at the universities of Lund and Uppsala before joining the Swedish Meteorological and Hydrological Institute in Stockholm. While there, he had served for a time as a radio weather forecaster. However, so many complaints came in about his strongly regional Småland dialect that he had to be assigned to other duties.

Gösta's accent was not a problem for the English-speaking contingent at Maudheim because he was fluent in English – and preferred to use it. He said he felt half British because he was conceived in England. From an early age he had recognized English as the language of science. Indeed his first scientific paper (1938) was in English although published in a Swedish journal. His hobby was polar history, and he had published an account of Richard Evelyn Byrd's four Antarctic expeditions.[5]

At mealtimes Gösta was a great raconteur. He told us that he had been assigned to investigate why observations from one particular meteorological station in Sweden differed radically from the surrounding stations. Through careful study he found that the

89

observer had avoided the chore of going outside by logging the records for the same date from three years before.

While telling stories at meals, Gösta routinely poured so much HP sauce on every dish that his middle initial – H (for Hjalmar) – instead became HP.

When the clock said 'go', one of the met men donned outdoor clothing and uncomplainingly ventured forth. In good weather, the observations could be done in a few minutes, but in bad weather the work could take an hour. In blizzards, the first task was to dig out the entrance, which quickly became covered by drift snow. The man always took a spade to make sure he that could dig himself in again. One day Gösta became stuck fast while attempting to wriggle through a narrow tunnel entrance. The occasion was no fun for him but gave the rest of us a laugh. To guard against becoming lost in a blizzard, when visibility was sometimes reduced to the length of an arm, the men had rigged hand-lines along the well-trodden routes to their instruments.

Gösta had special responsibility for the instruments on a 10-metre-high met mast. That could mean climbing up in any weather to clear snow or rime ice from each sensor. On coming down one day he became disoriented and – sensibly – decided to lie down until he was able to catch a glimpse of something he knew. Another day he lost a glove and returned indoors with white fingers. Luckily they quickly thawed out over the stove.

Once back in the hut, the duty met man had to shake snow off his wind-proofs, shed his outer garments, and then read an array of instruments recording wind, snow temperature and air temperature at various heights on the mast. The most remarkable feature of the local climate was the temperature inversion that occurred in calm weather. It was sometimes 10 degrees warmer at the top of the 10-metre high mast than at the bottom. The inversion was responsible for the mirage effects noted by so many polar travellers.

Once a day the meteorologists launched a radiosonde/rawin balloon. The radiosonde consisted of a small radio transmitter that sent signals of air pressure, temperature and humidity as the balloon ascended. On fine days the launch was straightforward enough, but in a blizzard it could be hell and needed additional volunteers. Hydrogen to fill the balloon had to be manufactured from raw materials. This involved mixing aluminium chips with caustic soda and water in a pressure cylinder – an inherently dangerous operation. Gas was generated immediately the ingredients came together, so if the lid of the cylinder was not screwed on rapidly, there was a risk of explosion and serious burns to those involved. If pressure built up too fast, the men had to choose between struggling with the lid or running for cover.

Launching a radiosonde balloon in a blizzard

The balloon was filled in a large room dug out of a snowdrift. The room had a lid in two halves to prevent the hole being filled by drifting snow. The small rawin transmitter was attached in the filling room, but the radiosonde, tied at the end of a long string, was held by someone on the surface to prevent it from hitting the side of the hole when the balloon was launched. Once the lid had been pulled aside, the balloon was set free. Its rapid ascent snatched the radiosonde from the outside man, and in strong winds could smash it against the ground. Such difficulties were overcome by trial and error over the first few months.

After each launch, Gordon Robin or Leslie Quar tracked the balloon from the rawin hut whilst Nils Jørgen raced indoors to monitor the radiosonde transmissions. Some balloons had to be tracked for up to two hours, rising to more than 20 kilometres above sea level before bursting. The coldest recorded stratosphere temperature was –91.3°C, a couple of degrees colder than the minimum ever recorded at the earth's surface.

Nils Jørgen Schumacher tracking a radiosonde ascent

8

FIRST EXCURSION

Throughout April I had been dropping hints about the need to explore the inland margin of the ice shelf before winter set in. Finally I secured permission to make a short journey with Peter Melleby and one dog team, though I did note: 'Giæver is like an old aunt fussing about the trip.' And well he might be. I had no experience of travelling over this kind of terrain, nor had Peter. Sunrise and sunset were only four hours apart and, away from the coast, we could expect colder temperatures.

Valter had brought to Maudheim several hundred snow stakes made from 2.5-centimetre aluminium tube cut into 3-metre lengths. We had no idea how abrupt was the transition between ice shelf and inland ice,[1] so I hoped to survey across the boundary in one or two places and plant stakes to mark the spot.

We would use a Norwegian dog sledge made from hickory and built according to the 1883 design of the Norwegian explorer Fridtjof Nansen. It was 4 metres long and 0.7 metres wide. Joints were lashed with rawhide thongs to allow the structure to bend under load. However, some concessions had been made to modern materials: plastic laminate was glued to the runners to reduce friction.[2]

We set off in calm, clear weather at 1100 on 6 May with five dogs, heading east. It was my first experience of dog sledging. As leader we had Tony, a shaggy and friendly dog from Spitsbergen. Peter used the centre-trace formation, with Tony alone in the lead and the others paired behind him on short traces spliced into the main trace.

We were on skis and holding a rope tied to the back of the sledge. So eager were the dogs that for the first few minutes we were towed at high speed. Then they slowed and we shuffled along beside the sledge without being pulled. There was a glycerine-damped compass, of the type used in Hurricane and Spitfire fighters, mounted on the left rear corner of the sledge. I could look down on it and propose a change of heading without moving from my place. Trailing from the rear crossbar of the sledge was a sledge wheel (a bicycle wheel with a distance counter), a wonderfully unsophisticated yet effective measure of distance travelled.

I revelled in the gentle breeze, the hiss of the runners on the snow, and the sight of the dogs with tails held high – at last we were doing what I had dreamed about. From that day on, neither Peter nor I ever used ski sticks when travelling with dogs – the trick of balancing without them was soon learned.

Peter was a taciturn companion, saying very little to me or to the dogs. This suited me because I was drinking in the silence and enjoying every minute of our progress. After covering 17 kilometres we came to the foot of the slope of the ice hill that we had seen from Maudheim.[3] It was well after sunset and we had begun to encounter crevasses. In the twilight, it was hard to judge whether the snow bridges were safe, so I called a halt and we made camp.

We had a double-walled pyramid tent of the kind that has been used on British expeditions throughout the twentieth century. Both inner and outer tents were tied to bamboo poles extending from ground level at each corner to the apex of the pyramid, where they were bound together. In principle, the tent was pitched simply by spreading the legs and pushing their four ends into the snow. A 50-centimetre flap extended outwards from the fly at snow level, and on it we heaped large blocks of snow to provide stability. Finally, guys on each face of the tent were pulled taut. Properly pitched on level snow, pyramid tents were then and are still the safest known. Inside the tent, another 50-centimetre flap extended inwards from the inner tent. Then we covered the whole floor area with a groundsheet. Cooking fumes were vented through a piece of radiator hose led through both walls near the apex. The tent had been manufactured by Camp and Sports Ltd at a cost of £43 17s 1d.

I crawled inside through the sleeve entrance and spread out our sleeping bags, while Peter fed each of the dogs a hunk of whale meat. By now it was pitch-dark and I lit a candle. We had a plywood food box and a cook box, each 60 x 24 x 23 centimetres of the type specially made to fit on dog sledges. Placed in line down the middle of the tent, they neatly separated our sleeping spaces while remaining accessible from both sides.

Meals were cooked on a Swedish Primus stove fuelled by kerosine. Peter had put blocks of snow between the walls of the tent and I sliced them into an aluminium saucepan. For this short journey we brought ordinary tinned food from the base supplies. On longer journeys, however, where weight would be critical, we planned to use dehydrated foods.

Ove Wilson had been at pains to ensure that we had medical supplies for most emergencies. A large emergency kit was kept on the sledge, and in addition, each of us had a personal kit containing:

10 morphine tablets
12 magnecyl codeine tablets
6 opium tablets
6 coramine-caffeine tablets
6 psykoton tablets (an extreme stimulant)
6 Vasodil tablets (to increase circulation in frostbitten limbs)
1 tube Vasodil ointment
1 tube anodyne ointment (for snow-blindness)
Wound dressings

I have never enjoyed being cold. It was −28°C outside and, after turning off the Primus, we could expect almost the same inside, so I was apprehensive. Peter was quietly amused on seeing my elaborate sleeping arrangements because, unlike me, he was well versed in how to live in cold climates. First, I laid a reindeer skin on the groundsheet with its fur side up, then placed on it a full reindeer sleeping bag with its fur side out. Finally, into the reindeer bag went two ex-US Army sleeping bags, one designed to fit inside the other. The bags were filled with down (40 per cent) and feathers (60 per cent).

I did not wake until a breeze shook the tent at 0730. After breakfast of porridge liberally laced with butter and sugar, we went outside to look at the surroundings. The dogs howled with delight as we emerged from the tent.

I found six narrow cracks with upturned edges running parallel with the ice shelf margin.[4] As the ice hill must be resting on rock, whereas the ice shelf was rising and falling with the tide, I took this as evidence of flexure at the junction. Presumably, the cracks formed when the snow surface was in tension during a falling tide. The upturned edges would develop on a rising tide, when newly formed snow bridges would be compressed between the sides of the crack.

We struck camp, harnessed the dogs and moved back onto the ice shelf. In the first few hundred metres we crossed some frightening crevasses, narrow at the top but opening out below to about 4 metres wide. Last night, because of darkness, we had been blissfully unaware of anything that big.

My aim now was to cut across the embayment at the eastern extremity of the ice shelf in the hope of finding a more abrupt break in slope. We stopped after dark and made camp after covering 23 kilometres. Here the tidal cracks looked the same as before. By the time we were ready for bed the air temperature was −35°C. 'Bloody cold. But weather holds, so we must press on.' Six weeks to Midwinter Day!

I woke several times during the night feeling cold, and so did Peter.

95

On emerging from the tent in the morning, I was shocked to find that the temperature was –39.2°C. But the weather was dead calm 'so we could not feel it'. The thermometer must have dipped to –40° in the night – the magic temperature at which the Fahrenheit and Celsius scales intersect.

Skiing in towards the land ice,[5] we found a small valley at the break in slope. Here I drilled in a stake and surveyed it relative to the slope. My idea was to repeat the survey after some months in the hope of calculating the rate of flow of the ice.

To harness the dogs, we had to take off our gloves to cinch leather straps. At this temperature my fingers were shot with pain and then, shortly afterwards, grew numb. It took half an hour of skiing to bring them back to life. However, my abiding memory of the day is of our vapour trail – or contrail, as aviators know it. The dogs' breath combined with ours left a kilometre-long line of fog hugging the ground behind us, stunningly beautiful as the sun rose over the southern ridge.

That night, after sledging parallel with the ice shelf margin for 24 kilometres, we again stopped for the night. As I was hammering in a tent peg, there was an alarming splitting sound that lasted seconds, rose in a crescendo, and ended with a crack like a rifle shot. I leapt away thinking that I had broken the snow bridge over a crevasse. I must have initiated a crack which then propagated because the surface was in tension. Next morning I found a 2-millimetre wide crack extending for 35 metres from the tent peg that had given me a moment of terror.

The temperature was now –37°C. Peter said: 'It is no idea to be out sledging in weather this cold.' He was right: we should wend our way home. His idiom *no idea* was a direct translation from Norwegian, and he stuck with it whenever he spoke English; it meant that something was a bad idea.

We walked some way up-slope on the inland ice to see if we could obtain a compass bearing on Pynten, the point at the mouth of Norsel-bukta. I hoped that it might be silhouetted in the afterglow of the sun, but we saw nothing. My dead reckoning would have to guide us home as best it could.

In our little camp, the next morning dawned clear and calm. At this time of year, that meant only one thing – it would be cold. I put a thermometer on the sledge and read it: –37.8°C.

Striking camp after breakfast, I reckoned that travelling 23 kilometres on a heading of 318° should take us to Maudheim.[6] The dogs did not like pulling straight into an orange-red sun that was skimming the horizon ahead; nor did we. We felt very lonely on such a vast and featureless plain of ice. It was not until half an hour after sunset that I saw, miraged above the horizon on a bearing of 320°, an image of the rawin hut. A modest enough structure, 5 metres high, it had the distinction of being the tallest building within 2,000 kilometres. It was more than an hour before the hut itself took shape ahead in place of its image in the sky.

We reached the dog spans at 1615, to the accompaniment of a wild chorus of howling from the chained-up dozens who would have liked to come with us. The sledge meter showed that we had travelled 95 kilometres, which was 3 kilometres further than my estimate before we left. We had achieved what we set out to do, which was humble enough, but it had also given me my baptism of fire in conditions worse than anything that we expected to encounter during summer travel. John Giæver was relieved to see our smiling faces and to see that we still had ten fingers and ten toes. In my snug little cabin, I realised that I could not have found a better teacher nor a more compatible tent-companion than Peter.

Ove Wilson, the expedition doctor, was short in stature and inhibited by a somewhat effeminate voice and manner. He had suffered from a peripatetic childhood. Born in Berlin in 1921, he had attended schools in Italy, Germany, France, Sweden, Canada, USA and Spain. His father was a Swedish-American engineer who became world professional figure-skating champion. Ove had a medical degree from Lund University and had served as a ship's doctor and later as a mountaineering doctor. His national service had been in the Swedish Army as a battalion doctor.

Ove was always looking for something to challenge or demonstrate his medical skills. At Maudheim he found himself as the general practitioner to 15 healthy men – hardly a heavy workload for a GP. But unlike any GP at home, he could not refer patients to a specialist except by radio: he must cope with every kind of illness or emergency.

The majority of Ove's patients had four legs. Sometimes, his X-ray machine had to be mobilized to check for fractures in legs nipped in battle. On one occasion while he was operating on a dog to remove a tumour from his leg, the poor animal died, possibly from an overdose of anaesthetic. Wedded to neatness in all things professional, Ove continued his surgery as if nothing had happened and then carefully sutured the incision before we removed the dog for burial.

Dentistry also came high on the doctor's list. He had foreseen this and wisely arranged to have a three-week course in a dental hospital, after which he was satisfied that he could handle anything. His patients were less persuaded. However, tooth decay proceeds just as fast in the Antarctic as it does anywhere else. It so happened that I

97

Ove Wilson

was the first to need treatment for a cavity, so a time and a place was agreed. On arrival in the dental surgery – his cabin – I was confronted by a professional-looking array of instruments and a 'dentist' eager to start. He had a tape recorder, which was a rarity in those days, and played classical music to soothe my apprehension. As I opened my mouth, he opened his textbook and placed it on a table beside me.

Ove was equipped with a dentist's drill that would not have looked out of place in a mud hut in Africa. Injecting Novocaine with a flourish, he proceeded to drill. Working cautiously, and frequently referring to the book, he made an effort to calm me by reporting that the operation was proceeding according to plan. However, so deliberate was his progress that when perhaps halfway through, the Novocaine no longer deadened the pain and I had to ask for a second dose. Finally his pestle and mortar appeared, mercury amalgam was prepared, and my newly drilled hole was no longer a cavity. More than two hours had elapsed since we began.

My diary notes: 'He is totally incompetent.' However, decades

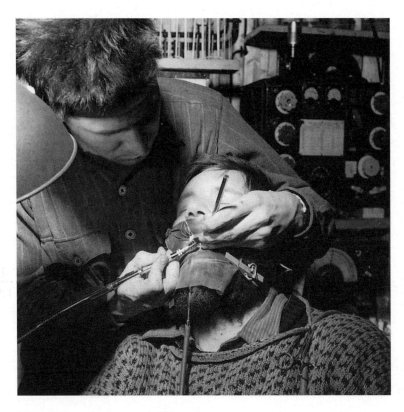

The author endures a tooth filling

afterwards, I have to admit that such a remark was unjust. Ove was slow, very slow indeed, but that came from his uncompromising adherence to the textbook. To my knowledge, none of his tooth fillings ever failed, at least not while we were in the Antarctic.

Ove, by choice, launched a physiological research programme in which we all served as guinea pigs. He was interested to discover what changes occurred as our bodies acclimatized to the cold and darkness – if they ever did. Once a month we were weighed. At intervals, we faced the indignity of having our ears pierced with a miniature dagger, after which Ove drew blood into a pipette. If the first stab did not draw blood, he would try again; this time it hurt. One day I offered to teach him how to do it 'properly'. I would stab him so hard that there would be plenty of blood at the first shot. To avoid the risk of penetrating through his ear lobe into an artery, I put a notebook behind his ear and let fly. With one hole where the dagger went in, and another where it came out and entered the notebook, there was

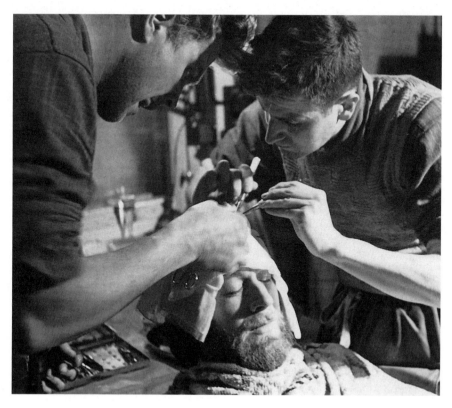

Valter Schytt (left) assisting Ove Wilson (right) to repair Nils Roer's scalp

plenty of blood. For a moment I was more concerned with first aid than with pipetting. Luckily, Ove laughed.

Our blood was spread on a glass slide, after which he spent hours doing red-cell and white-cell counts with a microscope. Early morning and early afternoon testing included blood sugar assays. In an attempt to understand why there were seasonal fluctuations in haemoglobin levels, he asked some of us to swallow large green iron pills to see whether extra iron would raise the levels when they were at their lower summer values. Fred Roots said that he was fed so much iron that he should have gone rusty.

Not satisfied with bleeding us, Ove asked us to submit to an infernal breathing machine. The purpose was to determine our basal metabolic rate. We were required to diet for a day, eat nothing after supper the night before, and not rise the next morning until he appeared at the cabin door wheeling his machine together with an oxygen cylinder. As we lay still in bed, our noses were clipped shut

100

Ove Wilson bleeds Peter Melleby

and we were gagged with a scuba diver's mouthpiece connected via a hose to the machine. After a floating tank had been filled with oxygen, we had to breathe normally until the oxygen was exhausted. Meanwhile a paper chart recorder showed the rate at which we were burning oxygen. Some of his guinea pigs were less enthusiastic than others, but I felt that we owed something to him.

In terms of working hours, Ove was a law unto himself, and this did not please the men in adjoining cabins. He used his tape recorder instead of a diary. Often in the early hours of the morning when others were trying to sleep, he would relate the story of his day. Afterwards he would listen to the tape to admire his entry, laughing from time to time at his own jokes. His colleagues, while fervently praying that he would fall asleep, nevertheless found themselves straining to hear what he said.

Mornings for normal people, however, were Ove-free, because he never got up for breakfast, only appearing hours later, bleary-eyed, for lunch.

Roer and Roots built a large igloo for magnetic observations about

Ove Wilson with his infernal breathing machine

500 metres north-west of Maudheim. The purpose was to record changes in the earth's magnetic field caused by streams of charged particles from the sun interacting with the earth's magnetic field. Owing to the sensitivity of the magnetometer, it had to be isolated from any ferrous metals that might affect the readings.

The trail to the igloo was marked with a closely spaced line of stakes. Nils and Fred took it in turn to spend hours inside the igloo peering into the instrument by the light of a candle. Sensibly, they had equipped the igloo with food and a sleeping bag in case of emergency.

On 16 May Fred went to the igloo after breakfast and said he would be back for lunch. Meanwhile, the wind increased to hurricane force and by lunchtime there was no sign of Fred. Valter and Nils prepared to mount a search party. Just then Fred walked in, having spent over an hour crawling on his stomach. Blinded by drift, he had fumbled for each of the stakes by swinging a spade ahead of him.

Safe in the hut, I found that I enjoyed listening to the wailing, high-pitched shriek of the storm winds as they resonated with the radio

Fred Roots (left), Peter Melleby and Ove Wilson X-ray a leg injured in battle

aerials above us. If asked why I loved it, my only explanation is that it contrasted so dramatically with the peace and security inside. Although the roof vibrated as the wind tried to tear it off, we knew that we were safe because the hut was half buried under snowdrifts.

Social occasions at Maudheim were invariably well lubricated with aquavit and other liquids. Very little beer was provided because the glass bottles sometimes burst on freezing. Norway's national day was on 17 May and it was the occasion for raucous celebrations and flag-waving. However, nationality did not matter because we all enjoyed an excuse for a party.

Early in winter, it was realized that with 15 of us on base, half of whom would spend months away during the summer, there could not be 15 birthday parties. We solved this difficulty by deciding to celebrate half-birthdays as well as whole birthdays. Unfortunately, I was born on 17 November, so my half-birthday was subsumed into Norway's national day.

The wind record was broken the same day. The barometer dropped abruptly after a slow fall and, within a minute, the wind rose to 70 knots. At this speed the RAF Austers, if they had stayed with us, would have been airborne.

9

SUNSET

Half of the sun rose on 21 May, sliding along the northern horizon, so we enjoyed a lovely coloured sunrise (or sunset) lasting three or four hours. I saw it because my surveying work was now beginning in earnest. Valter and I had set out a pattern of 22 stakes spread 1 kilometre apart over an area of 30 square kilometres. The furthest stake from Maudheim was just over 4 kilometres away. My job was to establish a triangulation network so that I could calculate the exact position of each stake in relation to the others. A repeat survey during the second winter would show what deformation had occurred in the interval. There was no way of finding the absolute rate of movement of the whole pattern because there was no fixed point of reference against which to measure.

Sometimes I drove a weasel to the stakes, but in cold weather it was often difficult to start. The penalty for flattening the battery was to lug it into the generator shed for recharging. If I spilled a few drops of acid on my wind-proof, holes appeared in it some days later. At other times I skied to the stakes but, carrying a heavy tripod and theodolite, I would arrive in a sweat. Damp clothes cool the body faster than dry clothes, so I paid a price for that too.

Early in the winter, in twilight, I could see the stakes through the telescope of the theodolite. Later on, it was pitch-dark and I had to hang hurricane lamps on stakes before sighting to them. This involved travelling long distances before surveying, and again afterwards to bring in the hurricane lamps. For observing, I could not use a bulky reindeer parka because, if it so much as touched the tripod, I would have to re-level the instrument. So I dressed in many layers of sweaters and a wind-proof anorak. The worst problem was keeping my fingers from seizing up. The tangent screws of the theodolite were metallic and small, so thick gloves were out of the question. My diary for 27 May reports: ' . . . impossible to keep warm with woollen mitts, 4 thicknesses of silk gloves, and catskin gloves . . . '

My breath froze on the eyepiece of the telescope, obscuring the view. I tried to remove the ice with a handkerchief, but that threw the

Pynten, the only point of reference for those confined to Maudheim

instrument off level; re-levelling took several minutes. I attempted to exhale sideways; that worked, until a puff of breeze blew my breath back. When all was ready, I searched through the telescope for the distant hurricane lamp. When I found it, the inverted image of the lamp was often dancing from side to side of the cross-hairs. There was commonly a temperature inversion, with cold air hugging the snow surface and warmer air above it. The slightest breeze could ruffle the layers and lead to near-mirage refraction.

Despite all the difficulties, the many long hours that I spent alone away from the base were some of the happiest I can remember. I was out of range of any sound from Maudheim, in total silence, at peace in the wilderness and at peace with the world. Often the great arc of sky above was filled with a thousand twinkling stars, brighter than anything I have seen in lower latitudes. On some days I was serenaded by the aurora, with its multicoloured curtains, dancing, shimmering, alive, grander than anything I could have imagined. From time to time, ripples flowed from one end of a curtain to the other, some fast and some lazily.

This symphony in the sky, I felt, was laid on for me; it would be an insult to leave before the final bars. But of all the sensations that came to me during those long hours alone, it was the silence that moved me most. Silence was the spirit of the place.

106

Late in the afternoon I would break the silence, gather in the hurricane lamps and head for the beacon, a light bulb mounted on a short mast at Maudheim to guide anyone outside in the dark. Sometimes an evening breeze wafted fog from the sea, and I knew that, if I misread the compass, I might never reach home. In these temperatures, already chilled to the bone, hypothermia would kill – fast.[1] But years before, as navigator in a warship, I had learned one good lesson about dead reckoning: calculate, then check the calculation and, finally, begin all over again. Life is too precious for anything less.

Our weasels had open cockpits and no heaters, although canvas cabs had been used by other expeditions. One day in the course of the survey I drove my weasel 96 kilometres in the space of 12 hours, but finished the day's work rigid with cold.

My colleagues seldom enquired how the day went, nor did I ask them how theirs went. Although we aimed to be courteous in our daily lives, and generally succeeded, some of the niceties of civilization

Lunch at Maudheim

seemed out of place in our stiff-upper-lip man's world. I suppose we believed that the only questions that will be asked on Judgement Day are: Did we do our jobs to the best of our ability; and were we willing to help others? With few exceptions, the answer would be in the affirmative.

It was the dogs who gave the greatest welcome to a returning traveller. Indeed, we could turn to them for solace at any time, especially the pups, who were growing fast. We let all pups run free for the first few months, so that they could explore their surroundings, learn to trust human beings and learn which of their elder brethren to trust or to fear. At first the instinct to explore kept them in and around the base and dog spans, but soon they became bolder.

Sometimes too bold. One day it was noticed that three of Belle's pups, now 11 weeks old, were missing. After searching on the fast ice with a weasel, I saw them heading east along the ice front of Norselbukta, their noses poking over the edge of the 20-metre-high cliff and uttering plaintive squeaks as they tried to move towards me. There was no safe way to round them up until Alan and Fred arrived together with their mother to add her bark to our bellows.

In the base routine, all except John Giæver took turns at domestic duties. This involved sweeping the floor (scrubbing once a week), refilling the kerosine space-heater that occupied the geometrical centre of each hut, washing up, disposing of rubbish and bringing in snow blocks for water. There was plenty of snow around, but within the tunnel system too much of it had been contaminated in one way or another during construction. Getting snow from outside meant, in the first place, digging open the main entrance to the tunnel system. This was a daily chore which some people tackled with more enthusiasm than others and, inevitably, there was an undercurrent of resentment if anyone failed to pull his weight.

Most of us learned that the best way to engender mutual respect was for each man to do rather *more* than his fair share. This paradox holds because many a good deed goes unwitnessed, so if a man does only his fair share, it will be perceived by his colleagues as being less than his fair share.

In practice, words were muted because we were all sensitive to the risk of discord on any matter that might diminish the friendly atmosphere. It was a measure of the determination of each of us to avoid falling out. If ever national rivalries had developed at Maudheim, most of us would have concluded that international expeditions were doomed. Luckily, we never encountered such things. There were tensions, but as often as not they were defused by light-hearted banter. While the best of friends, Ekström and Snarby

108

bombarded each other daily with rich affronts. All the time we knew that the base could only function effectively as a team.

Valter and I now made a good team. We were both intent on honing our language skills, so I had been speaking to him in Swedish, while he addressed me in English. This rather odd way of working continued until one day he said: 'Charles, I think it better we speak Swedish.' So I had my way, and for the next ten years, we always conversed in Swedish. In practice I used a mixed version of Swedish and Norwegian, tending towards Norwegian when addressing Norwegians and Swedish when addressing Swedes. However, Valter's English remained at least as good as my version of his language.

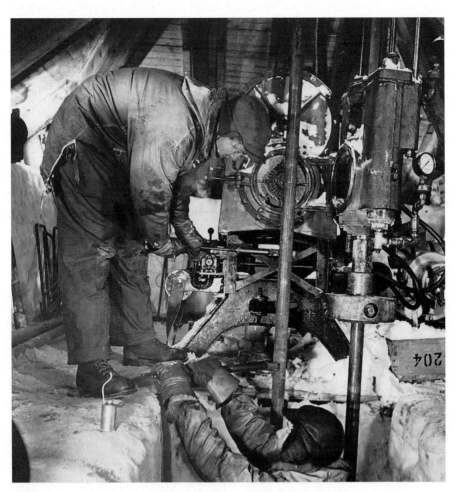

Drilling ice cores. I am in the pit while Valter unscrews a drill rod

We planned to spend much of the winter drilling. Our first task was to dig a great hole in the snow to make a 'cold' laboratory, and further days excavating to make space for the ice-drilling machine. Then each compartment had to be roofed over before the next blizzard.

When all this was done, we began by drilling into the ice shelf for temperature measurements, using relatively light weight extension tubes. By 6 June we had reached 63 metres, the deepest hole ever drilled in Antarctica. However, on that day the core barrel jammed and one of the drill-rod couplings broke – we lost 45 metres of drill rods down the hole. It was a disaster, and we had to restart the drilling from the surface. By 11 June we had reached 45 metres depth, and after lowering a string of thermistors to various depths, we called it a day.

The next task was to recover ice cores to learn, among other things, how and at what depth snow crystals metamorphosed into solid ice. We hoped to discover whether the crystals reoriented themselves at depth to facilitate deformation along 'easy-glide' planes. It was known that this occurred in temperate glaciers but, in the Antarctic, no core drilling had ever been done. At the same time we were to obtain ice temperatures and densities at various depths in the hole.

While some authorities of the day believed that Antarctic ice shelves were essentially just floating extensions of the grounded part of the ice sheet, others held that they were mainly the product of local snow accumulation, starting perhaps on a base of land-fast sea ice. Still others had presented evidence that they grow from below by the freezing of sea water. Our ice core would, we hoped, provide some answers.

The drill itself was a Canadian Longyear Company 'Straitline' rock drill generously donated by the manufacturer. It was powered by a 30-horsepower petrol engine, but the drill bit and core barrel had been specially made for bringing ice cores to the surface. During the long hours that we spent drilling, I was consigned to a 1-metre deep pit under the drill chuck, while Valter stood on the surface to attach 3-metre extension tubes as the hole was deepened. Each tube weighed 24 kilos, twice as much as the narrower tubes that we had used for the temperature hole, so by the time we got down to 40 metres – if we ever did – the drill string would weigh 1 tonne. Each time I had to grip it with a giant pipe wrench for several seconds after the hydraulic chuck had raised or lowered the string. My terror now was not about dropping the pipe wrench, but instead about dropping the whole string down the hole while Valter was attaching or detaching an extension tube. That could have killed the whole project.

110

Bath time. The water ration for bathing was 4 litres

On reaching the bottom of the hole, the coring device would take only a 1-metre core, and sometimes less, before jamming. Then the whole process of unscrewing the extensions, one by one, had to be repeated before we could get the ice core to the surface. It was a task of back-breaking boredom, repeated again and again, with the constant danger of disaster if either one of us should lose concentration for a second.

Once during a storm, I was alone in the drilling hut clearing snow from the machine when I discovered that snow drifting over the entrance had sealed me in. Valter came to the rescue and dug me out. Visibility outside was about the length of my arm but drift snow pasted our eyelashes together and made it difficult to see anything. In order not to lose contact, we held hands. I felt embarrassed by holding hands with my boss but, on this and other occasions, survival was the only criterion.

This incident was typical of the way we looked after each other. Knowing that someone was working outside in a blizzard, we kept an eye on the clock and did not hesitate to launch a search if we suspected that he might be in trouble. It paid off – later expeditions have had men freeze to death in similar circumstances.

One serious hazard of living under snow was carbon monoxide poisoning from inadequate ventilation and from leaky joints in an exhaust pipe. That happened to Valter on occasions, and to Peter, who took my place on the ice drill when I was out surveying the stake pattern. I was fortunate and never suffered the tell-tale headaches. The most likely explanation was that a continual updraught of fresh air came out of the drill hole, a result of the steady expulsion of air at depth as it was squeezed out of the snow mass by the weight of snow above it. I could feel the draught on my face and was grateful for it.

On occasions when the weather was particularly cold, we had to call in Knalle Ekström for help in starting the drilling machine. He had already demonstrated some bizarrely unconventional solutions to practical problems. On one occasion, to start the recalcitrant drilling machine he played a blowlamp on the carburettor air intake until the metal was a dull red colour and the carburettor itself burst into flames. At this point Valter and I felt like running for cover or grabbing a fire extinguisher, but Knalle calmly cranked the engine – and it started. The flames were sucked inside – Knalle knew they would be. 'We used to start tanks like that,' he said.

Taking each batch of ice cores into the cold lab, we used them to measure ice density, record visible strata, and cut thin sections with a microtome. Then each of us spent long hours peering down a microscope to measure the orientation of each and every crystal in the section. To keep moisture in our breath from condensing on the specimen, we had to breathe sideways through pouted lips. It was mind- and finger-numbing work. Shifts ended only when our fingers could no longer feel the thumb screws and when we knew that our body temperature verged on hypothermia.

The first step to recovery was to retreat into a warm hut for a cup of coffee. John Snarby kept fresh coffee on tap throughout the day and welcomed company as long as we kept out of the kitchen. This was not always easy because the kitchen was part of the open-plan living and dining area.

The base celebrated midwinter on 22 June, though with the sun only 5 degrees below the horizon at noon, there was more light on the horizon than I expected. This faded upwards into a vivid rose red, then a deep purple, and finally to the clear solid blue of the sky. The heavens were celebrating the solstice. We were also celebrating Christmas, on the grounds that many of us would be far away to the south on the real Christmas Day.

To begin the feast, John Snarby dressed in his white steward's

Valter Schytt measuring ice crystals in the cold lab. We breathed sideways to avoid condensation forming on the microscope slide

Midwinter Day, 1950. Alan Reece and Leslie Quar molest 'Mrs Rogstad' (Gösta Lilje-quist)

uniform and served *lutfisk*, a concoction of dried fish soaked in sodium bicarbonate. This is traditional Scandinavian Christmas food, and regarded as a delicacy, but the British members who tasted it indicated that almost any other food would be preferable. However, there was also rice pudding and meatballs. Alan managed to brighten the occasion by presenting a Christmas pudding that he had hoarded.

There was a good party in the evening. Although Giæver had forbidden record players on the grounds that repetition of a favourite record would lead to discord, Leslie and Ove had built a simple gramophone to play the one old record that someone had brought. Gösta Liljequist was dressed as 'Mrs Rogstad'. A secretly hoarded case of beer was opened; it must have been in someone's cabin to keep the bottles from freezing. A series of boxes carefully packed with Christmas goods had been rifled on the dockside in Göteborg and stuffed with brown paper. All that remained were party hats and a bottle of mustard.

The following day the unmarried members of the expedition spent three hours discussing the qualities that each of us would wish to find in an ideal woman. Assuming that the married men had already found theirs, they were not invited to join in. The younger members, including me, were dogmatic about the type of woman we would seek

114

to marry; but Giæver, our old sage, said that when the time came we would probably have no control of the matter. There was no measure of agreement between us, which was probably a good thing because it would save us from duelling unto death if ever such a woman appeared at Maudheim.

Egil Rogstad – Rog, as he was known – was one of the most popular men at Maudheim. His rugged Nordic face was dominated by a wide mouth and, as often as not, a broad grin. He never took himself too seriously and, through endless teasing, did much to maintain morale during the period when, by repute, cabin fever may raise its head. He had riveting stories to tell. Born in 1908 in Vingen, he had joined the Norwegian Army in 1926 (the year I was born). Later he served as ship's radio officer and, for a year, was leader of the Myggbukta weather station in north-east Greenland. During Hitler's blitzkrieg invasion of Norway in 1940, Rog was both an aircraft and ground radio operator before escaping to Finland, where he was interned. Escaping once again, he crossed into Sweden and thence via Siberia and Japan to Canada, where he joined the

Egil Rogstad

115

Norwegian Air Force in exile. Thereafter – still in the war – he served as radio operator in Iceland and Jan Mayen. After the war he spent a year in the navy before joining the Norwegian Airways Service.

Finding no joy in washing clothes, Rog calculated that if he wore each of his six sets of underwear for four months, he could avoid washing any of them for the whole two years.

His speciality was risqué and bawdy jokes, and he knew dozens of them. He would hound people mercilessly, particularly anyone looking gloomy, repeating the same joke we had heard before but refusing to let go until he had elicited a grudging smile. Rog was much too nice a person to be dismissed, so we all had to live with it.

All radio traffic was in Morse code. He had to send out meteorological reports every six hours, and handle all official traffic that flowed between Giæver and Norsk Polarinstitutt. Without the help of Leslie Quar, it would have been exhausting. Together they also handled private correspondence between us and our next of kin. Personal messages were rationed to 100 words per month each way. That may

Egil Rogstad tuning the main transmitter

116

not sound much, but there were times during the winter when we found it hard to think what to say in terms that would be understandable to people outside. *Theirs* was an alien world; we were in the *real* world – or so it seemed.

We lost interest in what was happening elsewhere. At any moment when Rog was not too busy, we could ask him to tune in to the BBC, but I do not remember doing so. Sometime in June he did mention that 60,000 North Korean troops had invaded South Korea, and later that 200,000 Chinese troops were driving back the United Nations forces, but the news elicited only a casual remark about the futility of war. Significantly, several of us had fought in a war that we had never regarded as futile. But here in Antarctica our isolation made the whole concept of war seem barren.

Leslie Quar was a delightful, easy-going 38-year-old from Croydon in Surrey. In his schooldays, Imperial Airways had been based at Croydon Aerodrome, and Les showed an early interest in aviation by landing a job with them on leaving school at the tender age of 14. When war broke out, he joined the Royal Air Force and was sent to Cranwell to train as a radio operator. In 1941 he was posted to the

Leslie Quar

117

Middle East and stayed there until the end of the war. Later Les was employed demolishing fortifications and U-boat pens in Germany. His varied career had made him into a versatile technician and an ever-cheerful handyman. We were lucky indeed that he had jumped at the unexpected opportunity of joining the wintering party.

The first week of July was the coldest yet. For days on end my diary reported: 'Fine and cold −40°C,' but on 2 July it began: 'Fine and cold −46°C'. It was no idea, as Peter would say, to try working outside. Three of Patches's pups died unexpectedly and Ove did a post-mortem in the crate at −35°C, claiming it as a world record temperature for an operating theatre. In the stomach of each of the poor animals he found wood shavings, steel wool, string, rope and straw.

Among the minor but pressing problems of polar life is whether or not a full beard is an effective protection against frostbite on the face. For my part, I revelled in the freedom from shaving and accepted the consequences. After a spell outside in a blizzard, a sheath of ice turned the beard into an effective windbreak. Unbecoming icicles of frozen breath hung from our nostrils. When an icicle was long enough, we could bite the end off and suck it for refreshment. Difficulties began when we came indoors for a meal. The ice could take ten minutes to thaw, in the meantime dripping on clothes or on the floor. If we were anxious to take a vacant place at table, falling chunks of ice would dilute and cool the soup. The shavers thought this was disgusting and of course they were right. However, outdoors they paid a price in terms of more frequent superficial frostbites of the cheek. As about half of our number had beards and the rest were clean-shaven, we never reached any consensus on the subject.

In an after-dinner discussion on 11 July, Gordon Robin proposed making a 3,500-kilometre trans-Antarctic journey to the Bay of Whales during our third summer season (1951–52). The purpose would be to measure the thickness of the ice sheet by seismic sounding. At first the idea caused disbelief or cynical amusement. Then he asked for volunteers and, quite unexpectedly, Fred Roots, Alan Reece and I offered to go with him.

'That idea stinks,' I wrote, 'as we are four British.' It was the first time that any national bias (or foolhardiness) had reared its head at Maudheim and, on those grounds, I was concerned. In the event, the project was scotched by the International Committee. What it did show was that we had already calculated, on the basis of each weasel's fuel consumption (in litres per kilometre per tonne of useful load), that such a journey was feasible. Ekström, however, assuming with some amusement that he would have to go along, doubted that the weasels were sufficiently reliable.

118

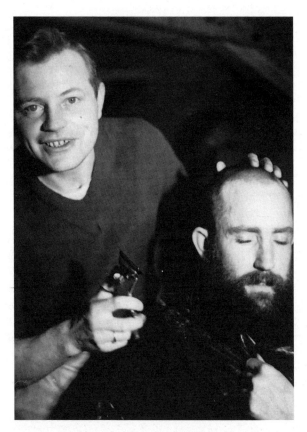

John Snarby clips Nils Jørgen Schumacher

Not to be outdone, Valter proposed a journey to Wohlthat Massif, 900 kilometres to the east of Maudheim. This was the most spectacular area photographed from the air by the German expedition in 1939. It was also the area that first attracted Professor Ahlmann because of signs that the ice sheet might be receding. Nils Roer, Fred Roots and I at once volunteered for the party. However, a journey of that distance would require two out of our three weasels, leaving only one for a seismic sounding journey proposed by Gordon Robin.

There was clearly a conflict of interest between Gordon and Valter as each of them tried to win John Giæver's favour and, failing that, to appeal to the International Committee. Nationality, however, was not involved; it was simply a matter of ambitious men not wishing to be thwarted.

All these concerns related to the third summer season. Plans for the second (1950-51) were more easily resolved, though they did involve some sacrifices. It was decided that there would be a geology/ topographic survey party consisting of Roots, Reece, Roer and Robin; and a glaciology party consisting of Schytt, Swithinbank, Wilson and Melleby. There was safety in numbers, yet each party could be divided into two when expedient.

It was evident that Roer could not work his theodolite stations without help, and field seasons are short in Antarctica and every man is expensive. However, each man was in the first place employed as an expedition member and in the second place as a surveyor, geologist, glaciologist and so on. The field parties were handled according to that priority.[2]

Although there was much discussion about the coming summer, it was still months away. The first sunrise was on 21 July but it was hidden by a week of blizzard conditions. My first good view of the sun was on 6 August, and I noted that it was high in the sky at noon.

On calm days, Valter and I measured and remeasured baselines on the stake network using a steel tape laid on the snow and tensioned with a spring balance. Insisting on an accuracy of 3 or 4 millimetres, we then applied a known coefficient of expansion to temperatures read from a thermometer attached to the tape. Each measurement involved both of us lying prone at the ends of the tape, reading off the graduations, adding the totals and, as often as not, rejecting measurements that did not tally.

Maudheim six months old. Snowdrifts have buried the huts up to the caves. We shovelled snow on to the roofs to improve heat insulation. The meteorological mast holds six anemometers and six thermometers. The low pyramid is the drilling machine hut

At other times, Gordon and I experimented with his seismic system. Our first job was 'refraction shooting' to determine the velocity of seismic waves in ice. This involved detonating charges made of TNT while timing the seismic waves to an array of seismometers (electrical seismographs) buried in the snow.

Next we used much smaller charges to seek seismic reflections from the base of the ice shelf and from the seabed beneath. Gordon usually set out six seismometers 10 metres apart while I drilled a hole for the explosive charge. The sticks of TNT had a hole in the middle, into which I inserted an electric detonator before connecting it through the seismograph to a spare weasel battery. When all was ready, Gordon set off the charge. There was a 'thump' muffled by the soft snow, and then silence. We did not know whether a shot had been successful until the film record was developed afterwards in the tent. After a number of experiments with different instrument settings, Gordon was able to say that the ice shelf at Maudheim was about 210 metres thick.[3]

10

SUNRISE

In the command hut, John Giæver suffered from insomnia. Noise, he said, was the bane of his life.

> One thinks of heavy feet on the double flooring, the scraping sound of furniture dragged through the room, strident discords from the radio section, the slamming of a door, conversation shouted from one cubicle to another, incessant humming and out-of-tune whistling for ever on the same phrase. The door slams again. The radio is turned on too loud with an infernal jazz or barbaric South African talk past all comprehension – but it is kept on for the sake of the noise itself. The puppies bark in the corridors like lost souls in hell. Rog roars out a verse of a tune, over and over again a hundred times, or dishes up a lengthy and pointless story for the hundred and first time, in Norwegian, Swedish and English. He drowns the radio with a solo roar of laughter. Then the door slams again... I can bear witness to the fact that London's air-raid sirens, mingled with a distant drone of German bombing planes, were more melodious than all this.[1]

Knowing that much of the success of life in our little community depended on interpersonal relationships, Giæver was an astute observer of the undercurrents. He asked several of us what we thought of the different nationalities at Maudheim. By now we saw our colleagues as individuals rather than representatives of their country, so it was difficult to generalize except in jest. Alan Reece said that the Swedes were tall and noisy. Giæver himself never managed to characterize the Scandinavians because they were all so different. But of the British he wrote:

> ... one can say that they were neither tall nor noisy. They became absorbed in the work itself with an impersonal attitude that was in sharp contrast to our own. Being apparently more

122

indifferent to their surroundings, they seldom betrayed any tendency to loss of humour or swift change of mood. I am sure they all slept well. Perhaps it is a fact that the British, over the course of centuries, have trained themselves to take a wider view of life than is usual among those of us from the small nations, with our more parochial habits of mind. Perhaps they are more disposed to take other races as they find them – whether these be bedouins of the desert, Mongols of the East, negroes, or again Scandinavians.[2]

Over a drink one day the Scandinavians discussed the extent to which personal relationships at Maudheim were surviving the strains of the long winter. One after another, each man claimed that everyone except himself had been the victim of winter psychosis. Clearly, subjectivity had triumphed over objectivity.

Some of my diary entries were uninhibited.

14 August: In the evening we argued whether Pynten is aground or not. Valter cannot argue without cursing the English language. I cannot argue without hurling insults at my opponents. Alan cannot argue.

15 August: Rog threw a jug of saft [orange squash] at Doc, and Alan suggested Rog should write out 100 times 'I must not throw saft at Doc.' Doc operated on Pluto's leg which is septic after a bite from Knoll. It took four of us to hold Pluto down . . . and he screamed just as a human, so loudly and furiously that we had to gag him.

16 August: Heard over radio that Princess Elizabeth had produced a daughter, so had a bottle of whisky at supper to celebrate . . . Giæver told many stories as he usually does on such occasions.

John Giæver had reported to *The Times* on the party we held to celebrate the birth of Princess Elizabeth's baby. Evidently Her Royal Highness was reading *The Times*, because soon we were delighted to receive a personal acknowledgement and greeting from her.

Valter and I stopped the ice core drilling on 26 August on reaching a depth of 50 metres. From here on we were to spend much of our time preparing for the sledging season. Then from May 1951 onwards, we hoped to continue the drilling.

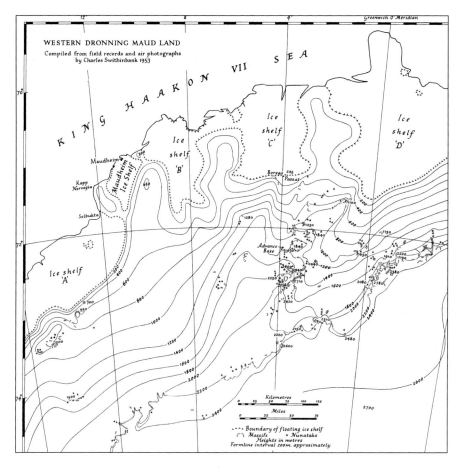

Map 6 The land as we knew it (1950/51). Except along sledging routes, the inland boundary of the ice shelves was sketched from aerial photographs

With the sun now rising steadily in the sky, we began to get in practise for the summer's travels. The geologists Roots and Reece left base on 9 September with their dog teams to reconnoitre a weasel route inland. Not to be outdone, Gordon and I left three days later with one weasel to extend our local seismic ice-depth sounding as far as the southern ridge.[3] Camped in the gentle depression at the hinge line (grounding line) 32 kilometres south-east of Maudheim, we were kept awake through part of the night by loud reports from ice cracking every few seconds, presumably as a result of a falling tide. Our presumption was confirmed when we noted a periodicity in the cracking that corresponded with tidal cycles. Gordon observed that the series of small cracks in the bending zone alternately opened and closed, again corresponding with tidal cycles. Finally I used the theodolite to demonstrate that the floating ice really was moving up and down relative to the grounded ice.

On the evening of the second day we saw two men approaching from the direction of Maudheim with a dog team. It turned out to be Peter Melleby leading Ove Wilson – our friendly vampire – to take blood samples. The following morning, Ove came into our tent with his instruments wrapped up in a dishcloth. We were cornered – and we were bled. Evidently we were to be pursued to the far corners of the land in the interests of physiological research.

We spent one day doing seismic shots at various points up and down the slope of the land ice, encountering some bridged crevasses 4 metres or more wide. Crossing them on skis was not a problem because the snow bridges were firm, though some of the dogs put their feet through. Whilst these crevasses were conspicuous, I found that the dogs had an uncanny sense of danger on coming up to the lip of any crevasse, even some that we had not seen.

By evening the air temperature was below –33°C. I knew it because the mercury was off the bottom of the scale. In May I had used a thallium-mercury thermometer designed for really low temperatures but this time we had not expected such cold weather. It was a healthy reminder that September is very early in the Antarctic spring. One advantage of having camped at –40°C on the earlier trip was that summer temperatures should soon feel balmy.

The next two days were spent surveying cross-sections of the depression in relation to the position of tidal cracks. We returned to Maudheim on 25 September. Gordon's seismic shots had shown that the ice shelf was between 210 and 290 metres thick and that, even as we approached the grounding line, there was still 100 metres of sea water beneath the ice.

The question now in our minds was whether the instrument would work with thicker ice that we expected to find inland. Excited by what we had discovered, Gordon and I set out the very next day to answer the question, this time following roughly in the tracks of the reconnaissance party in April. Heading about 105° from Maudheim, we reached the grounding line after 36 kilometres and began a steep climb up the slope of the inland ice. Driving the weasel, I had to change to first gear just to crawl up the hill. Luckily there were no crevasses, at least none that we knew about. Stopping late in the day at a point 47 kilometres from Maudheim, we enjoyed a magnificent view towards the sea from our tent. Having lived for seven months in a dead-flat, featureless landscape, *any* elevation seemed to offer a good view.

After making camp and completing a couple of seismic 'shots', Gordon reported good reflections from the bedrock beneath us. The ice depth proved to be 524 metres. 'Very surprising indeed', I wrote. In camp at a point 321 metres above sea level (according to corrected aneroid barometer readings) it meant that the bedrock was 203 metres *below* sea level. While this would be quite normal on an ice shelf, here we had no doubt that the ice sheet was resting on rock.

This was a stunning discovery with far-reaching consequences. We were learning that the surface topography of the inland ice sheet would not itself be an indication of the elevation of the rock basement. If we came across rock outcrops, of course, we would know their elevation above sea level, but we could make no assumptions about the level of the basement *between* outcrops. There might be subglacial fjords or inland seas extending hundreds of kilometres into the continent.

Gordon's seismograph, we realized, could answer such questions. But that would have to wait until the seismic journey planned for the final summer season (1951–52). Now we were bidden to return to Maudheim. That was easier said than done: there followed two days of high winds with fog, drifting snow and a temperature of –20°C. Confined to the tent, we talked, cooked and spent the time in our sleeping bags reading books. Only on the fourth day were we able to head for home, sometimes following our outward tracks but mostly steering by compass in poor visibility. The last part of the journey was in darkness, cruising in top gear at 20 knots and steering by the angle of the drift snow in the headlights. 'Most romantic', I wrote afterwards. However, we were constantly aware that a 10-degree error in direction could have taken us over the ice front into the sea. We both cheered when the faint twinkling Maudheim light appeared ahead.

It was now October and all of us were impatient to get going with the main inland sledge journeys. However, first there had to be some local depot-laying trips. These were to be followed by a reconnaissance party to find a route that was safe for weasels to establish what came to be known as the Advance Base. The place would not be occupied, but it would be stocked with fuel and food to provide for both field parties for the duration of the season. In addition to sledging rations, there would be some ordinary food for use by parties spending a few days there. Dog-sledge journeys could radiate outwards, returning at intervals to replenish their supplies. The intention was to site the Advance Base as far inland as possible.

Six men and four dog teams were mustered to undertake the first major thrust into the interior of the Norwegian sector of Antarctica. The six were Melleby, Reece, Roots, Robin, Roer and Schytt. I would have loved to go too but, as the baby of the house, I was not invited. My part was to carry on the base jobs that they would have done at Maudheim: feeding the remaining dogs, serving as semi-permanent mess orderly for the cook, and preparing equipment for the weasel journeys.

The departure of the reconnaissance party was chaotic, with dogfights erupting on all sides and much cursing. Their 32 dogs readily understood that something big was happening and they were hell-bent on contributing to the excitement. Each of the dog drivers had chosen a different formation to run their dogs. Roer used tandem traces, Melleby an extended fan, Reece and Roots variants of the centre trace. I guessed that this diversity was to some extent their response to a surfeit of unsolicited advice from Alan, who thought he knew best.

The dogs were international, the drivers were cosmopolitan, and the commands were unique to each team. Melleby started with the Greenlandic command '*Tama*, Kernek!' (his lead dog), Roer used the Norwegian '*Marsj*, Tony!', Roots called in Canadian 'Mush, Rachel!', and Reece yelled in the language of Labrador '*Weet*, King!'

Teams departed at intervals of a few minutes. Multilingual exhortations echoed across the ice shelf as the long train disappeared into the distance.

Left to my own devices, my diary reports: 'The base is very peaceful now. Get a lot more work done.' Rog claimed a historic first by transmitting one of my photographs by radio to Cape Town. The picture duly appeared in newspapers around the world.

Four days after the departure of the sledgers, they were in touch by radio. They had seen their first rock outcrop since leaving Cape Town ten months before – we sensed their excitement and shared in it. Roer and Robin, who were serving as a supporting party for their colleagues, were now able to hand over what they did not need. With a lightened load, they sped up to the nunatak. Stepping onto the rock, they became the first people to stand on terra firma in Dronning Maud Land. Roer took theodolite angles from the summit, Robin took rock specimens, after which they made fast time in returning to Maudheim. Roer was invigorated by the experience but said that Antarctic crevasses were more unpredictable than the minefields he had encountered in Finnmark five years before.

I well remember 16 October because it was the first day that I was able to strip to the waist while doing hard manual labour outside. From then on, when digging up stores or fuel barrels on sunny days, we worked in shirtsleeves or even shirtless – provided that there was not a breath of wind. The slightest air movement sent us racing back to don shirt and sweaters.

127

Hunting excursions to the sea ice were always exhilarating, slaughtering seals for the dogs – and emperors for our own delectation. Now there were also Adélie penguins, skuas and Antarctic petrels to herald the coming of spring – none of them was worth taking for the pot.

The first day on which the sun never set was 15 November. With the midnight sun came the reconnaissance party, returning to Maudheim 40 days after they had left. All of them sunburned, they brought news of a good site for the Advance Base among mountains 300 kilometres to the south-east of Maudheim at an altitude of 1,330 metres above sea level. They described coming across stunning panoramas of mountains that now they longed to explore. However, what shocked them was their inability to locate themselves on the sketch map that was made from German aircraft 11 years before. *Inaccurate* would be a charitable description; *artistic* would be nearer the mark. We never did fathom some parts of the map, nor did we understand how supposedly professional cartographers had perpetrated such a travesty of geography. No longer did we feel that we were to study a landscape with the help of a map. The land was effectively unexplored.[4]

On the return journey they planted 150 bamboo stakes with small flags, and also built 138 snow cairns to make the trail easier to follow. There were some crevassed areas but they did not believe that we would have difficulty crossing them. The day after the reconnaissance party's debriefing, we began to load the weasel sledges with supplies for the Advance Base. We would take all three weasels and no dogs. It would be a six-man party but, as a designated weasel driver, I was to be one of them. The others were Ekström, Melleby, Reece, Robin and Roots.

With 2 tonnes of weasel under me and another half-tonne of dog food piled high on the vehicle, I did not like the idea of crossing snow-bridged crevasses. After a sleepless night, I decided that the safest thing would be to drive the weasel in such a way that it would be impossible for me to fall to my death with the vehicle. I wanted remote control, but there remained only a few hours in which to design and build a system.

Weasels, like army tanks, were steered by means of two levers. Pulling one stopped the tracks on that side, so turning the machine in the same direction. As amphibians, weasels also had a rudder bar mounted over the stern. I discarded the rudder and mounted the rudder bar on the back of the driver's cockpit. Fixing a wire cable from each of the steering levers, I attached these to the ends of the rudder bar. Now I tied an alpine rope to each end of the rudder bar and led both ropes out behind the vehicle. Putting on skis, I could be towed with the rudder bar centred without exerting any pull on the steering levers. To turn, I simply pulled one rope harder than the other.

I needed an assistant to set the vehicle in motion before jumping out, and to pull the gear lever to neutral when we wanted to stop. Without him, we might be risking a runaway vehicle. Far from base, it would be embarrassing to see one's worldly goods disappearing over the horizon.

It was a crude system, but it allowed me to follow on skis at a safe distance behind the vehicle. If the weasel fell into a crevasse, I would simply let go the ropes. Remote control was too awkward to use all of the time, but I planned to use it for driving across known crevasses.

11

TRACTOR TRAIN

Our grand tractor train left Maudheim late on 20 November. I drove the lead weasel, with Reece as passenger, Melleby followed with Robin, and Ekström brought up the rear with Roots. With 500 kilos of cargo inside my weasel, Alan had a grandstand view sitting or lying on top of the load. Behind each weasel we towed a heavy cargo sledge carrying 2.5 tonnes of petrol, dog food, man food and camping gear. On my weasel, I proudly flew a Norwegian flag.

We drove all night, up and over the eastern saddle and down towards the next ice shelf, easily following the fresh tracks of the returning dog-sledgers. With the sun above the horizon around the clock, we preferred night driving because cooler temperatures made the sledge runners glide more easily. But the open cockpit meant that we ourselves grew colder with each passing hour. Not wanting to delay the train by stopping for a hot snack, we positioned tins of food on the exhaust manifold. I kept a tin of cocoa on the boil, occasionally replenishing with snow the amount I had consumed. One day the contents cascaded over the sparking plugs, and the engine misfired for some time afterwards. At other times the aroma of burning bread reminded me that my toast was done.

From time to time we stopped to establish depots to provide fuel for the return journey and food for dog-sledgers. Whenever I could see one of the snow cairns ahead, steering the weasel became much easier. Camping at 0500 the next morning, we had already covered 70 kilometres. We slept for a few hours and then set off again at 1400.

I was apprehensive because, according to Roots, we were about to enter a crevassed area. It was not long before we approached a bridged crevasse nearly as wide as the weasel was long. I rigged the remote control system and Roots put the weasel into gear. This was to be a spectacular demonstration of the merits of my invention. However, as the steering ropes became taut, I was pulled flat on my face while the weasel lurched across the crevasse with nobody in control. Luckily the snow bridge remained intact, which is more than can be said for my self-esteem. I recovered and raced forward, grabbing the steering ropes to regain control.

We had learned that apart from human error, the system could do what it was designed to do. Melleby and Ekström followed in my tracks without resorting to remote control. Some distance further on, I was quietly leading the procession when I glanced back and saw a commotion. The full length of one side of Melleby's sledge had dropped into a crevasse. I skied back to help, finding to my horror that the trail we were following was parallel with the crevasse and therefore in the worst possible direction for safe crossing. The dog-sledgers, with much lighter loads, had not known about this.

We had to unlash and unload the 2-tonne cargo, box by box, all the time wondering if we ourselves were stepping on a snow bridge. The empty sledge was then pulled out of the crevasse and reloaded – box by box. Not long afterwards the same thing happened again with the same sledge, and the whole tiresome procedure had to be repeated. My nerves were fairly shattered by the thought that I had already driven along the same crevasse. In this type of terrain, it was clear that triumph can lie inches from disaster. Nobody was to blame for this little adventure because nobody had noticed this particular crevasse.

It was a relief when we cleared the area and proceeded over the

Peter Melleby's sledge discovers a crevasse

131

gently undulating surface of this second ice shelf.[1] Some time later we had to stop for the first weasel trouble. Ekström's fan belt had broken, and he wondered why the designer of the vehicle had been so perverse as to make installing a new one nearly impossible without jacking up the whole engine. We decided to camp at this spot.

The following day we reached the far side of the second ice shelf and climbed once again onto the inland ice, where we camped near the nunatak discovered by the reconnaissance party. Not surprisingly, it came to be know as Førstefjell (first mountain). Most days we drove at night, not just to get better surfaces but also because, with a low sun, it was easier to judge the terrain ahead.

On 23 November I had another opportunity to use my remote control, this time to cross a 3-metre-wide snow-bridged crevasse. Everything went according to plan and I did not fall over. Then I led the procession over the last ice ridge to a spot where a gorgeous panorama of mountains unfolded before us. We were looking down on the scene, so we could see a score of rugged peaks spread out over a vast landscape, with many smallish nunataks and one high massif on the horizon to our right.[2]

Driving through the night in an open cockpit was tiring and cold. '0400 . . . stop to warm feet.' After running round the weasel ten times, I hopped in and headed for the pyramidal peak that was the chosen site of the Advance Base. Not surprisingly, the nunatak came

The aftermath of a blizzard on the first Advance Base journey. It took an hour to excavate the weasels from snowdrifts

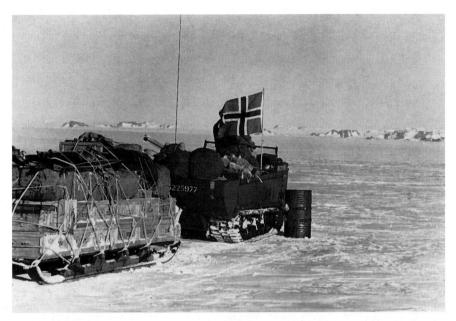

My first sight of the mountains

to be known as Pyramiden (the pyramid). On the last lap, 4 kilometres from the rock, Peter's weasel stopped with engine trouble. By this time I was straining at the leash, so Robin and I drove on to the foot of the nunatak and unloaded the sledge.

Then, for sheer enjoyment, I drove the weasel right onto scree at the foot of the nunatak. It was the first time that I had stood on solid ground since leaving South Georgia 12 months before. Moreover, it was a rare moment to enjoy the absolute certainty that a crevasse could not open under our feet.

The following day we climbed Pyramiden. The air was so clear that we could see well over 100 kilometres in all directions. Now I noted that as well as the regiment of peaks that we had seen from the ridge, there were tiny outcrops of a variety of shapes sticking their heads through the ice sheet. I guessed that what we were seeing might – if the ice were stripped away – turn out to be massive mountains. In due course, I hoped, our seismic soundings might reveal the real contour of the land beneath the ice.

As soon as all three weasels had unloaded, we started on the homeward trail. Our now speedier, lightened vehicles raced along at 15 knots. At most camp and refreshment stops, Robin set out his seismic gear and shot soundings. Some were successful, others not, but what

I drove my weasel on to the rocks of Pyramiden

we were learning was that it was not unusual to find more than 1,000 metres of ice beneath our feet. In view of our preconceived notion that the ice sheet must represent a relatively thin veneer covering the rock surface, this took us by surprise.

On the four-day return journey, two days were spent stormbound in tents. The final day we did a marathon drive of 215 kilometres in 16 hours, eventually steaming into Maudheim at 2000 on 28 November. On descending into the base, we found John Snarby serving a spaghetti dinner to the residents. Knalle commented: 'I did not drive all day just to be expected to eat worms when I came home.'

The journey had shown what the weasels could do, and at the same time had given us a better idea of how much fuel would be needed to undertake further journeys. On the heavily laden outward run, the weasels had quaffed 1.2 litres per kilometre (2.4 miles per gallon), while on the lightly laden homeward journey their consumption was about half as much.

We had ferried about 7 tonnes to the Advance Base but more was needed, so after six days we were off again, this time taking only two weasels. Ekström, Robin, Roots and I had done it all before but now we took Liljequist and Snarby for a 'holiday'. Both had full-time jobs at Maudheim, which meant that they might never see anything of Antarctica apart from the dead-flat ice shelf, so Giæver agreed to them taking a short break on condition that they found volunteers to do their jobs. I never knew how much arm-twisting was involved – but their jobs were done.

The Advance Base at Pyramiden

We left Maudheim at 1000 on 4 December. I led, with Gösta and Fred sitting on 200 kilos of whale meat behind me. Knalle followed, with Gordon and John Snarby sitting on 300 kilos of whale meat and towing about 1,700 kilos. At the top of the eastern col, where another sledge had been left, that too was attached behind mine. Now I was towing a total of about 3 tonnes.

When we reached the crevassed area, I drove by remote control, while Ekström chose to zoom across crevasses praying that he would reach the far side before the snow bridge let him down. We both succeeded, but as the weather was now clear we saw many bridged crevasses that we had failed to see last time – it was sobering to realize how lucky we had been. I found one crevasse, quite big enough to swallow a man, that we had all unwittingly walked over without skis on. Once clear of the bad area, we camped in calm sunshine and enjoyed seal steak, tinned potatoes and tinned cabbage for supper.

Peter Melleby had operated the radio on the earlier trip but now the job fell to me, because he was not with us and few men knew the Morse code. I had not tapped out messages in Morse since my navy days four years earlier but, despite slowness caused by cold fingers, I made contact with Rog at Maudheim without difficulty. Thereafter we communicated daily, with me sending position and weather reports, and Rog replying with news and weather forecasts. One piece

My load on the second Advance Base depot journey (5 December 1950). The two bottom layers of boxes on the leading sledge contain whale dog food, while the top layer consists of stockfish (dried cod) in sacking. The smaller boxes on the second sledge contain sledging rations for men

136

of news that cheered us all was that *Norsel* had crossed the equator – southbound. There were to be supplies, new faces and letters from home.

But we of the sledging fraternity would be far inland at the time and would miss everything. Indeed, by the time we returned to base and opened our own incoming mail, *Norsel* would again be in the Northern Hemisphere. The earliest time that a letter mailed to me from home in December 1949 could receive a reply from me would be in March 1952—some 27 months later. If some had been invoices, would I find creditors waiting on the dockside with handcuffs? It was not something that brought me sleepless nights.

On the third day we left Robin and Liljequist in camp to make seismic soundings while the rest of us ploughed on to the Advance Base. Much new snow had fallen since our last visit, so ploughing was an apt metaphor—we used low gears and left behind deep furrows.

After unloading our cargo in the shadow of Pyramiden, we raced home, covering the 300 kilometres to Maudheim in two days. On parts

Gordon Robin sorting electric detonators. The cylindrical TNT charges (right) will have detonators inserted in them

137

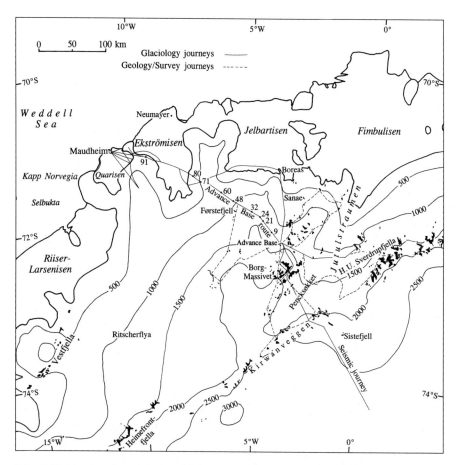

Map 7 The land as known now. Of the 150 stakes (flags) on the Advance Base route, the map shows only those mentioned in the text. Ice front changes since 1950–51 (Map 6) are due to ice movement and the calving of icebergs. Apparent changes in the inland boundary of the ice shelves are not real. Whereas the 1950–51 boundary was estimated, this one is taken from satellite images. The official Norwegian place names were not made available until 1961. Neumayer (Germany) and Sanae (South Africa) are permanent research stations

of the route the sastrugi were 20–30 centimetres high, making for a very bumpy ride. The next day I wrote:

> My weasel has run 800 miles over this ghastly surface with a tremendous load without a single fault. Five tons moved 200 miles, bloody marvellous!

Ten days were spent making everything ready for the longer dog-sledge journeys ahead. The glaciological party consisted of Valter, Ove, Peter and me. Valter and Peter would each drive a team of ten dogs. I was relieved to learn that Valter planned to share a tent with Ove, because both of them were incorrigible chatterers. Peter and I, in contrast, spoke when necessary but seldom chattered; we shared a tent in peace and drank in the silence of the wilderness. With some petulance I wrote that Valter 'wants everything done for him', while Ove was preparing medical bags for sledging, 'a job he has had 9 months to accomplish . . . we would do well to leave without him.'

We finally left Maudheim – with him – at 0200 on 19 December. The whole population came out to see us off. Valter's team, overcome by the excitement of the occasion, launched themselves into a vicious dogfight. As Giæver put it later: 'Valter is the only man I know who can be angry and drive dogs at the same time . . .'[3]

Valter had a sledge wheel attached to the back of his sledge to measure the distance travelled. Both sledges were fairly lightly-loaded because we planned to pick up supplies from depots along the way. The surface was smooth and the runners glided easily. Although we Europeans were brought up to believe that the sun moves from east to west across the sky, here – at night – we watched it moving from west to east along the southern skyline. The air temperature was $-4°C$, though day temperatures during the last few days at Maudheim had on occasion risen to $-1°C$. That, by our standards, was almost tropical.

It was a calm and clear night with the southern hill bathed in purple mist, the eastern hill pink and the snow sparkling with a rainbow of colours. We had waited a year for this moment and now savoured the thrill of finally getting down to work.

The geology/survey party set out from Maudheim some hours after we did. Fred Roots, describing the merits of their various dog-hitching methods, wrote:

. . . one conclusion, at least, could be drawn: the 'fan' hitch was undeniably superior for entangling spectators. One driver . . . found his whip to be more effective in controlling the bystanders than his team. When the air cleared, Reece was standing for-lornly, out of breath . . . watching his team and sledge disappear towards the Advanced Base, doggedly determined to get on with the field work, driver or no . . . Roots was hanging grimly to a rocketing sledge that was not noticeably hampered by an iron-shod brake dug deep into the snow and the inert forms of two puppies who, unable to maintain the pace, were being dragged on their sides.[4]

139

Valter proposed to follow the Advance Base trail for the first 150 kilometres before branching off into unexplored country. He was aiming for a circuitous route to the east to take in as much new land as possible. What we might discover none of us knew, though eventually we had to reach the Advance Base – or perish. To have some point to head for on the way, he chose the northernmost nunatak on the German map, though with little faith that it would be where the map said it was. The place had been named Boreas after one of the two Dornier Wal flying boats used by the German expedition. A nearby nunatak was Passat, named after the second flying boat.

The first day we covered 28 kilometres in 4.5 hours. Skiing beside Peter, my own job while under way was to record the exposed height of each of the many bamboo trail markers. By repeating the measurements every time anyone passed by, we would establish the rate at which snow was accumulating on the surface. This should be roughly the same as what meteorologists measure as 'precipitation'.

Camping at the foot of the eastern col, we began a routine that was to continue throughout the summer. The first task was to feed the dogs, each of them ravenous after a hard day. Then Peter and I pitched our tent, and Valter and Ove theirs. Peter and I shared the job of piling snow on the outside flap to weigh the tent down in case high winds might try to lift it. At this point our duties diverged. Peter disappeared inside one tent and Ove into the other. Their job was to start making supper while Valter and I launched into our glaciological studies. Valter dug a 2-metre deep pit to study the structure of the snow while I used an auger to drill a hole to measure the temperature of the snow at depth. We reckoned that several metres down, the seasonal fluctuations of temperature at the surface would be damped out, giving a rough guide to the mean annual air temperature. We would soon know whether or not that assumption was justified, because the meteorologists at Maudheim were measuring air and snow temperatures throughout the year.

My other job was to take meteorological observations three times a day, and whenever possible to transmit them to Maudheim using an international numerical code. I sent our position, temperature, pressure, wind strength and direction, visibility, cloud cover and cloud type. Peter, whose speed on the Morse key was better than mine, generally transmitted the message.

Our radio was a far cry from what people use today. I stayed outside the tent and had to pedal furiously on a generator to provide power while Peter sat in the warmth inside wielding the Morse key. My task was relatively easy while Peter was just listening, but transmitting was another matter. The drag on the generator was exhausting,

140

and I knew that, if I slacked off, the message would not get through and Maudheim would ask us to repeat it. I longed for the invention of a radio powered by the sun.[5]

By the time Valter and I had completed our outside work, we could plunge into a nice warm tent to find our sleeping bags neatly laid out and our supper all ready. It was an admirable routine that satisfied everyone.

The next day's sledging brought us onto the inland ice. We covered 27 kilometres in five and a half hours before camping at an altitude of 300 metres at 'Flag 92' on the shoulder of the southern hill. Here the temperature was –9°C and there was a moderate breeze from the south. Since leaving Maudheim, the visibility had been unlimited.

We had brought along small quantities of fresh provisions to use before launching into the sledging rations. By the time I had finished my work, Peter had prepared a fine meal of freshly fried seal meat with bacon and rice to go with it.

On 20 December I skied ahead over the crevassed area, following the weasel tracks and getting 'some unpleasant shocks to see what I had driven my weasel over four times'. This time the weather was clear and I could see many crevasses that had not shown up in the semi-whiteout of our earlier crossings. Often I thought of Brian Walford's aircraft and how useful it would have been to have it with us. Whenever we chanced upon a crevassed area, we could launch the little machine to find a safe route.

The view from above, as I learned years later, is infinitely more revealing than from the ground. Deprived of an overall view, surface travellers cross thousands of snow-bridged crevasses without ever knowing it. Most of the snow bridges remain intact, but when they do break under the weight of a man or a sledge, anything can happen and lives are at risk. We were lucky.

Mike, one of our puppies, had collapsed late in the day and was dragged under the runners by his harness. For the last half-hour we had carried him on top of the sledge load. Eventually camping at Flag 131 on safe ground at 0345, men and dogs were exhausted after eight and a half hours on the move – too tired even to do our camp work.

The blue outer covering of our double-walled tents absorbed so much of the intense radiation that we slept on top of our sleeping bags, practically naked, with the tent door wide open. Even so we found it too hot.

Valter and I did our camp work the next morning – in reality the next evening, because we were travelling at night and sleeping by day. On looking out, Valter saw through binoculars that the other main sledging party – Roer, Robin, Roots, and Reece – were in camp some

141

way behind us, having left Maudheim later. Now it was Midsummer's Day, and I regretted that 'we have only got this far. Utterly stupid. We should have left Maudheim 6 weeks ago'.

On getting under way, Valter's team was in chaos because Faith was on heat and attracting too much attention from her male colleagues. Following behind, Peter and I were also in trouble trying to hold our own dogs from catching up. It took half an hour for the pace to settle down. Here we diverged from the Advance Base trail to have a look at an inlet on the south side of it.

After a further 20 kilometres we came to a grounding line marked by the usual small crevasses and active tidal cracks. Climbing onto the land ice, Valter stopped after an hour because drifting snow had cut visibility to 100 metres. We made camp in a moderate gale, the first time we had done so. To avoid any risk of the tents being carried away before they were up, we secured a climbing rope from the loaded sledge to the apex of the pyramid, only removing it after all the guys were taut and heavy blocks of snow had been heaped on the flaps.

As we emerged after a good night's sleep, the weather was fine and calm, the temperature a balmy –2°C. Valter decided that there was nothing of interest in the direction we were heading, so we turned east to return to the trail. After lunch we saw the geology/survey party – each man with his own dog team – crossing our bows from left to right, so we turned in their direction. Yesterday's blow had stripped all soft snow from the surface, with the result that now sharp ice crystals began cutting into the dogs' feet.

By the time we reached our colleagues, they had stopped at Flag 71, one of the depots established on the weasel journey two weeks earlier. Peter's dogs ran right up to Alan's team for a joyful reunion. Peter said, 'Alan, aren't you in my way?' The thought of anyone blocking the way in this wide featureless expanse gave us a good chuckle.

It was Christmas Eve and we stopped to exchange news and views. Nils Roer had a battery radio to receive time signals for his survey work, and sometimes listened to world news. He reported that apart from the battles in Korea – for which he had only contempt – nothing was happening. We knew it could not be true but were determined not to sacrifice the bliss of our ignorance.

Gordon and Fred, who both had mouth organs, treated us to a painful rendition of 'The First Noel'. Ove, who had a fine voice, joined in. Never was a Christmas carol played so badly yet sung so nicely in such an incongruous setting, there in brilliant sunshine on the broad snow ridge. Fred could get two of his dogs – Rachel and Curly – to join in, though whether expressing their pleasure or their distress, we could not tell.

142

Of more immediate concern was the fact that the geology/survey party's puppies, like ours, could not keep up in harness, so they had been let loose to follow the sledges. We all knew that at the age of six to nine months they should not have been pulling sledges, but owing to the loss of so many dogs on *Thorshøvdi*, we needed to train them early.

After an hour, our colleagues headed off towards the Advance Base and we camped beside the depot. The next day we headed north-east into the unknown and, probably for that reason, our spirits rose. Crossing the high point of a ridge,[6] we found ourselves travelling steadily downhill. After covering 23 kilometres we camped for Christmas. Now we were 260 metres above sea level and the air temperature had dropped to −13°C.

Valter and Ove invited us over to their tent to share Christmas dinner. The meal consisted of luxuries taken from the depot – boiled ham, scrambled eggs, rice pudding, stewed mixed fruit, condensed milk, bread, butter, jam, shortbread and a bottle of whisky. It was our last fling before settling into the unchanging menu of sledging rations.

After a long sleep and a slow start because of doubtful weather, we set off again at 2315. Soon we found ourselves descending over giant, smooth steps about 4 kilometres apart. Racing down six steps without encountering a single crevasse, we spied three heavily crevassed blisters to the north, places where subglacial bedrock knobs must be trying to force their way to the surface. They were incipient nunataks, or 'nearly-nunataks' as I liked to call them. At 0300 we recognized all the usual signs of crossing a grounding line – active tidal cracks in a smooth valley, then a short climb of 5–10 metres onto the level surface of an ice shelf, where we camped.[7]

We knew that one day these ice shelves would be given names and put on a map, but now we could only call this one – the third encountered on our journey – Ice Shelf C.[8]

12

INTO THE UNKNOWN

Far away to the east we spied a solitary small peak on the horizon. Could it be Boreas, we wondered? The next day was calm but it was snowing hard and a lack of contrast made it dangerous to travel. We simply would not see crevasses unless a snow bridge gave way, in which case it would be too late. We stayed in our tents, Valter and I writing up notes, Ove and Peter reading paperbacks. When the weather cleared for a short while, I made sun observations with the theodolite to fix our position, incidentally finding the magnetic declination to be 17 degrees west. That meant that for every bearing taken with a compass we had to subtract 17 degrees to arrive at the true bearing.

It was not until 29 December that we were able to get under way again, and even then the contrast was poor. We appeared to be travelling parallel with the northern margin of steeply rising inland ice to the south,[1] but after covering 20 km we were again overtaken by a blizzard. This time it lasted two days and brought a fresh gale.

On sledging journeys, particularly in cold weather, we attended to calls of nature as rapidly as possible. Walking 50 metres downwind, we would dig a shallow hole in the snow and squat over it. It helped to hold on to a shovel. Blizzards could reward a slow performer with pants full of snow, and there was a risk of frostbite in awkward places.

Returning to the warmer tent with snow clinging to outer clothing, we had to brush ourselves down quickly. Snow in the crannies of our underwear melted, and we felt soggy and cold until things dried out.

The enforced idleness had made sledging rations feel more than adequate. Each of our food boxes weighed 23 kilos and held rations for 20 man/days. The contents were modelled on the ration scale then in use by FIDS.[2] The actual food content of the box was 15.6 kilos, the rest being the box itself and packaging. This was a planned diet that, to save weight on the sledge, avoided foods containing water. We had plenty of water, albeit in solid form, right under our feet. There were no ordinary tinned foods because all of them contain more water than solids.

Passat (left) and Boreas (right) from 3,100 metres above sea level, facing south.
Borgmassivet can be seen on the horizon 120 kilometres away

Pemmican was the only item that would not be stocked in a good food shop. North American Indians have made pemmican for centuries by drying buffalo or deer meat and pounding it into a powder. The powdered meat is then mixed with hot fat. When the mass of fat and meat cools, it is cut into cakes.[3] Our pemmican was made by Bovril in England from beef and pork. It consisted of protein and fat in about equal proportions and had the texture of very hard cheese. We chipped it out of the tin into boiling water and stirred it up with butter to make a rich soup. The thickness of the soup could be adjusted to taste by adding potato powder or pea-flour. Pemmican soup is so rich and fatty that, consumed in warmer climates, it can induce vomiting. Here, however, it was just what we needed.

The total daily ration for each of us was 780 grammes (27.5 oz) dry weight consisting of:

145

	Grammes
Pemmican	160
Butter	136
Biscuits	106
Porridge oats	65
Milk powder	45
Lump sugar	92
Cocoa	23
Pea-flour	23
Potato powder	23
Chocolate	68
Onion	12
Coffee (instant)	7
Tea	12
Marmite	6
One vitamin tablet	2

The staples were oatmeal porridge for breakfast, biscuits and chocolate for lunch, and pemmican with pea-flour or potato powder for supper. The calorific value of the ration was said to be 4,066 Kilocalories per man per day. For us, it was rich, nourishing, and satisfying – particularly after a hard day's sledging.

Confined to the tent by blizzards, however, we were beginning to wonder whether our food supply would last long enough for us to reach the Advance Base without going on short rations.

The advantage of using dogs rather than mechanical transport is that one travels with enormous reserves of edible supplies: man food, dog food, and ultimately the dogs themselves. To spin out the rations, we tried stockfish to make *bacalao*. Even after soaking overnight, it still took a lot of chewing. It tasted of ammonia because the dogs had taken pleasure in scent-marking the bales.

When the wind let up on the first day of January 1951, we had a great deal of digging to do. The dogs never seemed to mind being buried – snow protected them from the elements. All we could see were low mounds at intervals of 3 metres along the wire span but, as we emerged from our tent, one by one the mounds erupted, shook off the snow, and stood up with tails wagging. It was a heartening sight. Both tents were heavily drifted up and the sledges were smoothed over with snowdrifts.

Finally under way at 2200, we saw that a second, smaller nunatak had appeared from behind the nearer one. Could it be Passat? Now the land ice 5 kilometres to the south of us was criss-crossed with spectacular, close-spaced networks of gaping crevasses on its steep slopes. We hoped that by the time they reached the ice shelf, these chasms would be deeply buried under snow.

After five hours of slogging through sticky snow resulting from the recent storms, once more we camped in a rising wind. This time the bad weather lasted four days, with blinding snow being swept along by winds of up to 50 knots. We began to wonder whether we must learn to live with this, because travelling blind was out of the question.

It was 6 January before we set off again. Just after the lunch stop, Ove was making a trail ahead when, suddenly, the full length of the right runner of Valter's sledge broke through a snow bridge and heeled over. With an almost superhuman effort, Valter lifted that side of the sledge, only to realize that the other runner was on the same snow bridge. Ove had not even known there was a crevasse. Peter immediately swung our dogs to the right so that, seen or unseen, we would be crossing the crevasses at right angles.

As we approached the nunataks it became clear that we really had found Boreas and, behind it, Passat. I led on skis through a maze of crevasses on the west side of Boreas with Pluto, Valter's lead dog, close on my heels. We stopped only 250 metres from the vertical rock face. Here there were tidal cracks, and in order to prove that they really were active, we pitched our tent astride one of them and set about measuring its width every hour or so. Serenaded by sounds like rifle shots as the ice deformed, it did not take long to satisfy ourselves that we were exactly at the boundary between land ice and floating ice.

Boreas was surrounded on three sides by a giant windscoop, evidently caused by winds bouncing off its upstream face. They had hollowed out a sort of empty moat 50 metres wide. The outer limit of the moat was a 15-metre-high vertical ice cliff. Although windscoop is the common term for these features, they are at the same time radiation hollows due to heat radiated from the rock face on sunny days.

Towards the downstream end, the windscoop gave way to an icefall and then to a general chaos of crevasses as the glacier swung in to fill the void behind the nunatak. It seemed almost incredible that the finger-like plug of Boreas thrusting through the ice must represent the summit of something much bigger, most of it hidden beneath the ice. The exposed sides of the nunatak were almost vertical and its horizontal dimensions were smaller than its height, which I measured by simple trigonometry to be 200 metres.

Valter was clearly in shock from the crevasse incident. Fifty years on, the scene of his close call with destiny is still etched on my memory. Such events are part and parcel of exploration – but not one that we relish. Ove advised Valter to rest while Peter made a meal.

Meanwhile, Ove and I were bent on exploring the surroundings,

147

knowing that the weather might change again. Neither of us being alpinists, we decided not to climb Boreas but instead to ski over to Passat, which looked smaller and possibly climbable. It took 15 minutes to traverse the 1,500 metres or so that separated the nunataks. Fortunately there were no crevasses because the ice flowing from inland was under compression, evidently dammed up behind the outcrops.

Passat was made of diorite sill material and it too had a big windscoop, but here the moat held water. There was one lake 20 by 150 metres and it appeared to be about half a metre deep. We quenched our thirst with clear, virgin water. It was then not difficult to scramble onto the rock.

Climbing without difficulty, we were astonished to come across yellow, orange and grey lichens clinging to bedrock surfaces. There were also luxuriant mats of a green, long-haired moss in sheltered spots. Here, we realized, was an Antarctic oasis.

One of the duties of explorers is to bring back any observations or specimens that could be of interest to other scientists. Taking this responsibility seriously, Ove spent half an hour prising off representative samples of every variety of moss and lichen before gently loading them into his rucksack.

The windscoop of Boreas, with our tents behind

On reaching the summit, we noted that, according to my aneroid, we were 115 metres above the lake and probably 150 metres above sea level. There was a spectacular view in every direction. The main glacier from inland passed just to the east of Passat, presenting a memorable picture of icy chaos and confusion trending about 20 degrees west of north towards an ice front that must have been 100 kilometres away.

Another obvious duty of the first visitors in a new land is to bring back a map. Nils Roer, of course, was the expedition's professional surveyor, but he would not be coming this way, so we would have to bring home a sketch map based on our own observations. With this in mind, I spent two hours taking compass bearings to every feature in sight, far and near.

Our survey routine was to ask a companion to write down the bearings, repeating each one back to the observer to make sure that the note-taker had heard correctly. Today it was Ove's turn. Bored by the slow pace of my observations, he turned over some loose rocks. All of a sudden he exclaimed, 'Look, Charles, we are not alone!' I did not know what he was on about but, seeing his excitement, I bent down to see where he was pointing. There were dozens of tiny, fast-moving red, brown and black mites running for cover. Living under the rocks, they had been rudely disturbed by Ove's curiosity.

Grabbing a film container, Ove ever so gently brushed the mites and some of their eggs into it. The insects were less than 1 millimetre long, so could very easily have been damaged. Looking under some other rocks, at first I did not notice the mites because they did not move. But after a minute or two in the sunshine, they slowly came to life, moving one leg carefully, then another. After thawing completely, they began to run around. We soon realized that they wanted to get back into the shade, being only comfortable within a very narrow range of temperatures.

For the rest of my angles we were both in a high state of excitement. Finally starting down from the summit, we carefully broke off small pieces of the dominant types of bedrock and put them in our backpacks. A solitary snow petrel (*Pagodroma nivea*) wheeled overhead, eying a strange and unfamiliar species (*Homo sapiens*). No doubt the birds were breeding nearby because there was no other nunatak closer to the coast.

Back at camp, it slowly dawned on us that the mites Ove had collected represented probably the first living land fauna discovered between Snow Hill Island (57°W) in the west and Gaussberg (89°E) in the east. These two places are more than 5,000 kilometres apart.

It had indeed been a worthwhile excursion. Years later, the mites were shown to represent not only a new species but also a new genus;

and according to custom, they became known as *Maudheimia Wilsoni* – a tribute to Ove and a tribute to serendipity.[4]

Meanwhile, Valter had been using the theodolite to determine the position of Boreas. It was 71°18′S, 03°56′W, which was 36 kilometres south of where the Germans had put it. We estimated that the summit was 250 metres above sea level – the Germans had mapped it as 1,400 metres.

The next day all four of us went to explore Boreas. It bore the appearance of a volcanic plug, but could be part of a once extensive sill. The smoothed, polished and striated surface of the bedrock indicated that the surrounding ice, at some stage in the past, had been at least 200 metres above its present level. Snow petrels were living and presumably breeding among rocks high up on the north face (the sunny side). We also found lichens and mosses in abundance.

Valter was interested in what the lichens could tell us about climatic change. We soon found that they were growing on rock faces right down to the lowest level that was exposed. He knew that, even in warmer climates, lichens take many decades to spread outwards from their first foothold, so this indicated that the ice surface could not be retreating. If it were, there would be a band of clean rock below the colonized rock.

On that morning, in other words, we established the fact that the general recession of the glaciers in the north had no direct counterpart in the inland ice of Dronning Maud Land. Valter's mentor Professor Ahlmann had bidden us to seek such evidence – and now we had found it. This was the first of many observations that told the same story. Not until much later could we also state that the inland ice itself was not increasing.

Our plan now was to head straight for the Advance Base, a journey of 110 kilometres that would involve a climb from 100 metres to 1,330 metres above sea level, heading almost due south. That meant facing into a katabatic wind,[*] but now the sky was almost cloudless, the visibility unlimited, and the temperature –9°C. This sort of temperature was ideal for travelling because the sledges glided easily, without the stickiness of new snow or the sandpaper-like surface of really cold snow.

We seemed to be ascending a wide, stepped glacier.[5] To the left was a long ridge[6] punctuated by nunataks and small, isolated mountains.

---

[*] Air cooled at a higher level flowing downhill under the influence of gravity.

Sledge tracks on leaving Boreas (left) and Passat

To our right was a smooth highland that appeared to be a continuation of the broad ridge on which Førstefjell lay.[7]

Except when we had to help the sledges along by pushing, I was finding that dog sledging was a most relaxing form of travel, because the dogs tired before we did. This left plenty of time for other activities. At each camp we took bearings of every outcrop in sight. Used with the sledge wheel readings, these would provide all that we needed to make sketch maps. This compass-and-sledge-wheel technique, with theodolite angles whenever possible, had been a standard method of reconnaissance mapping in the Antarctic for half a century.

At each camp site, Valter progressively dug himself out of sight down a snow pit. No earlier Antarctic expedition had been able to distinguish annual layers by studying snow strata. Valter, however, with his experience from Swedish Lapland, was soon able to tell how much snow had accumulated between one summer's layer and the next.

I myself ground away with the hand auger to drill holes for snow-temperature measurements. Although the annual temperature fluctuations would be damped down at 3 metres' depth, they would not be eliminated, so we planned to drill 10-metre holes in a few places during the season to yield a correction factor for the shallower readings.

As we climbed steadily up-glacier, the 3-metre temperature read – 17°C on 8 January, –21°C on the 9th, and –23°C on the 10th. Finally

Looking for a place to cross a crevasse

we hauled into the Advance Base at 0430 on the 11th. There was no sign of the other parties – evidently they were off and away to the east.

Valter allowed three days for resting the dogs and repacking the sledges for our next journey. During the rest period, we set up and surveyed a line of stakes across a nearby tributary glacier to measure its rate of movement.[8] We noted that Nils Roer had already measured a precise baseline in the same area to serve as the starting point for his main triangulation network. He was later able to complete a continuous triangulation network that extended 300 kilometres to the east of the Advance Base and 150 kilometres to the south.

We were off again at 2345 on 18 January with nearly half a tonne on each sledge, heading south-east to reconnoitre the high mountain area that we had seen ever since leaving Boreas. Fred Roots had named the massif The Fortress, which Nils Roer translated as Borgen.[9]

With soft fresh snow and an uphill climb, the dogs were struggling and we had to help by pushing the sledges. Both teams were exhausted after three hours during which we climbed about 100 metres but covered only 7 kilometres, so we camped.

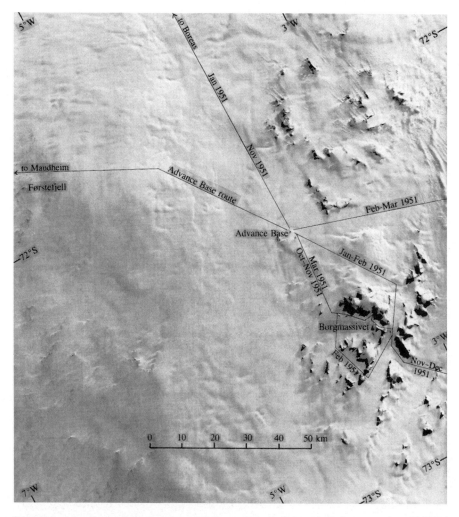

The Advance Base area showing sledging routes of the glaciology parties. NASA/ Landsat image from an altitude of 900 kilometres. Note that the frame of the picture –unlike a conventional map – is aligned 29° east of north.

At breakfast after a good sleep, the silence of the wilderness was shattered by the unmistakeable sound of a single-engined aircraft taking off. At first we were astonished, but soon realized what this implied. *Norsel* must be back at Maudheim, this time carrying aircraft belonging to Wiederøes Flyveselskap, a Norwegian company. They were to undertake aerial photography to add detail to Nils Roer's surveying. The aircraft must have taken off from the Advance Base – we prayed that they had brought mail from home. We also hoped for

153

a visit, or at least a friendly wave but, although they could not have missed our tracks, they headed off in a south-westerly direction.

On emerging from the tent on the third day of this uphill struggle, I was brought up short by a glance at the sun. It was framed by two brilliant haloes, the inner at a radius of 22 degrees and the outer at 46 degrees.[10] The inner halo was touched on three sides by tangential arcs – the whole picture having a soft, ethereal beauty. Earlier we had been treated to the first rainbow that we had seen since leaving Maudheim. Soft white rime crystals decked the sledges and, after completing our routine observations, we got under way in fog – steering on a compass heading.

The slope ahead was becoming steeper, so reluctantly we started relaying – taking half a load ahead and then returning for the other half. After two and a half hours we had gained another 100 metres in height but men and dogs were exhausted, so we had no choice but to camp.

The next day the aircraft passed low overhead while we were sleeping, heading south-east. Although I had been taking bearings at every stop and we could see massifs or nunataks on all sides, it was still impossible to make sense of the German map. We were now close among the mountains, and soon reached the foot of a pass with magnificent views of mountains perhaps 200 kilometres away. To anyone coming from the haze of an industrial country in the Northern Hemisphere, 200 kilometres seems a long way, but here, with clear air and very little moisture in the atmosphere, it was commonplace.

While Valter was digging his pit, Peter and I scaled a ridge on a nearby mountain whose smooth faceted faces buttressed a thinly ice-capped summit.[11] At intervals we took rock specimens for the geologists, who might never come this way. From the top, we looked back towards our camp far below, where the dogs were enjoying a well-earned rest. I felt they needed reassuring that we had not evaporated, so I cupped my hands and let out a couple of long, wailing wolf howls. 'Aooo, aooo!' Not many seconds passed before their answering howls reached us, echoing through the mountains. We too felt reassured – we belonged to the same team, and they knew it.

On 27 January, after taking sun sights with the theodolite to pin down our position, I noted 'First sunset at midnight.' It was five weeks past midsummer; soon it would be too dark to travel at night as we had been doing. The snow temperature was –28°C, a reminder that at this altitude winters must be harsh. The air temperature too was beginning to fall – now it was –14°C.

At the summit of the pass,[12] we were at 2,030 metres above sea level. Here Valter and Ove parted from us in order to broaden the reconnaissance. They headed south-west down a broad valley,[13] while

154

Borgmassivet seen from 4650 metres above sea level, facing south

we turned north-west to parallel the side of the main massif. It was
good to be alone with Peter, the easiest of travelling companions,
never flustered and never complaining.

Cooler weather had brought better snow surfaces, so we decided to
travel and work by day rather than at night. After sledging through
another pass between mountain blocks,[14] we discovered the largest
windscoop that I have ever seen. It was on the south side of the pass
at the foot of a steep escarpment.[15] The windscoop itself was more
than 1,500 metres long, 200 metres wide and 40 metres deep – a moat
to end all moats. We camped beside it, praying that we might be
spared the sort of winds, accelerated by the narrow pass, that must
have carved it out. Here we searched for signs of changes, finding that
although the ice level had been higher in the past, there was no
evidence that it was now falling.

Another of our objectives was to study how active the mountain

Camp under the north face of Borgen (22 January 1951)

glaciers were – in other words, to see how fast they moved. Some 5 kilometres from the windscoop was a neat little glacier below an icefall supplied from the summit plateau of the main massif. We harnessed the dogs and sledged across, camping in the middle of the glacier close to a series of 3-metre wide crevasses. The surface was hard so that, as long as we kept off the snow bridges, there was no danger in walking around without skis. Moreover, we could use the crevasses to dispose of our rubbish.

Surrounded by cirque walls, we were in an echoing amphitheatre. Every dog bark or shout came back to us as it would in a whispering gallery. At a glance, it was clear that this was a slow-moving glacier and, although I measured a baseline, drilled in a few stakes and measured angles to them, I guessed that in the space of a few months the rate of movement would be too small to measure. And so it proved.[16]

On 6 February we sledged 8 kilometres to the north-west, finding a delightful camping site on a snow patch in the middle of a low nunatak.[17] To camp here was immensely satisfying, because for weeks we had been living in fear of crevasses. Here, at least, we were safe.

156

Valter Schytt measuring snow density in his daily 2-metre-deep pit

Cautious by nature, I drilled to bedrock – the snow was only 2.5 metres deep.

Spanning out the dogs, we realized that more than 15 months had elapsed since any of them had touched bare ground. So to amuse them, we presented each one with a rock. They were not amused and gave their rock the widest berth that their chains would allow. It dawned on us that rock was so unfamiliar to them that the poor animals feared that it might attack them. Peter and I laughed unsympathetically. Then slowly, over the next half hour, sniffing intently, the bolder dogs crept towards their 'predator'. Finally, with a swipe of a paw, they challenged it to battle. Gradually, they came to understand that rocks generally capitulate without a fight. After this it was not long before calm was restored and each rock was well-used in place of a lamp post.

The great windscoop, looking up-glacier. Peter Melleby stands at the edge of the moraine

The great windscoop, looking down-glacier from the same camera position

Icefall camp

13

SUSPENSION BRIDGE

During the night we were struck by a curious series of hurricane-force winds interspersed with moments of eerie calm. The gusts were so violent that we feared for the tent – if not for our lives. For half a minute before each blast struck us, we could hear a roaring crescendo from the 500-metre high rock wall upwind of the camp. We both put on all our outer clothing and boots before re-entering our sleeping bags. If the tent were carried away, we planned to stay in our bags. I soon understood that we were under attack by a series of giant vortices caused by the swirling of an easterly storm over the mountain. Luckily, the tent and its occupants survived. At least it gave us confidence that pyramid tents are not easy to destroy.

The next day we met up with Valter and Ove, who were surveying ice movement stakes a short distance to the west. They were on the edge of a 2 x 5 kilometre area of bare blue ice, the first extensive snow-free area that we had come across. It was smooth enough, I remember thinking, for landing wheeled aircraft.[1]

Seeking to explain the origin of this patch of ice in a land of snow, we measured the exposed height above the ice surface of each of the stakes. Anyone returning the following year would be able to repeat the measurements to determine the rate of ablation.[*] Over the few days that we were on the icefield, it was too small to measure.[2]

We struck camp on 10 February and headed for the Advance Base. This time it was all downhill, and we covered the 33 kilometres in seven hours. In the course of our circuit we had found much of interest, and had confirmed that there was no vertical zonation in the distribution of lichens. Glacial striations and smoothed rock faces, on the other hand, indicated that at some stage in the past the ice had been several hundred metres thicker.

---

[*] The processes by which snow, ice or water are lost from the surface. We found that sublimation – the direct conversion of ice to vapour – was the dominant process.

At the Advance Base, we quickly discovered that the aircraft had brought a small supply of beef, fresh potatoes and fish cakes, so we had a welcome change of diet. We intended to rest for two days, but bad weather intervened and held us there for five days. I decided to take a bath, the first for seven weeks. This involved clearing everything out of the tent except for a Primus stove and an empty biscuit tin. Starting with snow, it took an hour to melt 3 litres, and by that time the tent was like a steam bath. Stepping into the tin, I scooped up water in a mug and poured it over my head. After soaping, I had to rinse off with the same water. I felt refreshed and invigorated, and put on clean underwear.

Ove took blood from us, but spilt the samples all over his sleeping bag while trying to cook at the same time. 'So wants to do all the morning values again tomorrow.' My own small consolation was to serve as vampire for his own specimen.

We read and reread books, calibrated instruments, and repacked the sledges for the next trip. Now disillusioned with the radio because it was heavy and seldom gave us any contact with Maudheim, we decided to leave it behind, although this was strictly against Giæver's orders.

Pencilling a note for the geology/survey party to place on record that we were heading east with provisions for 21 days but no radio, we got under way on 16 February under a clear sky. The dogs had benefited from the enforced rest and now bounded ahead. After half an hour we saw Ove turn and ski back towards Pyramiden. 'As usual he has forgotten something, this time his gloves . . . ' Ove was a dear friend to all of us but prone to these minor misadventures. We teased him mercilessly but fortunately he remained good-humoured. Anger would have damaged our friendship but teasing seemed to enhance it.

Although it was uphill, we covered 20 kilometres in four hours. On reaching a saddle, Pyramiden disappeared from view and we were treated to a splendid panorama of new features to the east. On camping, the atmosphere was crystal-clear; it was almost dead calm, and the air temperature was -25°C. I was convinced that we could see the tops of mountains 300 kilometres away, and to this day I do not doubt it.

Now, with darker evenings, we had to light a candle to read by or to write up notes. Peter read avidly and had learned to carry enough books. When he had finished with whatever Norwegian books he had brought, he simply started on my books in English and, when those ran out, went on to Valter's and Ove's books in Swedish. While he and I spoke Norwegian all the time, he could read English books as fast as I did. He was undoubtedly the most erudite man on the expedi-

Snow patch camp, where the dogs were confronted with 'predators'

tion when it came to translating idiomatic English into Norwegian. Moreover, when a difficult Norwegian word was to be translated into English, he would come out with the right – even if obscure – English word.

It was dead calm when we woke up the next morning. Rime ice from our breath coated the inner tent, so it must have been a cold night. Outside, diamond dust – microscopic ice crystals floating in the air – endowed the scene with a rainbow-sparkling mist.

Soon after starting, the snow became deeper and softer and the sledges seemed heavier. By the end of the day the dogs were only making 50 metres before the drag on the sledge brought them to a standstill. We had to call a halt after only 10 kilometres.

Day after day, I noticed that the dogs showed every sign of suffering from lack of food. All of them ate faeces – no doubt counting on some trace of recycled nourishment. Their own or any other dog's faeces were equally welcome, though most prized of all was human faeces. Ove rewarded his favourite dogs by defecating in front of them. However, I was concerned that there might be some risk to my person from dogs seeking to ensure that their snack was steamingly fresh.

One of my daily chores—drilling a hole to measure ice temperatures

When on the move, the last pair of dogs in harness got the best rewards – if they acted quickly. On the rare occasions when a bitch gave birth in harness, she ate her pups if hungry neighbours had not already snatched them.

For four days from 18 February we had to relay with half-loads, a back-breaking chore, no more fun for the dogs than for ourselves. The snow was soft from frequent snowfalls and much of the time we were in whiteout. Unable to see anything but whiteness, we seemed suspended betwixt snow and sky. Without any scale factor, I mistook a discarded matchbox 6 metres from the tent door for a sledging party 1 kilometre away.

There followed an enforced lie-up because of high winds. In my notes I reported that I might have altered the zero adjustment of our

We built snow cairns to guide our return

Sledge tracks in soft snow. Under these conditions we had to carry half-loads, returning for the other half

precision aneroid 'by dropping it'. Luckily, the next calibration proved that it was undamaged.

Only on the 23rd could we get going again with a full load on the sledges. It was evident that we were heading down into the broad valley of a major ice stream, for ahead lay echelons of enormous crevasses. However, they were so wide and so well bridged that we had little difficulty in running between them. Battling an easterly wind towards the end of the day, we climbed out of the ice stream onto a ridge 1,050 metres above sea level near a pair of nunataks.[3] Rising 100 metres above the level of the ice stream, we camped at a point where, for the first time, the summit of Pyramiden just showed above the pass from whence we came.

Snow-bridged crevasses. Here they are conspicuous – probably 3–4 metres wide and 30–40 metres deep – but sometimes they are completely hidden under smooth snow bridges

Ahead lay an ice stream wider and grander than the one we had just crossed.[4]

Rows and rows of clean transverse crevasses, kilometres long and perhaps 50 m apart . . . looking in the oblique light for all the world as a giant's ploughed field.

But the furrows were deeper.

Behind this scene rose great snow-capped mountain ranges, orange in the sunlight; and to the left of them, an enormous orange moon appeared from behind an ice ridge 200 kilometres away. A deep, dark blue suffused the northern sky; above it there was an orange band. Perhaps the deep blue came from the far-off sea reflected as water sky, or perhaps it was just the approaching night – an earth shadow opposite the sun.

The next day, 'Exactly the same miserable windy cold clear weather.' We laid a depot of five days' provisions for the homeward journey and marked it with a tall snow cairn. Intending to return along our outward tracks, we knew that they could be obliterated in a storm, leaving only the snow cairns to guide us.

Descending to the ice stream in overcast conditions, we encountered rows of crevasses about 30 metres wide and, as they lay across our course, there was little choice but to take our lives in our hands and cross them. The width of some of the crevasses was beyond anything I could have conceived, each with a smooth, deeply sagging snow bridge. For anxious seconds of every crossing, our whole train, from lead dog to sledge wheel, was moving over the hidden abyss. Later in the day we found ourselves among low parallel ridges in the snow, most about 0.5 metres high. At first we thought they were sastrugi, but then Valter stopped his sledge abruptly on realizing that we were poised on the Antarctic equivalent of a suspension bridge. The crevasse was about 40 metres wide. Worst of all, we were right in the middle and travelling along it. Valter had been alerted on seeing an open chasm just ahead of his lead dog.

We turned round and went another way as quick as we could, imagining that if one fell in a crevasse of these dimensions one would not stop until face to face with the devil himself.

I recollected that Roald Amundsen had named a similar crevassed area *Fandens Dansesal* – the Devil's Ballroom.[5] Between the worst areas there were ridges trending in the direction of glacier flow – about 30 degrees east of north. Most were relatively free from crevasses, so after

166

sunset we camped on one of them to lick our psychological wounds. I comforted myself with the thought that snow bridges as wide as those we had crossed must themselves be so heavy that adding the weight of a sledge should be insignificant.

On 26 February we came across the tracks of several sledges running parallel with our own, evidently quite old. That the only other travellers in history should tread the same path as ours was a chance in a million, because none of our routes had been pre-planned. We had known that the geology/survey party was heading 'east', but many different routes would fit that description.

Moving close to and parallel with a 40-metre wide crevasse with a deeply sagging snow bridge, we met two open crevasses trending right across our path. They were 10 metres wide and we could see down to a fallen snow bridge 20 metres below the surface. There was nothing for it but to retrace our steps again and try to go round the area.

The next day we experienced something akin to a hurricane. The wind noise steadily increased to a roar that drowned the usual whistling of the tent guys. The upwind side of the tent bulged inwards, bar-taut, and on the lee side, snow built half way up the roof. Peter went out to feed the dogs and was blown off his feet. The ventilator at the top of the tent became iced up, and as soon as we cleared it, ice blocked it again.

'But inside the tent', I wrote, 'it is warm and comfortable, and has been so all the time; and we know the canvas will hold out.' Peter and I were enjoying the simple pleasures of life. Watching the Primus flame and waiting for our supper became one of the high points of our existence. We had a device (made by Primus as an optional extra) that turned the stove into a space heater. It was a brass dome peppered with holes and could be suspended over the flame. Intercepting the rising column of hot air, it glowed red and radiated so much heat that we had to turn the flame down. I have husbanded ours ever since – an invention never to be forgotten.

By noon the following day the wind had dropped but the sky remained overcast, and there was a total whiteout. Travel in these conditions could be suicidal, so we stayed put.

The first of March dawned clear, calm and 'warm', though the thermometer read −16°C. We made fast time all day on a hard-packed surface, covering 20 kilometres in four hours and camping near a small mountain towards which we had been heading for two weeks.[6] Approaching it, we crossed many crevasses but they were well-bridged, so there was no problem. Looking back, we could see the giant transverse crevasses that gave us trouble three days ago. They were dead straight and at least 5 kilometres in length. I guessed that they must be on very deep ice – moving as a single block over a very large area.[7]

On rising, Peter and I started out on skis towards the nearest part of the nunatak while Valter and Ove headed towards the far end. We crossed three crevasses 20 metres wide and, without a rope to hang on, I remember feeling decidedly less secure than when we were following the sledge. The last 200 metres into the rock consisted of bare blue ice riddled with small crevasses, so Peter and I crawled on hands and knees to avoid sliding into one of them. The rock was granitic, highly deformed at a variety of scales and weathered on the surface. We climbed a steep ridge with a 200-metre vertical cliff on one side and 'an unstoppably steep snow slope on the other'. Reaching the summit, we were 500 metres above the ice-rock contact and 1,600 metres above sea level. From here we looked down on a windscoop 200-300 metres wide at the foot of the north face; it was 50-70 metres deep, deeper even than the windscoop that we had seen a month ago.

I took bearings as usual and also a complete panoramic round of photographs. There were many smoothly rounded hollows pitting the bedrock, most of them with dimensions of 10-30 centimetres. They reminded me of potholes in the bed of a stream beneath a waterfall, but here they were probably due to chemical weathering. A few of the holes contained sharp pebbles of an alien rock type. Swirled around by hurricane winds, these must have served as tools to accelerate the weathering process. Some potholes and crevices harboured flower-shaped black lichens and also a fine-grained red variety. Rich green moss banks were flourishing in sheltered corners.

Traversing the ridge, we came to a vertical cliff. Not wishing to return the way we had come, Peter and I abseiled down, one at a time, though Peter readily admitted that he had never done it before. Keeping track of our dead-reckoning position, we had a good laugh on realizing that we must be roughly on the same meridian as Picca-dilly Circus.

As the sun was setting, we roped together and glissaded down to where we had left our skis. From all the signs, I concluded that here too the surrounding ice had formerly been hundreds of metres thicker. But again there was no indication of any recent retreat.

The 3-kilometre run back to camp was icy but downhill, so we freewheeled at high speed, 'too fast we hoped for the crevasses to swallow us'. We had been away eight hours.

Valter and Ove were excited by the results of their own excursion, having returned to camp with mites, mosses and lichens. The mites were of the same species that Ove had found on Passat. That animals could survive winter temperatures of perhaps −50° or below was astonishing.

Our colleagues reported with some relish that they had traced a wide crevasse right up to the camp and that it probably extended right under our tent. Peter and I had not noticed the signs. However, we were too tired to consider moving.

With only five days of food remaining, we realized that we had reached the limit of our range, so the next day we set off to return to the Advance Base. Carefully circumnavigating the worst-crevassed areas, most of which we could now see, we made very fast time, putting 30 kilometres behind us in five hours. 'Horribly cold pitching camp after dark' – the temperature was –27°C.

On 4 March we covered another 30 kilometres, which rewarded me with blistered heels,

> but am twisting my socks round slowly so that the hole is not on the heel. Shortly the top part of the sock and the foot part will cease to be one.

Next day we reached the food depot but had to stop before negotiating the nearby crevassed area because of poor contrast. Three days passed before we could move again. We had run out of all man food except oatmeal, so had to make do with porridge twice a day. The dogs, plainly undernourished by our powdery whale pemmican, were 'tired and indolent now after so much bad food, and they are very cold, shivering pitifully'.

Our sleeping bags were of the kind known as 'mummy' bags. They enveloped the body like an Egyptian mummy, being wide at the top and tapering towards the toes. Our heads were inside and, when fully zipped, there was a breathing hole just big enough for nose and mouth.

One night I was woken by muffled shouts. Peter seemed to be suffocating but, as it was pitch-dark, I could not understand why. He was in a panic, and agonizing seconds passed before he understood what was wrong. He had turned over in his sleep and woken with the zip at the back of his neck. He was so shaken that

> now he does not take his head inside, but instead wraps up in a scarf and dons a leather helmet just as if he is off for a motor cycle ride.

It was 9 March before we got away, after a lot of digging to excavate tents and sledges. Negotiating the crevassed areas without incident, we started on the long climb towards the pass leading to Pyramiden. The snow was soft but we covered about 20 kilometres in seven hours and a similar distance the following day. Although our loads were equal, Valter's dogs were almost crawling, so Peter and I drove ahead. After half an hour we had left them a kilometre behind – to their amazement and ours.

This caused some ill-feeling that lasted for the rest of the season. Valter wanted Peter to carry some of his load. From Peter's point of view, Valter's team was confused by his constantly chattering with Ove; we saw dogs looking back over their shoulders to see who was being addressed – themselves or Ove. Moreover, they had become demoralized by being subjected to almost continuous shouting, whereas Peter's seldom heard more than a quiet word of encouragement.[8]

With hindsight, we should have been more considerate, but it was not a matter of life and death. Luckily, the sight of Pyramiden gave all the dogs renewed vigour and we reached the Advance Base at 1230 on 11 March.

14

THE ACCIDENT

We saw two tents at the Advance Base, so we assumed that the other party must be there. Hearing us, Gordon Robin came out and told us that he had been alone for eight days. Then came his bombshell. He handed us a radio message telling of a terrible accident at Maudheim in which Knalle Ekström, Leslie Quar and John Jelbart – a new arrival – had been drowned. Stig Hallgren, another new arrival, had spent many hours on an ice floe before being rescued. This had happened on 24 February and the base was in disarray. Three lives had been lost out of only nine at Maudheim.

How could this happen? We had left Maudheim as a safe haven, free, we thought, of risks. Surely it was we – the sledgers – who might not return; we who were putting our lives at risk by crossing thousands of crevasses with our fingers crossed?

But now everything had been turned on its head. There was no mechanic to look after the diesel generators on which Maudheim depended for radio communications. Rog was running one generator for an hour a day – they could not risk more. There was no longer anyone to stand in for Gordon on the Rawin set for the daily radio-sonde flights. Maudheim, in other words, was desperately short-handed.

Fred Roots, Alan Reece and Nils Roer had left the Advance Base on 3 March for an exploratory journey to the south. Giæver had asked Gordon and Peter to return to Maudheim immediately. Late though it was in the season, Valter, Ove and I could continue our work.

Now I would have to drive Peter's team without him. But by this time the dogs were so well trained that I had no qualms about taking them on. We would allow a couple of days for rest and give them small pieces of whale meat, seal blubber, and stockfish, ' . . . a moment of paradise for them, but it is about 100 times less than they need'.

Gordon invited all four of us into his tent for a hearty supper of seal meat, potatoes, peas, pears and apricots – a nice change from sledging rations. He had been making himself useful by excavating the whole Advance Base – all 4 tonnes of it – and moving everything to a new site clear of snowdrifts. He had contacted Maudheim three times, a feat that we had thought impossible without an extra man to pedal the generator. Demonstrating, he sat on a box and pedalled furiously while at the same time tapping out a message in Morse code.

Valter decided that he, Ove and I would return to the main massif to add some finishing touches to our earlier work. Meanwhile, Gordon and Peter would put together a scratch dog team consisting of Billy, Sue and Whisky – three dogs left here by the geology/survey party – Sigur from Valter's team, and Kakortok, Kajo and Belle from Peter's team. That left me with Kernek as lead dog, Amiako, Krane, Mike, Nafalik and Rapasak, all of them Greenland dogs.

On 13 March Gordon and Peter headed north; Valter, Ove and I south on a rather sticky surface. The first time I called Peter's – now my – dogs to get up and go, Kernek looked over his shoulder as if to say, 'Who do you think you are?', but a moment later, 'Well, I know what you mean!' Whereupon he jerked the trace taut and the others followed. From that moment on I had no difficulty in making myself understood. We made over 20 kilometres and climbed 300 metres in the space of four hours; evidently both teams had benefited from the rest.

Rather than having a pyramid tent all to myself, I had decided to use one of the small pup tents that we kept for emergencies. It was quick and easy to erect but had no fly. It was not even high enough for me to sit cross-legged on the groundsheet without hitting the ceiling. Although the temperature was −26°C outside, my Primus made the inside quite comfortable. However, as soon I turned off the stove, the tent cooled rapidly and I had to seek shelter in my sleeping bag. Before fastening the sleeve entrance, I looked outside and saw the first aurora of the season:

> Wide searchlight beams darting up from the horizon, subdividing and widening again as they approach the zenith, where they hover for a bit and then fade out.

Pressing on the next morning, Ove found two different lichen species on a tiny nunatak. The bare rock rose only 1.5 metres above the snow surface and the whole nunatak was only about 10 square metres in area. Now we had even more evidence that there was no ice retreat.

On reaching the blue icefield, Ove and I drove off together to remeasure the stakes that Peter and I had set out on a small glacier seven weeks earlier, leaving Valter alone with the pup tent to remeasure his own survey network. My stakes showed no discernible movement. When we returned to Valter's camp on 18 March, his survey had also drawn a blank. It was, however, useful to have discovered that glaciers in the mountain area were sluggish in the extreme.

With very light loads on the sledges, the three of us headed north at breakneck speed. This was the sort of running that the dogs really enjoyed. I sat on my sledge all day long to prevent it from overtaking the dogs. It was –29°C when I crept into the pup tent.

As we were approaching Pyramiden the next day, we saw two figures climbing the northern ridge, silhouetted against the sky. This was a surprise because the geology/survey party had left with supplies for a month and they should still be away somewhere to the south. Rounding the corner of the nunatak, we saw two tents and innumerable dogs. It was not until we had spanned out all of our dogs that I went over to their tents to see who might be there.

Nils Roer imparted the shocking news that Alan Reece was blind in one eye after a rock splinter flew into it while he was chipping out a rock specimen. They had returned in order to catch Ove before we headed north. Although Alan had been in great pain for days after the accident, he and Fred were now climbing on Pyramiden to pass the time. It was not until after dark that they returned, having spent the day roped together and climbing an ice face where a slip might have precipitated them 300 metres to the foot of the mountain.

On examining Alan's eye, Ove said there might still be a chip of rock there, but that he could not attempt to extract it until we were back at Maudheim. Meanwhile, there was no reason why the party, including Alan, should not embark on another journey south. We tried the radio but there was no answer, and anyway there was nothing that anyone else could do to help.

What a miserable run of bad luck this expedition seems to be having! Perhaps we will be known at home as the 'ill-fated' NBSX. All six of us supped together on seal meat, potatoes, and whisky, then talked non-stop until midnight.

The next morning:

Fred invited me in for breakfast with his gang. As usual [when at the Advance Base] he had produced some superb food. Featherweight cakes, and a sumptuous omelette, of enormous dimensions, and coffee. We spent the morning sorting out things that we must take home. The absolute minimum of course.

Valter and I each agreed to carry 100 kilos of rocks for the geologists.

173

My total sledge-load was 370 kilos, or 53 kilos per dog, and Valter's was about the same.

We left the Advance Base at 1400 on 20 March and made good time to Flag 9, where we camped after dark in a temperature of –30°C.

Pluto, one of Valter's dogs, got loose in a fight at feeding time and ran away in the direction of the moon. Valter had beaten him cruelly, with the result that he was the only dog in either team who would not come when called.

> This trip I am living in luxury, alone in a pyramid tent. The space is enormous, and the company delightful. I cook and eat and sleep as I like.

Although Valter and Ove pitched their tent about 50 metres from mine, my ears always told me when they were awake and when asleep. Silence of more than a minute's duration meant they had gone to bed.

The next morning, Valter decided to turn back to search for Pluto, while I elected to go on. Pluto gave himself up the following day, tired

My dogs follow Schytt and Wilson. Iron-hard sastrugi like these were common on the Advance Base route. Traces of months-old weasel tracks still show (22 March 1951)

and shivering. Meanwhile, I had driven far ahead. When I stopped for lunch there was a 15-knot wind at –32°C. It was bad enough for me but the dogs were really suffering: underfed, underclothed, emaciated, and so close to the ground that they caught the drifting snow. We were struggling uphill and their morale was steadily falling.

Kernek was a good-natured dog but never a dynamic leader. At one point when he was tired and I was tired, I became so exasperated at his vacillation that I beat him with the handle of the whip. He was confused and bewildered.

Immediately I was struck by the injustice I had done him. I had lashed out at a friend who, in spite of being near to the point of collapse, had given me his trust and his loyalty. Mortified by what I had done, I dropped to the ground beside him – and grovelled. Cowed as he was, Kernek saw the tears in my eyes, understood that this was my apology, and licked my face.

Fifty years on, I still feel ashamed that I lost my temper. Kernek never let me down again, and I do not believe that it was from fear of the whip. All of us were operating at the limit. I took off my skis and, cursing the weight of the rocks, pushed the sledge from behind. Finally, even with all eight of us straining, the sledge would not move. The poor beasts fell to the ground, curling up in an attempt to keep warm. Except for Amiako, who was a marvel of energy, I had to drag each dog to his place on the span – they could not or would not stand up.

I fed them their ration of this fantastically inefficient and unpalatable whale powder, but they only ate half of it, for they got cold, and had to curl up at once to keep the very life in their limbs.

By now I was convinced that the poor performance of our dogs was directly attributable to an unfortunate decision of the International Committee. They had sought to save money by not buying dog pemmican. Dog pemmican was similar to man pemmican but had a higher protein content (65 per cent protein and 28 per cent fat). It was being used successfully by other expeditions, including FIDS. Betting on a whale concoction that had never been tried before had proven foolhardy. Our dogs were getting a bare survival ration – no more – and for that we paid a heavy price.

When Valter and Ove caught up with me, Valter lost his temper and swore that I had the lighter load. I offered to compare what we carried – box by box. In terms of stubbornness, there was nothing to choose between us. The conflict was never resolved. We both had to relay half loads before returning for the rest.

Finally reaching the depot at Flag 21, we found most of it deep under snow. For the sake of the people following us, we dug everything out and once again made it a conspicuous landmark. Restocking our own sledges with enough dog food to reach the next depot, we attempted to drive ahead. But it was not long before we were once again relaying and then, exhausted, camping where my dead reckoning put us at Flag 24. The temperature was –27°C, the wind 25 knots. In terms of wind chill, that was equivalent to –46°C in still air.

The dogs were given a treat – stockfish and blubber from the depot – and it was good to see them happy. Happiness is relative, though we do not always see it so. The following day was spent relaying half-loads. The trail markers, all of which were more than a metre high when planted in November, had now almost disappeared. Come what may, we had to keep on course in order to find the next depot. Valter's dead reckoning was superb; on one occasion Ove, after searching with binoculars, found the next stake between his own skis. A mere 5 centimetres was showing above the snow. At the end of the day my ski binding broke and we camped in a temperature of –33°C.

By 26 March we were at Flag 32 and on a downhill slope. Now back to carrying full sledge-loads, we covered 26 kilometres in six hours. For the next few days we could look forward to reaching depots where we would be able to feed the dogs just a bit more than usual.

I was still drilling holes for ice-temperature measurements in places where we had not done it before. Early in the season, the 1-metre temperatures were always warmer than at 3 metres because the deeper thermometer was reflecting the cold of last winter. Now at the end of the season it was reversed, with the 3-metre temperatures reflecting summer values.

Two weeks earlier, when I told the dogs to stand up after a rest stop, they all did so. Now none of them stirred. I had to start the sledge by pushing it at the same time as commanding *Tama*! One by one they stood up and began to move, desperately slowly, until nudged from behind by the cowcatcher – the curved rod at the front of the sledge. Without my pushing they could not even haul the load over sastrugi.

Valter had a still worse time starting up:

But he exhausts himself by screaming until he is hoarse and has completely lost control of his emotions, and has whipped his dogs cruelly. Now I go forward to help him start it after each flag halt.

Our next camp was by the well-stocked depot at Flag 71:

176

We gave the dogs the feast of their lives, because they need it, and because there is much food here. Every one of them got two [whale] pemmican rations and about 3 fish rations – that is to say we gave every one as much of either as it would eat. Poor beasts. They were bewildered. Tonight they will all have tummy aches. There are three big boxes of assorted manfood. First we feasted our eyes. It was delicious, just standing and looking at it all, chewing dried figs and dipping one's hand in here and there to take out something to cook up. For supper I have eaten three tins of Swedish Army potted rations. Now I am waiting a couple of hours for that to sink down while I prepare a thick creamy rice pudding upon which I shall take a large amount of raspberry jam and sweetened condensed milk. Then I shall sleep – at any rate until I wake up to be sick.

On 30 March we covered 26 kilometres in six hours of driving, all downhill, to camp at the ice-shelf grounding line. After crossing the ice shelf we left the trail to find a safer route to avoid the area where Peter's weasel sledge had opened crevasses. We did find a place where the crevasse belt was only 500 metres wide but it still meant crossing some snow bridges more than 10 metres wide. Passable for dog sledges but definitely not for weasels.

At this point, our progress was so desperately slow that we decided to dump the geologists' rocks for collection later. We knew that nobody was proposing to work on the specimens during the winter, so nothing would be lost by leaving them to be brought home with a weasel depot-laying trip in the spring.

We finally steamed into Maudheim at 1230 on 5 April. The dogs had seen the radio masts a long way off. They could have pulled a tonne over the last 500 metres. Instead, they dragged me with the ice-axe brake fully on, 'and pretty fast going it was too'.

My first – and joyous – task was to span out the dogs and give each of them a large chunk of whale meat and seal blubber. Considering what we had put them through, they never showed the faintest sign of resentment. We were friends for life.

The atmosphere was subdued when, one by one, we slid down a snow chute into the tunnels. Giæver seemed greatly relieved to see us alive and well. Our arrival increased the population – to 12. Top priority was to read the mail brought south by *Norsel*, and each of us spent a day doing little else. We read a sheaf of newspaper reports – many of them entertaining. The *Irish Times* said that the ship was bringing us '10,000 lbs of throat pastilles to encourage singing as a substitute for smoking which might be dangerous'.[1]

Stig Hallgren

Our Maudheim colleagues seemed still to be in shock from the fatal accident. There were two new faces: Bjarne Lorentzen, a cook who had replaced John Snarby, and Stig Hallgren, a Swedish film-maker. Stig was the one who had lived to tell about what happened when the weasel with his three companions had plunged over the ice front. Had we come back in January, we would have met the third newcomer, John Jelbart, a 25-year-old Australian physicist who had come to help with the glaciological programme. He had only been at Maudheim for seven weeks before drowning with Ekström and Quar on 24 February.

Lorentzen was a cheerful, wizened little man from Lødingen in the Lofoten Islands. Born in 1900, he was a year older than John Giæver. Most of his life had been spent at sea, in whaling, fishing and overseas trade. However, he quickly adapted to life at Maudheim and, as a professional cook, found that catering for our small numbers was an easy job.

Hallgren was 25 years old and had film-making experience in Argentina, Brazil, Denmark, Finland, Norway, Sweden and Uruguay. Like Valter, he was a large man; that in itself may have been an asset when he was plunged into sea water at $-1°C$.

Norsel had arrived at Maudheim on 6 January. Besides the new winterers, she brought Professor Sverdrup, the overall director of the expedition; Dr Brian Roberts, representing the British committee; Lieutenant Lloyd Foster of the Royal Navy, British observer; and Captain Reinhold von Essen of the Royal Swedish Air Force, Swedish observer. Guttorm Jakobsen was captain and his brother Torgils was chief engineer.

The Norwegian air unit was made up of pilots Kåre Friis-Baastad and Anders Jacobsen, photographer Sigvard Kjellberg, and mechanics J. Jensen and W. Andreassen. They brought two single-engined aircraft, a Norwegian-built C-5 for aerial photography and a Danish KZ-3 training aircraft for shorter flights. Experiencing miserable weather during *Norsel*'s short stay, they only managed three flights inland. To cap it all, Friis-Baastad took Liljequist as passenger on a flight towards Kapp Norvegia. Misjudging a low pass on his return, his wing-tip hit the snow and the machine cartwheeled. Liljequist was concussed but the pilot had only cuts and bruises. The aircraft was a write-off. An unsatisfactory flying season had ended in ignominy.

An error of judgement. Both occupants survived

179

Giæver told us that three weeks after *Norsel* had left Maudheim, Ekström and Hallgren repaired one of the weasels and, late one evening, decided to take it for a test drive. As the weather was calm and clear, Jelbart and Quar decided to join them. They would drive down to the quay to pick up some seal meat that had been unloaded from *Norsel*. On the way, they ran into a bank of fog rolling in from the sea. Ekström, always a fast driver, saw the water ahead too late to stop the machine before it plunged over the ice cliff. Hallgren related afterwards how three of them quickly drowned, though he himself was able to swim to a small ice floe. But for the fact that he wore a sheath knife, he too would have drowned. There was nothing to hold on to, so he stabbed the knife into the floe and hauled himself out. Later he slid into the sea again and swam to a larger floe.

At 0100, Rogstad, the only man then awake on base, had seen the fog and become concerned about the weasel party. After waking Giæver, he set out on skis, with Lorentzen, to follow the weasel tracks. There was no trace of the party but he heard Hallgren calling from an ice floe out in the bay. Promising to rescue him, Rog raced back to Maudheim and woke everyone. The only possibility was to dig up a small dinghy that was deep under a snowdrift and manhaul it to the ice front. This they did, lowering it down the sheer cliff into the sea. Giæver and Schumacher got in and rowed out to Hallgren, who by this time had been walking round his ice floe for nearly 13 hours, knowing that if he sat down he would freeze to death.

When the three of them had been hoisted on to the ice shelf, they abandoned the dinghy because there was no way to lift it. Hallgren insisted on walking unaided the whole way back to Maudheim with the others. His only bodily injury was slightly frostbitten toes.

With the base complement reduced to six, they knew they had a bad time ahead. Giæver was so despondent that he informed Sverdrup that the loss of Ekström 'probably makes further weasel transport impossible. . . . If Maudheim radio should become silent, the reason is motorstop.'[2]

It took the party some weeks to begin recovering from shock. Then Giæver wrote: 'Yet life must keep its course and be carried on, even where death has taken its toll. The war had taught us that.'[3]

The survivors faced another hazard of their troglodyte existence deep under snow – carbon monoxide poisoning. It came either from stoves or from exhaust fumes leaking along the snow corridors from the diesel power station. The best-known story of carbon monoxide poisoning in an Antarctic setting is told by Richard Byrd, who lived alone under snow on the Ross Ice Shelf.[4] I once experienced it in a tent in Iceland. The insidious feature is that the gas is undetectable by our human senses, being colourless and odourless. It leads to headaches, nausea and confusion, and can be fatal. With dulled senses, people seem unable to analyse the reasons for their own debility.

While the field parties were away, this touched everyone. Worst affected were those who never ventured outside, and least affected were the meteorologists, who had to go outside every few hours. The new faces who burst into the corridors when *Norsel* arrived on 6 January were struck by the apathy of the residents. Brian Roberts wrote: 'It was almost as if we were unwelcome intruders upsetting their routine and disturbing the quiet of their home.'[5]

The newcomers at once understood the carbon monoxide problem and built ventilator shafts to extract the bad air and replace it with clean air drawn into the corridors from the surrounding snow.

By the time our little group had returned to Maudheim, there was little sign of any pervasive lethargy. We soon fell into the now well-practised winter routine.

15

THE SECOND WINTER

It was Valter's intention to extend the ice core drilling, if possible, to a depth of 100 metres, while I had to resurvey the whole stake network to see how much deformation there had been since the previous winter. But our start on these projects was delayed by a series of blizzards, sometimes with gusts of hurricane force.

I was also anxious to resurvey the stakes that Peter and I had planted at the ice-shelf grounding line a year ago. Hallgren, eager to see what was involved in Antarctic travel, volunteered to come with me. We left Maudheim on 25 April with a 250-kilo sledge-load hauled by Rapasak, Sally, Milagtose, Amiako, Singarnase, Mike and Krane, now substantially recovered from their appalling diet of the summer. I steered on a compass heading of 111° and we camped in pitch-darkness at 1800 after covering 32 kilometres. Stig said it was a long time since he had been so tired and so hungry – he felt like eating five days' rations. However, unaccustomed as he was to the high fat content of pemmican, he was unable to swallow his full ration.

We completed the surveys the following day and, after a couple of days lie-up in high winds, packed up and started up the slope of the inland ice to investigate the lie of the land. Crossing a number of large but well-bridged crevasses, we reached a point 300 metres above sea level and camped in clear weather at a temperature of –24°C. The next day we continued climbing to about 600 metres above sea level. The dogs were pulling well and, on reaching the summit, we were rewarded with a shimmering image of Førstefjell 150 kilometres away to the east.

Reckoning that we were then 70 kilometres from Maudheim, we had a good night's sleep before heading for home at 0830. Rapasak proved to be a fine leader and, as soon as were going downhill, Stig and I had to hang on for dear life. The dogs knew where we were going. After four hours I caught a glimpse of Pynten on the horizon, so we knew that we were pointed in the right direction. Approaching the crevasses, Stig skied ahead and soon learned how to test a snow bridge. We crossed seven or eight big ones, from 2 to 7 metres wide.

Rapasak showed an uncanny awareness, stopping at the lip and refusing to step on the snow bridge until I forced him. Then we took each crevasse at a rush, the front of the sledge crashing down onto the middle of the sagging bridge before the dogs reached the far side. To my diary I confided: 'I did not like it at all.'

On reaching the ice shelf, we had covered 40 kilometres in six hours. Stig suggested that we should continue – I sensed that he was missing the comforts of Maudheim. Steering on the afterglow of the sun, Rapasak lost his sense of direction – he was exhausted. So we stopped for a rest, eating chocolate and sweetened condensed milk before pressing on. Stig skied ahead, steering first on Sirius and later on the Maudheim light, which we saw faintly flickering on the horizon. The stars swung round and finally the Maudheim light blinked out. It was pitch-dark and we really needed something to head for.

Overhead was the aurora, white curtains tinged with red and blue, ripples racing along them from one part of the sky to another. Knowing that a meteorologist would have to come outside for his routine observations at 2100, I flashed my small torch on the off chance that someone might see it. Some minutes later, a couple of brilliant lights flashed in our direction – they had spotted us. By that time, Krane was so tired that I let him loose to follow behind. Rapasak eventually overtook Stig and, as we approached the spans, he fell into Peter's arms. Peter had been waiting for us and was surprised to see that Rapasak was in the lead.

We had covered 70 kilometres in 13 hours and the dogs were too tired to eat. Stig and I went inside and feasted on double ham and eggs, 2 litres of beer and 1 of milk.

The beer had come with *Norsel*. Giæver allocated 120 bottles to each man, though Roer, Roots and Wilson had not ordered any and had to do without. Consumption was recorded by each man marking ticks against his name on a list posted by the dining table. I still have the list; the small number of ticks against three of the names are a poignant reminder of the men whose lives were cut short.

As Stig and I slept off our weariness, the weather broke and it was 9 May before I could begin the stake survey. I took every opportunity to continue, but entries in my notes reveal the infrequency of days when it was possible. On average, I only succeeded in working outside about once a week.

Norsel had brought a year's supply of *Aftenposten* and *Svenska Dagbladet* up to the day the ship had left Oslo. Throughout the winter, Bjarne dutifully placed a daily newspaper on the breakfast table. It was exactly one year out of date, but that did not concern us because

Bjarne Lorentzen shopping for the day's meals

we had missed the whole year's news. Like people arriving at work anywhere, the day's news gave us much to discuss. Although there was nothing to stop us raiding the store to peer into the future, cheating was frowned upon.

Norway's national day came round again on 17 May and I recorded the menu: soup, smoked salmon, smoked mackerel, silverside, roast chicken with roast potatoes and fried fungus, then an enormous alcoholic sponge cake covered with thick whipped cream; plus whisky, aquavit, punch, port, and Guinness.

Bjarne Lorentzen was unfailingly cheerful and we were well-satisfied with his cooking. He told Giæver that he had never been so happy in all his life. Later we discovered one element in his happiness – he had quietly taken to sampling aquavit from one of the boxes outside.

Spontaneous concerts occurred from time to time, with Rog playing a piano accordion, Gordon a recorder, and Bjarne – not to be outdone – strumming on a stringed instrument that he had made from a broomstick, an empty food tin and a piece of wire. The rest of us joined in the singing. Though there was some dissonance between the instrumentalists, it did not matter because we were all having fun.

Giæver had become worried about the non-return of the geology/

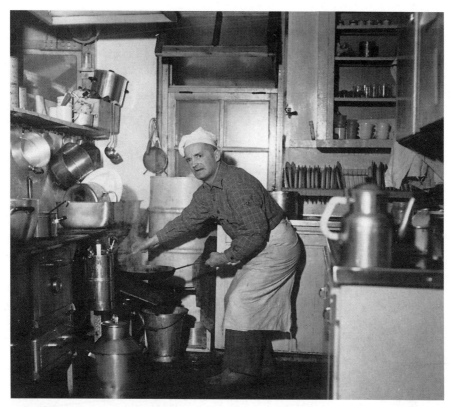
Bjarne Lorentzen preparing dinner

survey party, so on 24 May he despatched a search party comprising Valter, Ove and Peter with two dog teams and provisions for 21 days. The sun had set for the winter five days earlier, so following the trail was no easy matter. On the sixth day out, they met up with the other party at Flag 91, 60 kilometres from Maudheim. Giæver was greatly relieved when all six arrived in pitch darkness on 30 May. They were fit and well.

Roots, Reece and Roer had travelled far and wide. Their eastern journey with Gordon Robin had reached as far as 01°30′E. After Gordon left them to return to Maudheim with Peter Melleby, they had sledged far to the south, reaching 73°30′S. Alan Reece had shown enormous courage in carrying on after his eye injury. Reaching Maudheim eight weeks after we did and a week after the last sunset, they had endured blinding blizzards, extreme temperatures, and darkness that often made it impossible to follow sledge tracks. However, they and their tired but gallant dogs were well. Their morale was high as they revelled in the satisfaction of a job well done. They had been in the field for 163 consecutive days.

Giæver half-scoldingly commented that they, with the perverse attitude of mountain-climbers who think it fun to carry heavy loads up big hills, seemed to have been enjoying themselves while those at base were worrying about them.

One rather incongruous new arrival with *Norsel* had been a pair of motorcycles. Unpacking one of them, I became the first person ever to experiment with this form of travel in Antarctica.[1] The Swedish Husqvarna company had presented the expedition with two Model 27, 120 cc machines with hinged ski attachment.[2] The skis were sprung, so that on a hard road they would rise clear of the ground. On snow, however, I could put part of my weight on the skis, bringing them down to the surface. Now the machine was supported in four places – two wheels and two skis. If a wheel skidded and the machine was

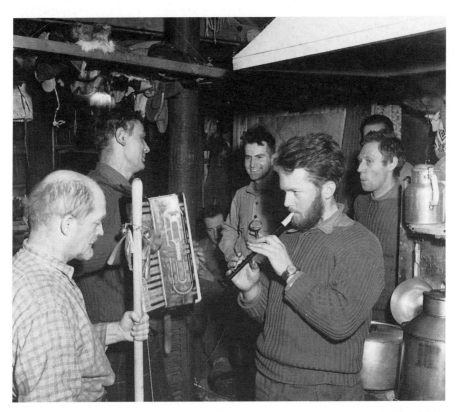

Impromptu concert. Standing (from left): Lorentzen, Rogstad, Wilson, Robin, Liljequist

getting out of control, I put all of my weight onto the skis and then hoisted the bike back to an even keel with the handlebars.

The ski attachment was not an experimental rig but a standard optional extra designed for use on icy roads in winter. As far as I was concerned, the bike was a great success and I was never thrown off, even when negotiating 40-centimetre-high sastrugi. I used the machine throughout the winter. A spare tyre was cut up to make treaded rubber soles for our smooth-soled ski boots. We enjoyed the incongruity of finding Husqvarna footprints in the wilderness.

The stake survey was a repetition of all that I had done the previous year, with the same problems of handling frozen instruments with numbed fingers in inky darkness. Often as I peered through the theodolite telescope, refraction made the inverted image of the stakes dance wildly – until my condensing breath blotted out the picture altogether.

Yet all the time I knew what a privilege it was just to be here. Sometimes visions – totally out of context – flashed through my mind: of milling crowds back home – imprisoned, as it were, in cities; of their daily grind back and forth to satanic mills; of great wars and petty conflicts.

Not that I harboured any contempt for my fellow men; rather it was a sadness that they could not share – perhaps could not even comprehend – my elation in this environment. I was alone with the firmament, while they might not even once in a lifetime find an opportunity to stand in awe, pray to the heavens and cast their eyes up to the eternal stars.

Dreaming of the sublime in this environment was a paradox too lovely to ignore and too profound to explain, though I was far from the first to be moved by it. Fridtjof Nansen put it this way:

> Anything more wonderfully beautiful than the polar night does not exist. It is a dream-like sight. It is a light-poem of all the finest and most delicate tones of the soul.[3]

For my part, the agony of cold meant that no trance could long endure. After an hour or two of reading angles in temperatures around $-45°C$, I was well aware that hypothermia was stalking me. If I ever succumbed, I would be dead long before anyone found me, so I packed up to go home, sometimes on skis and sometimes on the motorcycle.

Back in the hut, Alan Reece – still blind in one eye – and Fred Roots were quietly getting on with the task of making dog rations for all sledging parties for the 1951–52 field season. Giæver's revised

Midwinter Day, 1951. Schytt congratulates Lorentzen on his cake

recipe consisted of whale meat boiled up with oatmeal and margarine. We agreed that almost anything would be better than the powdery stuff we had been using.

Meanwhile, Ove was reporting to his former teacher Professor Sven Larsson of Lund University Medical School on the state of Alan's eye. The indications were that the damaged eye was beginning to affect the other eye, though Ove did not reveal this to Alan. In mid-July Professor Larsson said that Alan's damaged eye must be removed if he was to have any chance of saving the sight of the good eye.

Ove had never even witnessed an eye operation. But now there was no choice. He set to work preparing a set of instruments for the purpose, modifying some dental tools and making a number of completely new instruments by filing and polishing pieces of welding wire. Peter built an operating table out of old boxes and fashioned an oxygen mask out of weasel spares.

Then Ove began to train his 'theatre' assistants, which he did with extraordinary thoroughness. Hallgren was chosen as anaesthetist and was made to practise by injecting people with vitamin solutions. Fred

Roots was to assist Ove in the most delicate task of all – actually removing Alan's eye. Valter was taught the duties of theatre nurse, handing the right instruments to Ove when he called for them. Rog learned how to monitor blood pressure and muscle reflexes. Gösta would monitor heart rate and keep records.

Sterility was an insoluble problem. Ove could only do his best. The operating theatre was the open space between the rows of cabins in the command hut – a most unsterile place. Aprons and face-masks were made by cutting up sheets – then sterilized by boiling them in Bjarne's biggest saucepan. As Ove put it, ' ... we had everything a small hospital has, if one leaves out the feminine element'.[4]

Neither Alan nor the rest of us were supposed to know of these preparations, but Alan must have guessed, as I did, that something was up. On 18 July he was told that the operation would be in a few days. He took the news calmly – what else could he do?

The final preparations looked every bit as professional as a hospital training film. There was a long and thorough scrub-up with nail brushes, soap and boiled water, and then, hands held high, all concerned donned sterile rubber gloves. I had been briefed to take still and moving pictures, so I was called into the operating theatre at the same time as Alan. Now Alan was strapped to a mattress to restrain any violent reflexes and Hallgren inserted the needle.
Ove's written report says it all:

Slowly but surely Hallgren submerged our patient in ever deeper sleep. My operating knife made the first incision in the pupil. Roots assisted with swift and cool precision, Schytt passed the instruments with absolute assurance, Rogstad followed the blood pressure. Gösta Liljequist kept the records and took the pulse, Hallgren maintained the anaesthesia always at the right level. The tension was tremendous. Suddenly I found the first eye muscle, which I retracted by means of my home-made instruments. Directly after, I had severed all the eye muscles. The most dramatic moment came when I was looking for the optic nerve. The only audible sound was the ticking of the film camera in the background. After a while I was able to sever the nerve and take out the eyeball, then tie up the muscles and close the wound.[5]

After two hours and forty minutes of tension, it was all over. Alan was carried to his own bunk and slept. The next day, we all visited his cabin to congratulate him on his remarkable courage. Ove too enjoyed universal praise for his masterly management of the surgery. Alan's left eye was now safe.

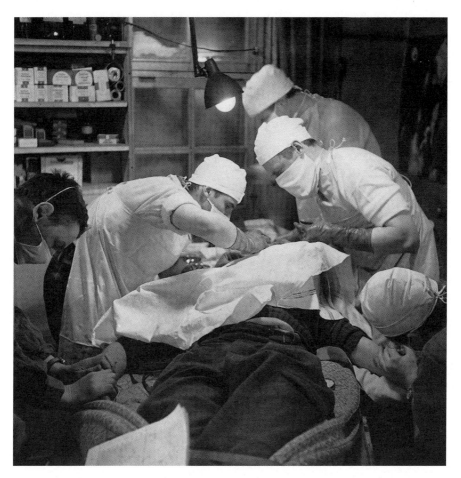

High drama – the operation to remove Alan Reece's injured eye (21 July 1951)

To prevent his good eye from becoming 'lazy', Alan was made to read a book the very next day. He found it uncomfortable but said it did not hurt. Within a few days he had made a complete recovery and Ove could see no reason why he should not take part in the coming summer's fieldwork.

The coldest temperature ever recorded in Dronning Maud Land was on 9 August – the minimum thermometer read −47°C. I went out on the motorcycle to do some surveying. Although the machine was kept outdoors, it started on the first kick without any pre-heating. The Swedish manufacturer must have learned something about cold starting that we in Britain would do well to emulate.

Alan Reece two days after his eye operation

Valter and I had resumed ice-core drilling in May but, because I was preoccupied with the stake survey, Stig Hallgren suffered most of the back-breaking drudgery of handling the drill rods. I took chips of the ice core to John Giæver to put in his drinks, telling him, 'This piece fell as snow on the day that the Germans under Bismarck invaded France 80 years ago' or 'This bit fell when Napoleon was at the gates of Moscow'.

> . . . deep-frozen air bubbles burst in small, crackling explosions. My modest cocktail is diluted with water; but simultaneously a little cycle of 150 years is concluded in the glass before me.[6]

After many an anxious moment, Valter and I finally reached our goal on 16 August by extending the hole to 100 metres' depth. It was then by far the deepest hole ever drilled in Antarctica. At this point we reckoned that the risk of jeopardizing everything by accidentally dropping the drill string outweighed the value of going deeper. We lowered a light bulb to the bottom, marvelling at the tiny spot of light coming from a point within the ice yet far below sea level. The fact that we could see it at all showed that the hole was straight. More by luck, we knew, than skill.

Robin was able to fire some seismic shots at the bottom of the hole to check on the velocity of sound waves at various depths in ice, now of known density. Finally we lowered a string of electrical thermometers down the hole and filled it in with snow.

Valter and I endured many freezing hours at the microscope in the cold lab. We were able to draw important conclusions about the transformation of snow into ice and to throw light on the origin of the ice shelf itself. A steady increase in density with depth led to a transition from snow to ice at a depth of 60–65 metres and a maximum density of 0.88 at a depth of 100 metres. The core revealed two distinct layers, the top layer 70–75 metres thick, made of snow that had accumulated in situ on the ice shelf; and the bottom layer made of ice supplied from the inland ice sheet. Finding a change at that depth was consistent with my own estimate of a rate of movement of about 280 metres per year.[7] A very steep temperature gradient in the bottom half of the ice column ruled out the possibility that sea water was freezing to the ice water interface. We concluded that the ice at the bottom was melting.[8]

While all this was going on, for week after week we used ice axes an hour or two at a time to excavate a shaft to a depth of 12 metres so that we could study the snow strata. Valter was able to identify the different annual snow layers as far back as 1934, and to determine that the average annual accumulation (or precipitation) at Maudheim was equivalent to 365 millimetres of water, roughly half as much as it is in the east of England.

As soon as the duty orderlies realized that the dense snow in the shaft was better for making water, willing hands took part in the excavation. It sidestepped the chore of digging open the main entrance and avoided the need to go outside in a blizzard.

John Giæver was finding the second winter harder than the first. He seldom moved from his cabin and often missed meals. He quoted one of his Svalbard friends, the legendary trapper Henry Rudi, as saying:

A two-year polar wintering is comparable in many ways with a marriage lasting at least ten times as many years. But the polar experience lacks, to a tiresome degree, all the redeeming features of marriage.[9]

However, John had begun writing the official account of the expedition and that helped to keep him from being overcome by lethargy. He was also a skilled seamster, spending a lot of time sewing skin-mitts

Story time. L to R: Rogstad, Hallgren, Wilson, Giæver, Schytt, Liljequist, Lorentzen and the author

and skin-socks for the sledging parties and even offering to repair our worn-out clothing. He was always available to give advice if asked, but I never felt him breathing down my neck. We had become very good friends.

One day Gordon and I did our biggest ever seismic refraction shots. Detonating a 20-kilo charge of TNT made a satisfying bang and alarmed everyone except those of us who knew what was going on. I suppose at the back of our minds we all harboured some dread of the shock wave that might herald the calving of an iceberg right under our feet.

My survey of the stake pattern was finished in September, at which point we remeasured the baselines to give scale to the whole triangulation network. Assuming that the rate of deformation had remained constant, we could interpolate not only the baseline lengths but also the angles to any date between the two surveys. We planned a third survey the following summer to check on this assumption.

16

THE SEISMIC JOURNEY

After spending much of the winter overhauling the two remaining weasels, Peter and Gordon finally declared them fit for the summer ahead. But Gordon had something more dramatic to announce: he wanted to build a house – as he called it – on one of the sledges. The idea was to avoid the chore of pitching a tent every night and every time he needed to develop a seismic record. Moreover, living on the sledge would provide more space than a tent.

On securing Giæver's agreement to what some saw as a hare-brained idea, Gordon and Peter started building. The cargo sledge was 1.25 metres wide and 4 metres long. Using its full dimensions, they fixed a rectangular framework over the sledge and covered it with a tarpaulin nailed to the frame with battens. A thinner canvas was hung on the inside. Now we had the equivalent of a tent with fly, though it was vastly more spacious and almost high enough to stand up in. To ensure that no snow would find its way in, they installed a sleeve entrance. The floor was made of plywood, and there was a small hatch through which we could jettison rubbish. To sleep three in comfort, they erected two sprung bedsteads along one side. He and Peter would each have a bunk, while I, the junior member, was consigned to the floor. On completion, Fred Roots christened the structure a caboose, after the term for the workmen's living quarters towed at the end of long goods trains on the Canadian prairies; and the name stuck.

One of the contingencies for which we prepared was what to do if weasel batteries became flattened while trying to start in cold weather. With two weasels it was easy, but mechanical failure might leave us with only one. I thought it might be possible to build an emergency generator by cannibalizing the spare motorcycle, which was still in its crate. It was quite a challenge. I stripped the machine down to leave just the frame and the engine, then mounted a spare weasel generator in the back fork and connected it with a drive belt. The contraption worked well and we took it with us.

We were all kept busy, Alan still making dog food for all parties, then, together with Nils and Fred, rebuilding sledges, sewing tents,

Making dog food. Alan Reece (standing) and Fred Roots (kneeling)

repairing dog harnesses and completing a hundred and one other jobs to ensure that everything was in tip-top condition. Dog teams were taken out for exercise and training whenever the weather was fine.[1]

This time we could not linger inland. Giæver ordered all parties to be back at Maudheim by the first week in January 1952 at the latest. Anyone returning much later, as we had done last summer, would find the base deserted and learn that *Norsel* was northbound, never to return. We would be stuck here for eternity. All of us took the warning seriously – we *had* to get back in time.

A topographic survey/geology party consisting of Fred Roots, Nils Roer and Stig Hallgren was to visit areas untravelled the previous season. Finally, a small glaciology/geology party comprising Valter Schytt and Alan Reece would return to the Borgen mountain area, partly to remeasure stakes that we had put out last summer and partly to look at the geology.

Since all parties were to assemble at the Advance Base, the dog-sledgers left Maudheim in a fairly random order. Owing to storm following storm in quick succession, it was not until 27 September that Valter, Fred and Alan were able to set off with three teams. Nils and Stig left base the following day, each with his own team.

Before the seismic traverse could begin, Gordon, Peter and I had to make a depot-laying journey – as we had done last season. With one weasel having been lost in the accident, everything depended on keeping the other two running. We left Maudheim on 30 September with both weasels loaded and towing heavy sledges. One new task – which we did not entirely welcome – was to carry a number of drums of aviation fuel. Reinhold von Essen, who had been the Swedish observer on *Norsel*'s last visit, proposed to bring a small team from the Royal Swedish Air Force to continue the aerial photography. He had asked for a fuel depot to be carried inland in order to extend the range of the aircraft. Of course we wished him well, but we were hard-pressed to carry what was needed for our own work.

On reaching the crevassed area, we found Fred Roots camped alone and waiting to help us across. For our sake, he had scouted 10 kilometres or so on either side of his camp to find a better crossing place. On his advice we proceeded eastwards, following the contour of the inland ice to a place where the crevasses appeared well-bridged. Luckily they were, and we continued on our way with Fred and his dog-team following in our tracks.

One day my weasel engine burst into flames from an electrical fault, and if the fire extinguisher had not performed, we would have lost the weasel. Fortunately the damage was minor and I was able to make repairs on the spot. Shortly afterwards, in crossing rough sastrugi, one of my bogie wheels broke and I stopped to replace it. The next problem was the water pump in Peter's weasel. It had broken and it took all of eight hours to replace it. However, we were able to shed the load of aviation fuel at an agreed place near Førstefjell. A depot at this point, two thirds of the way to the Advance Base, should be easy for the airmen to find and must certainly enhance their operating range.

Continuing, we unloaded our last depot at Flag 31 on 7 October. Twice I had to stop to dismantle my carburettor and clear iced fuel lines that had stalled the engine. Peter had stripped his second gear, so he struggled through a complete replacement of his gearbox and a bogie wheel as well.

Such was the price we paid for keeping the machines running. We carried a large supply of spare parts but lived in constant fear that some new problem would arise. We knew that we were overstressing the engines – weasels were never designed for hauling loads like ours. Neither Gordon, Peter nor I had any training as mechanics, nor in dismantling complex carburettors, nor in replacing a whole gearbox while exposed to the elements at –35°C. We taught ourselves simply because there was no alternative. Necessity is the mother of invention – capitulation in our circumstances would compromise the very purpose of our being here.

Having shed the cargo loads, we started homeward after dark, following the sledge tracks at high speed in the beam of the headlights. Coming across Valter and Alan heading south, we stopped to chat and then drove on. Later, we found the surveyors – Nils and Stig – camped at Flag 48. Tired after our long day, we camped with them. Here, as planned, Fred Roots left us to rejoin the survey party.

The next morning we were off early and made good speed. Stopping at depots to refuel and to pick up the rock boxes that we and the geologists had been unable to carry home in May, we kept going until sunset, continued by moonlight, and reached Maudheim at 2330. Some hours earlier, Schumacher had seen our headlights coming over the hill while we were still 40 kilometres away. We had covered 200 kilometres in the course of a very long day – we were tired and very hungry.

Now Gordon, Peter and I prepared to launch ourselves on the seismic journey, aiming to penetrate as far inland as time, terrain and the weasels allowed. Ove Wilson would accompany us as far as the Advance Base, where he would await Valter's return from the mountains with Alan Reece.

We spent a week on weasel repairs. One day I grovelled for 13 hours while greasing the bogie wheels and oiling everything in sight. Our plan was to take both weasels and 11 dogs. Beyond the Advance Base, Gordon would drive the dogs ahead of the weasels. In theory at least, he would spot any crevasses in time to warn the weasel drivers.

We left Maudheim with high hopes on 18 October. The sky was almost clear but in the open cockpit of the weasel, the temperature of –17°C felt bitterly cold. I drove the lead weasel, flag flying, towing a 2-tonne sledge-load and, on a long rope behind that, the caboose. Gordon rode as passenger to say where to stop for seismic soundings. Peter followed with the second weasel towing 2.5 tonnes. Last of all came the dogs, pulling a lightly loaded Nansen sledge, driven for this part of the journey by Ove, who was now a keen dog-sledge driver. Stopping four times that day for seismics, we camped at the grounding line after 33 kilometres.

The domestic arrangements worked well from the start, although

197

with four of us on board we had to be more careful about the space that each could call his own. With the sleeping bags rolled up at one end of the caboose and the seismic recorder in a corner, there was plenty of room left for preparing meals on the floor and also for developing the day's seismic records.

Weight was less critical on this journey than it had been with dog-sledging, so we could afford to carry small quantities of normal tinned food. However, all foods containing water – as tinned foods do – take much longer to thaw and prepare than dehydrated foods, so we generally stuck to sledging rations cooked on a Primus stove.

Ove and I slept on the floor under the bunks. While we envied the sprung bedsteads above, on hot days we were glad that the floor was the coolest part of the caboose. When we awoke after the first night, the caboose was vibrating, the canvas flapping, and we estimated that the wind speed was 50-60 knots. We were grateful to have secured our mobile home with taut guys. However, what mattered and what pleased us was that nothing gave way. Perhaps it was just as well that our new home was being tested before we travelled far from Maudheim.

The next day it was blowing 60-70 knots. Responding to a call of nature, I went outside but was blown off my feet and had to crawl back on hands and knees. On the third day I found the weasels full of drift snow. It was not until 24 October that we were able to move again, after digging out the weasels. One good thing was that – unlike tents – the caboose was so massive that it deflected snowdrifts away from itself and needed very little digging out after a storm.

Belle had pups during the storm; they froze to death. The following day we managed to do five seismic stations. Each evening at bedtime, Gordon set an alarm clock to wake us and it became clear that he intended to maintain a cracking pace. The previous season, the glaciological party had generally felt the need for eight hours in bed. True, on that journey we often spent all day on skis, whereas now we were riding the weasels. Without enough sleep, however, my diary entries became abrupt and there was not much conversation about anything beyond the task in hand. 'It is no idea to go without sleep,' as Peter put it when out of Gordon's hearing. Fortunately, the occasional bad weather days allowed us to catch up on sleep. Together we were determined to bring home the richest possible harvest of scientific results.

We took turns at cooking. The duty cook rose when the alarm clock rang, cooked the breakfast and, when it was ready, wakened the others and handed each of us a steaming bowl of porridge liberally laced with butter and sugar, and a mug of cocoa.

We quickly developed a set routine for who did what. Gordon

Peter Melleby (left) and the author in the caboose. Our faces are tanned by sunburn and soot from the Primus stove

stretched out cables and dug shallow holes for six seismometers evenly spaced along a straight line. Peter connected up the seismometers. I recorded the weasel mileage, read an aneroid barometer and measured the height of the nearest trail marker. I then drilled a hole for the seismic charge, inserted the detonator, taped it into the TNT and lowered the charge into the hole.

At this point Gordon would disappear into the caboose to prepare his instrument and I would connect the shot cable to a spare weasel battery. The final act was when Gordon, with his recorder running, pressed the firing switch. There was the muffled sound of a rifle shot, and that was it.

At many campsites on the inland ice, I set up the theodolite to measure the direction of surface slope. Ove held up a 3-metre graduated staff and, walking away from me, stopped after every 100 metres so that I could sight onto the staff through the telescope. Gordon would later compare my results with his own calculations of the subglacial bedrock slope based on the different times of arrival of the ice-bottom echo – measured in milliseconds – at each seismometer.

Once or twice we made the mistake of leaving the seismic cables out overnight in case we had to repeat shots in the morning to confirm uncertain results. If there was drifting snow during the night, we found

199

the cables buried under a hard wind crust. Digging trenches to extract hundreds of metres of cable took several hours and, on occasions, a spade severed the cable, adding further hours for repairs.

By 2 November we were opposite Førstefjell, where we had left the aviation fuel a month before. Here we prepared for a short excursion with the dogs and one weasel to the nunatak. Ove and Peter decided to leave the bitch Dinah at the depot because she was on heat and causing chaos in the ranks. Turning towards the nunatak, Gordon, Peter and Ove skied ahead to scout for crevasses, while I followed towing one sledge and the caboose. Camping quite close to the rock, Gordon and Peter prepared the shots while Ove and I climbed to the summit. There we found the rock cairn that the reconnaissance party had built a year ago. Ove discovered lichens and I noted abundant signs that the nunatak had been overridden by ice at some stage in the past. The direction of ice flow at that stage – north-west – was evidently the same as it is now.

Gordon was anxious to obtain unequivocal evidence that his reflections were coming from rock rather than from some reflecting horizon within the ice. The most convincing evidence would be to obtain, from a series of soundings, an ice-bottom profile that, if projected, would outcrop at the edge of the nunatak. We spent a whole day doing this. Although the shallower soundings were more difficult, the results were convincing. The ice thickness was only 70 metres where we had made camp.

Returning to the Advance Base trail, we expected to hear Dinah barking at our approach. But there was silence – and she was gone. We could only surmise that, feeling abandoned, she had pulled out the stake to which she was chained – and made off. There were indications that, before leaving, she had gorged herself on stockfish from the depot.

Now down to 10 dogs, we resumed our journey. Snow conditions, and particularly the size of sastrugi, varied from day to day and from place to place, depending on the slope of the surface and on recent weather. Sometimes the weasels were struggling in low gear and, when this happened, Ove and the dogs easily kept up with us. But even when we led at full speed, they were never far behind.

High sastrugi in some places caused Ove's sledge to overturn. Each time he had to reload and lash it. Even the weasel sledges were having a hard time on side slopes, and we were concerned for the weasels themselves. My weasel already had a bent leaf spring, and we had no spares.

One of the advantages of weasel travel had always been that we could power the radio from batteries, thus avoiding the torment of the hand generator. A couple of days later we heard on the radio that Dinah had arrived at Maudheim none the worse for wear. In less than two days she had travelled 200 kilometres, stopping briefly at each depot for a meal. Giæver reported that in her excitement she had rushed around greeting everyone before falling down Valter's 10-metre shaft. John proposed to leave her there to cool off, but Bjarne climbed down and hoisted her back to the surface. John suggested over the radio that the seismic party should send mail with the next escaping dog.

Temperatures at this stage of the journey were around –20°C, and my drill-hole temperatures indicated that the mean annual temperature must be about the same. However, we had become so hardened to low temperatures and windy conditions that it made no difference to what we did outside.

We reached the Advance Base late in the evening of 8 November. In three weeks we had covered 307 kilometres and measured ice depths at about 40 places; the deepest ice recorded was 1,847 metres. More remarkable was that, along four-fifths of the distance travelled from Maudheim, the bedrock under the ice proved to be below sea level. If, by magic, the ice should vanish before our eyes, we would be staring across a 30-kilometre wide strait to an island – the 'Førstefjell island.' Beyond the island would be nothing but ocean. The site of Maudheim would be over the horizon and far out to sea.[2]

Ove now looked forward to camping alone under the shadow of Pyramiden until Valter returned from his mountain excursion. Peter left him with the Greenland dog Nanok for company. Afterwards, Valter and Ove planned to return to Maudheim via Boreas and Passat to collect further live specimens of the mites.

The seismic party began repacking for the journey ahead. On each weasel sledge we put fuel drums, dog food and man food, so that if either sledge was ever lost in a crevasse, we would still have the essentials. As a final back-up, we put survival rations on the dog sledge.

Finding some of John Snarby's bread that had been sent here a year ago, we hung it under the ceiling of the caboose to thaw. On taking it down later to spread butter on the slices, I could have sworn that it had just come out of the baker's oven. It was light, soft and smelled fresh. I thought we could suggest storing the world's grain surpluses here to provide for lean years and poor harvests. Could we solve famine? Not, I surmised, without more foresight than is generally found in politicians.

A note from the survey/geology party asked us to carry a load of dog food to a nunatak beyond the mountains that they had marked on a sketch map. We were already heavily loaded, but knowing that their range of operations was even more dependent on weight than ours, we took it.

We left the Advance Base on 9 November in almost tropical weather (–4°C). As far as the seismic work was concerned, from here on we would be breaking new ground. Gordon wanted to press on inland as far as time and weasel fuel would permit. More detailed work could be done on the homeward trail when we could see where we stood in relation to Giæver's deadline for reaching Maudheim. For the first day or two, we would be travelling on the same route as last year's glaciological party – south-eastwards as far as the 2,030-metre-high pass through the mountains.[3] From that point onwards Gordon would have to drive the dog team ahead to spot crevasses.

As navigator, my job was to take bearings at every station so that their positions could afterwards be plotted on Nils Roer's maps.[4] As often as possible, Gordon or I read three aneroid barometers. They were being mercilessly bounced on the weasel, so we read all three in the hope that if one failed, the other two would show it. We would afterwards use the observations to determine the surface topography of the ice sheet and our altitude above sea level.

Into the unknown. Gordon Robin leads the way through the mountains to spot any crevasses ahead of the weasels. Appropriately for an Australian, his 12-metre whip was made in Sydney from bullock hide

Another of my duties was that of meteorologist. On average five times a day, or whenever practicable, I had to record the air temperature, wind direction, wind speed, visibility, pressure, the amount and type of cloud, snowfall, and optical phenomena like solar haloes.

Wanting to make fast time, we stopped for only two seismic stations before reaching the pass. Ove had earlier reported that Amiako was unwell, so we let him out of harness and carried him on top of a weasel sledge. Turning south-westwards, we set out to follow the trend of the broad valley flanked by rocky ramparts that we had seen a year ago.[5] After following it for 7 kilometres we were 200 metres below the level of the pass. At this point we forked left down a distributary valley that the survey/geology party had traversed last year.[6] It trended towards 150°, which was just about the direction in which we hoped to continue.

After another 8 kilometres we came out of the mountains onto a wide but gently sloping glacier trending south-west–north-east.[7] Mercifully, Gordon and the dogs had found no crevasses. Continuing between two small nunataks,[8] we built a snow cairn and left the dog food requested by Fred Roots, together with a depot for our own return. Three snow petrels took an interest in us, the first we had seen since leaving Pyramiden.

Ahead, we found ourselves looking out on a vast depression unbroken by nunataks. It was so vast – perhaps 50 kilometres wide –

We headed south-westwards along the broad valley flanked by rocky ramparts

203

that we recognized it as what the Germans had named Penck-Mulde.[9] From here on, we planted pieces of dunnage in the snow at intervals to ensure that we could follow the same route homeward even if the weasel tracks were snowed under. A couple of hours later we stopped to camp.

The following day, 13 November, Gordon planned a specially thorough series of observations, to include refraction shooting to determine the velocity of seismic waves. This allowed me a whole day to dig a pit and make all the observations that Valter had done last season: describing snow strata, calculating the density at various depths and measuring ice temperatures.

There was little wind, so it was quite pleasant work although it was snowing gently, and a watery sun sported a multi-hued halo. Late in the day we admired some quite spectacular anvil-shaped standing-wave clouds over the mountain ranges that we had just come through.

17

FARTHEST SOUTH

Continuing downhill, we reached the bottom of the great depression. Here we were evidently in the middle of a major ice stream trending parallel with the smaller one that we had crossed on coming out of the mountains. We were now 1,540 metres above sea level, but Gordon reported that the ice depth was a whopping 2,340 metres. This meant that the bedrock beneath our feet was 800 metres below sea level. Considering that we were 350 kilometres from today's coastline, we had to face the stunning fact that the 'seabed' here was deeper than it was off the coast. At first it was hard to believe that Gordon had got it right. However, we reconciled ourselves by visualizing what a typical Norwegian fjord might look like if it was hidden beneath ice 2,000 metres thick – as many of them were 20,000 years ago: it would look like this.

As we forged ahead, it was clear that we were climbing out of the depression. This was confirmed when the next seismic shot put the bedrock 270 metres above sea level. However, only 10 kilometres further on, the bedrock was back to 400 metres below sea level. We began to understand that while we were having a roller-coaster ride over the bedrock, the topography of the ice surface bore only the faintest trace of what was going on underneath. It was as if a blanket had been stretched across the landscape, hiding everything except the high points where bedrock was close to the surface or came through it as nunataks.

An abrupt escarpment loomed ahead, perhaps 40 kilometres away.[1] It appeared to buttress a plateau, and we speculated that the plateau might possibly continue unbroken from there all the way to the South Pole. To the left of our heading, the escarpment was unscalable, with 300-metre high rock and ice cliffs. We recognized this as the plateau shown on the German map as Neumayer-Steilwand, although we chose to use the Norwegian version – Neumayerveggen.[2]

Peter's weasel was some kilometres behind when I realized that he had stopped. I unhitched my load and drove back to see what the trouble was. His fan belt had broken and, as this could take time to repair, I towed his weasel and sledge forward to mine. Gordon, who was way ahead with the dogs, turned and came back to the weasels. We had intended to depot one of the weasels somewhere near here anyway, so decided that this was as good a spot as any. We would continue with my weasel pulling both cargo sledges and the caboose.

We laid a depot for the return journey and spent some hours cannibalizing Peter's weasel for spare parts. Besides engine parts, we took a leaf spring in case the bent one on my weasel should actually snap. If our last weasel failed, the dogs would really come into their own: we would be left with no alternative but to retrace our steps the whole way to Maudheim carrying nothing but survival gear and our scientific results.

I thought that, for the record, it would be worth calculating exactly what we were asking the weasel to do. Including the weight of the three sledges (one being the caboose), I was towing just over 3 tonnes. Although we would progressively discard some of the seven fuel drums

Looking west across the big ice stream. Borgmassivet is on the horizon to the right

on the sledges, by any standard we were starting with a prodigious load. Could we get away with it?

We had never been able to start moving heavy loads by slipping the clutch. The driver had to back up, rev the engine and let fly. As the towing wires jerked taut, the weasel was jerked almost to a standstill but the sledge runners had broken their bond with the snow and we were moving. The weasel tracks – operating at the limit of traction – were slipping but the long train was on the move. In places I had to meander between sastrugi up to 1 metre high; this kind of terrain put a great strain on the weasel as well as on the sledge lashings.

Peter and Gordon went ahead with the dogs, while I followed some distance behind. Peter spotted dog-sledge tracks crossing ours and heading east. This could only mean that the geology/survey party had come this way, and later we reported the news to Maudheim by radio.

We were climbing now, albeit gently and in steps, but the weasel certainly felt it. Seismic shots told us that the bedrock was above sea level and that – like the surface – it was continuing to rise. As we approached the escarpment, we saw that the gentlest slope lay in a 10-kilometre-wide gap between Neumayerveggen and a group of small nunataks.[3] Much of it was crevassed, but dead ahead we saw a small gap, and on it we pinned our hopes.

We camped at the foot of the escarpment on 17 November, which was my twenty-fifth birthday. I was delighted to be rewarded with a box of chocolates and a special meal of pork, beans with onion, tinned pears, coffee and a dram.

As we started out next morning, the weasel was labouring and I had to change to low gear. From a distance, I had guessed that we might have to zigzag up the slope, but in the event we were able to take it head-on.

It was still a struggle. Finally reaching level ground at the top, we found ourselves on a plateau 2,500 metres above sea level.[4] We turned right to head 145 degrees, in the hope of reaching the deepest ice in the shortest distance.[5] However, Gordon at once began having difficulty finding any ice-bottom echoes at all, and this problem continued. Evidently, reverberations from collapsing snow layers were drowning the echoes. We surmised that it was due to the softer snow prevalent at this altitude. Gordon tried 'air shots', which were known to work under some conditions. This meant raising the charge several metres above the snow surface in the hope that its broader shock wave hitting the surface would give a better result. It didn't.

Communications with Maudheim were better than ever they had been on dog sledge journeys. Peter was getting through almost every day. On 19 November we learned that *Norsel* had crossed the equator.

Ploughing onwards for another 30 kilometres, we laid a depot of food and fuel for the return journey. The mountains behind us were gradually dipping below the horizon, but at this point we could still see a couple of high points on Neumayerveggen and also a nunatak to the east, which, we named Sistefjell (last mountain), as it was probably the last piece of rock that we would see before starting homeward.

Leaving the depot on 21 November, we forged ahead, stopping at intervals for seismic stations, but Gordon's grim face after he developed each batch of records told the same story – no detectable echo. It was 80 kilometres further on before he reported any success – an ice depth of 1,844 metres. The paucity of results depressed us, but if the effort paid off sometimes, we felt it worthwhile. We were, we believed, the first people ever to try measuring ice depths on the high plateau of Antarctica – and we had succeeded.

Still wary of crevasses for the sake of the weasel, Peter or Gordon had been skiing ahead because in this featureless landscape the dogs had become difficult to steer. However, as we had not seen any crevasses and the surface here was flatter, I said that I was happy to lead with the weasel. This speeded our progress because the dogs now had something to sight on. Gordon rode with me, and every 3 kilometres we stopped to plant a dunnage stake. To take a compass bearing, I had to walk several paces away from the weasel because the magnetic field from the engine upset the readings. After taking the bearing and moving on, all I could steer on was clouds, the shadow of the sun or the direction of sastrugi. A useful check was to take back-bearings on the stake behind. If I remembered to look at my watch, our latitude could be checked by setting up the theodolite to take meridian altitudes of the sun.

The surface rose in long, smooth steps and, even with my eyes shut, the engine noise told me when we were climbing. The dogs were never far behind, but at this stage Milagtose was listless and obviously unwell, so we let him ride on the weasel. After covering a further 30 kilometres, Gordon called a halt. Although there was sufficient weasel fuel on the sledges to continue heading inland for a day or two, he chose instead to allow time for an exhaustive series of experiments to find out why we were not getting bottom echoes. Setting up the theodolite, I took a series of sunsights to establish our position.

It was 24 November 1951, we were 620 kilometres from Maudheim and 2,710 metres above sea level. Strangely, the German map indicated a surface altitude of 4,200 metres near here. While aircraft estimates are notoriously unreliable, we never did understand how the Germans could have got it that far wrong. Perhaps Josef Goebbels, the Reich

Our farthest south. The author (pulling string), Robin and Melleby with Kernek

'minister of propaganda and enlightenment', felt that a degree of exaggeration was good for the nation's morale.

Still a meteorologist at heart, Gordon announced that we had reached the 700-millibar level – the pressure of the air we were breathing was only seven-tenths of the pressure at sea level. We felt triumphant at getting this far, and planned an unhurried stay.

First, we laid out the seismometers in different directions and varied the size of explosions. We tried lowering the shots to different depths in several drill holes. We tried making cavities at the bottom of drill holes by setting off one charge and then hanging further charges in the cavity.

I dug the deepest pit that I had ever dug away from Maudheim, reaching a depth of 2.74 metres. Feeling that the word pit was too humble, in my notes I called it a shaft. We drilled an ice-temperature hole from the bottom of the shaft. Given lots of time, we eventually got down to 12.2 metres. At that level the thermometer read $-40^{\circ}C$, suggesting that in winter, temperatures at the surface below $-60^{\circ}C$ must be common. The coldest temperature in the hole showed a vanishing trace of last winter's cold wave: it was $-42.6^{\circ}C$ at a depth of 7 metres.

The visible strata down one side of the shaft showed six distinct layers where the density of the snow was next to nothing. I could poke my fingers into the spaces and scoop out what few loose crystals there were. We speculated that the seismic explosions might be triggering the collapse of these layers and that the resulting noise could be drowning any faint reflections from the bed of the ice sheet. One possible solution might be to collapse the empty layers before shooting. It was worth a try, so we drove the weasel back and forth like a lawnmower over the seismometer line until we had a kind of runway 6 metres wide. Then we set charges at the bottom of the ice-temperature hole.

Finally, Gordon emerged from the caboose to pronounce the experiment successful. The ice was 2,000 metres thick and the bed of the ice sheet was 720 metres above sea level. The result had been worth waiting for.

On 29 November we learned that Valter and Ove had arrived back at Maudheim, well satisfied with their work in the mountain area.

Three days later, we lined up in front of the weasel for an official 'farthest south' photograph. Not having a self-timer, I used a piece of string to trigger the shutter so that all three of us could be in the picture. After a celebration dinner, Gordon served each of us a tot of rum. Then he proposed a toast to King Haakon. I followed with a toast to King Gustav, and Peter toasted King George. Thus did we uphold our international credentials.

With unconcealed pride, Gordon asked Peter to transmit to Maudheim:

To Giaever. Have raised the Norwegian flag,[6] and toasted kings of Norway, Britain and Sweden in position 74.3 degrees south, 00.8 degrees east stop Commence return tomorrow stop Weasel and dogs in good condition. Robin.

Starting homeward on 1 December, we made fast time because the stakes made it easy to keep on track and we did not have to stop for compass bearings. Drilling some shot holes to 12 metres, we made successful soundings where none had been obtained before. This was not without risk to the drill, because soft snow falling on top of the core barrel tended to jam it. The solution, we found, was to line the top 2.5 metres of the hole with a larger tube. Then, by lowering the drill string through it, much less snow was scraped by the drill rods from the sides of the hole.

We tried hardening the sides of the hole by pouring petrol down and igniting it. The petrol went on burning for some time and it was strange to feel a plume of warm air coming out of a hole in the snow. I made a dangerous mistake by pouring petrol into one hole believing that an earlier dose had burned out. An explosive shaft of flame shot upwards, and in snatching the can away, I splashed burning petrol over my arm.

Remembering that as a child I had been drilled in what to do – and what not to do – when clothes catch fire, I jumped clear, fell on the snow, and rolled on my arm so quickly that not even my anorak was holed. Self-immolation was not what I had in mind. I was more careful after that.

Although most of the dogs appeared to have benefited from the rest at our turning point, poor old Milagtose died the next day. We now had eight dogs, and hoped to bring them all back to Maudheim.

We had enjoyed more days of clear weather on the plateau than at lower altitudes, presumably because fewer of the coastal weather systems penetrated this far inland. Day temperatures were generally around –20° to –25°C, which by now we found quite pleasant, but one night the thermometer dropped to –38°C. There were varying amounts of cloud but, throughout our stay, visibility was unlimited.

In traversing 150 kilometres before we left the high plateau, Gordon was able to measure ice depths at five places. The greatest depth was 2,450 metres at a point where the ice surface elevation was 2,530 metres. Although at this stage we could see Sistefjell, the sounding meant that beneath us was a trough reaching almost to sea level.[7]

By 7 December more peaks appeared and we could see a nunatak to the left of Sistefjell.[8] Between these two nunataks was a gently sloping glacier flowing north-eastwards.[9]

Reaching the head of the big escarpment on 10 December, we descended the upper section before stopping just off the western extremity of Neumayerveggen. We were delayed for some hours next morning by a 25-knot wind with drifting snow, but in the afternoon I managed to obtain a good temperature profile down to 9.5 metres. At that depth the temperature was –31°C – already a full 10°C warmer than it was at our turning point. As usual, we used the hole for seismic shots, after which Gordon reported an ice depth of 2,130 metres.

On this day 40 years earlier, Roald Amundsen and his four compatriots had reached the South Pole. We celebrated by feasting on fried corned beef, bread, rice and tinned pears. Afterwards we drank a toast to Amundsen. When this did not seem enough, we added toasts to Amundsen's companions Olav Bjaaland, Helmer Hansen, Oscar Wisting and Sverre Hassel.

On reaching Peter's abandoned weasel, we spent some hours taking more parts, including one complete track. Then, pulling gently with

Gordon Robin offers to sell spare parts (12 December 1951)

the good weasel, I turned the machine on its side and took from it a complete mainspring and one bogie assembly. We were now determined to get the surviving weasel back to Maudheim and even perhaps to England, as a memento of the three vehicles that had made possible not only this but also every other journey.

We made five successful soundings in crossing Penck-Mulde. On reaching the depot that we had laid for the geology/survey party, we found a note from Fred Roots reporting that they had picked up the food on 18 November and continued their journey homewards.

Re-entering the mountain area on 15 December, we were amazed to find deep ice in places where – or so it seemed – one could almost reach out and touch the rock. In a pass overlooked by 700-metre-high cliffs, we found 1,650 metres of ice.[10] Put in perspective, that meant that the highest summit in the British Isles could sink without trace beneath our feet. We never did get used to the prodigious scale of the landscape.

Day temperatures were now back to around –15°C, making outdoor labour comfortable. Turning right into the long north-east – south-west trending valley and climbing to the high pass, we still found 730 metres of ice at its highest point. Stopping frequently along the way for soundings, we did not reach the Advance Base until 20 December.

Seeing two tents ahead, we decided to play a trick on the occupants. Gordon went into the caboose so that when Roots and Reece came out to greet us, all they saw was me. At this point I called to Gordon to announce our arrival. He emerged yawning – to make believe that while one of us was driving, the other was bedded down in the caboose. The geologists were quite impressed with our apparent life of ease. Peter arrived with the dogs half an hour later.

Fred reported that Nils and Stig were already on their way to Maudheim, having extended the triangulation southwards and tightened up its geometry. Fred and Alan had followed a circuitous route 120 kilometres to the north-east, successfully sampling many small nunataks.

Fred prepared a feast for the five of us, serving *Får i kål* (mutton in cabbage) followed by raisin tart and, while gorging ourselves, we exchanged stories of our travels.

Gordon, Peter and I spent one day doing seismics to the north of

Fred Roots cooking at the Advance Base

Pyramiden and another day sounding along the line of stakes that Valter had surveyed to measure the rate of ice movement.

At this stage we knew that we had plenty of time and adequate depots for the journey ahead of us. Let the weasel fail if it must – we would still bring home our records and the remaining dogs. The geologists, however, would have been extremely unhappy to find us without the weasel. They had about half a tonne of rocks for us to carry back, and we were able to load every one of their priceless specimen boxes onto the cargo sledges.

On 22 December we heard that *Norsel* had arrived at Maudheim after a fast passage through the pack ice. That meant mail and new faces, but for us it meant simply that we could be certain of sailing home this season. The third year's food supply at Maudheim could stay where it was – deep under snow.

Before leaving the Advance Base, we moved all the remaining food boxes and a sledge onto Pyramiden to prevent them from being snowed under. Though we ourselves would not need them, somebody in years to come might. We had no reason to believe that the food would significantly deteriorate in the course of a decade or two.[11]

The weather was fine, so Fred Roots entertained us to a picnic lunch of pea soup with bread, butter and jam while sitting in the sunshine on the sledges. Climbing to the summit of Pyramiden, we built a rock cairn and in it left a note for posterity outlining what we had achieved and listing the 13 men who had visited the Advance Base. Though nobody spoke, each of us felt nostalgic at leaving such a wondrous landscape. In a sense it had become ours. No visitors in a thousand years could ever share what we ourselves had shared – the privilege of being first.

But all good things must come to an end. We set out for Maudheim at 1730 on 23 December, leaving Roots and Reece to follow by a different route. The daytime weather had become too warm for the dogs and there was a tendency for snow to stick to the sledge runners, so we decided to switch to night travel.

The following day, 24 December, we made two successful soundings before stopping for Christmas dinner according to Scandinavian custom. The meal began with rice – another Scandinavian tradition – and continued with ham, potatoes, chocolate, coffee and gin.

On Christmas Day we were still within sight of the mountains but nearing the highest point on the trail. Like every other day, it was a working day – the ice depth proved to be 1,450 metres. Peter contacted *Norsel* and the crew gave us an impromptu concert of carols. This shook me into realizing that our life of isolation was nearing its end.

Amiako, who had been a passenger on the sledges and was still weak, was despatched on the 27th. Having left Maudheim with 11 dogs, we now had seven.

As we were the last travellers along the Advance Base route, one of us had to measure every single snow stake in passing so that we would have at least a 12-month record of the rate of snow accumulation at very many points. At each depot we were able to take our pick of tinned foods. However, by this time I had become so accustomed to porridge and pemmican that I had little hankering for variety. I felt that the hour or so taken to thaw a tin of Norwegian meat balls was hardly worth the effort.

It took 16 days to reach Maudheim, not because of any serious breakdowns but because of Gordon's commendable urge to squeeze the maximum amount of work into the time available. Our jobs had become so routine that we behaved like automatons. However, one day I did make a mistake that could have been my last. Our spare weasel battery, which was normally kept on a different sledge, had been unwittingly stowed close to the seismic explosives. As I was taping an electric detonator into sticks of TNT, I suddenly became aware that the bare wires from the detonator were brushing across the bare terminals of the battery. I cursed myself for not checking beforehand – and thanked providence that my hands were still attached to my wrists. A moment's inattention could have become the worst mistake of my life.

The Swedish airmen had asked us to mark their fuel depot near Førstefjell with a cairn of snow blocks in the form of a cross 10 metres long, 1 metre high and 1 metre wide. With all three of us slaving away at it, the cross was completed in under two hours. The next day a twin-engined Beechcraft flew over us at low level, obviously following sledge tracks towards the Advance Base.

Roots and Reece caught up on 30 December 1951 and stayed a few days to help with the seismics. The following day the wind was blowing at about 25 knots, so we spent it inside catching up on rest. The air temperature outside was now only –7°C. Fred and Alan joined us for supper to see in the New Year, and we listened to the BBC at midnight. Sunburn and grime, I noted, had changed each of us so much that I doubted whether our closest relatives would recognize us at first glance. We all had beards but Alan's was as luxuriant as Michelangelo's Moses.

We heard an aircraft again on 2 January but could not see it because it was above a cloud layer. For the next couple of days we worked our way slowly along the trail, stopping frequently for seismics. Fred and Alan followed in our tracks. Each of them had a vested interest in ensuring that no weasel breakdown could stand in the way of their rock boxes reaching Maudheim. They eventually left us on 4 January 1952, practically within sight of Maudheim.

At this point we diverted to the top of the eastern hill from where Maudheim could be seen through binoculars. The altitude of the summit was 276 metres above sea level but the ice depth was 420 metres. That meant that – just as we had learned from all soundings over the southern hill – the bed of the ice sheet was well below sea level. If we could simply remove the ice from the face of the earth, we would now be far out to sea. Perhaps, long ago, when the ice shelf first advanced over the ocean, this part of it had run aground on a seabed shoal. No longer flowing on a frictionless bed – the sea – it built up through successive layers of snow to form the dome that we were standing on.

Returning to the saddle next day, Peter found that rather than having the dogs trailing far behind my speeding weasel, they could ride as passengers. So we tethered some on top of the sledge-loads and some in the weasel. Rapasak was terrified when the train began to move, so he was taken off and allowed to run behind. The others quickly learned that lying down and watching the world go by was a most agreeable form of travel.

As our journey drew to a close, I noted the contrast between the condition of our dogs and the pitiful state in which the same team came back to Maudheim at the end of the previous season. The difference was that throughout the seismic journey, they had only hauled light loads and had plenty of time to rest while we did our work.

We drove into Maudheim just after midnight on 6 January 1952.

Dog sledging the easy way – for the dogs (5 January 1952)

216

We were tired but, more important, we felt triumphant at having achieved what we set out to do – *and* nursed the weasel home. We had been lucky with the weather: in a journey lasting 80 days, there were very few on which we had been unable to travel or at least to do useful work in camp. Of the 240 observations of horizontal visibility in my logbook, 84 per cent gave it as unlimited. In the cold clean clear air of Antarctica, as often as not that meant that it was limited only by the curvature of the earth. Where else, I wondered, where else could that be true?

18

NORTHBOUND

We who had come in from the outback were precipitated into a place of bewildering and frantic activity. The seismic party had been the last to return to the fold – all the other sledging parties had preceded us. Aircraft were flying overhead and our colleagues were preoccupied with last-minute measurements and with packing whatever items were too valuable to abandon.

Ove told me of his adventures after being left alone at the Advance Base on 9 November. Heedless of the risks of travelling alone, he had embarked on a solo excursion to the north. Climbing several nunataks, he searched for mites and lichens. Ove and Nanok together were hauling a light sledge carrying sleeping bag, pup tent and provisions for ten days. Finding plenty of lichens but no mites, they returned to the Advance Base after five days.

In order to survive in comfort while waiting for Valter, Ove had pitched a pyramid tent, crawled inside and made a cup of cocoa. Falling asleep, he awoke to find the tent on fire, his sleeping bag on fire, a blue-grey sky above him, a howling wind and drift snow pouring in. Evidently he had left the Primus stove burning and it had flared up or capsized. He leapt up and used his sleeping bag to put out the fire. His fingers were burned but also stiff with cold in a breeze at –15°C. Luckily there was a spare tent in the depot and, after pitching it, he moved in, by that time chastened and wondering how he could explain away the disaster.

He spent the next 24 hours stitching and patching the remains of his sleeping bag with surgical tape. He realized how fortunate it was that all this had happened at the one place where there was a spare tent.

Before leaving the Advance Base, Valter had resurveyed the stake line that he had set up in mid-January across a broad tributary glacier nearby. Quick calculations with his slide rule gave the same kind of parabolic ice-velocity profile that is normal on mountain glaciers in the Northern Hemisphere. The fastest stake had moved at the sluggish speed of 41 millimetres per day, equivalent to 15 metres per year.[1]

There was an interesting sequel to these measurements. Nils Roer found that the sum of the angles in his triangles extending outwards from the baseline adjacent to Valter's survey did not add up to exactly 180 degrees, even after allowing for the curvature of the earth. The discrepancy amounted to very few seconds of arc but, for a meticulous professional, it was embarrassing. It turned out that he had observed angles from one end of his baseline on one day and from the other end on the following day. The discrepancy, he now saw, must be due to ice movement during the interval. Professional surveyors, of course, are not used to baselines that deform while they are being measured, but this is exactly what was happening. When later he asked Valter for the precise rate of movement of the baseline, Nils was profoundly relieved to find that his triangles could be adjusted. It was a heart-warming example of the mutual assistance that we were able to offer each other on many occasions.

Ove had succeeded in keeping alive the many mites that he had collected on his return visit to Passat. They were nurtured on pieces of rock from their native habitat and kept in a snow tunnel. He was very excited about the possibility of carrying live specimens to Lund University to carry out experiments on their reaction to light and their tolerance to cold. Another excitement was that, at Ove's request, *Norsel* had brought a glass eye for Alan Reece. It was quite a good match and was soon inserted in Alan's empty eye socket.

Norsel, we learned, had left Norselbukta to do a radar survey of the coast to the east. Giæver, Schytt and Roer had gone with the ship. There was an open shore lead and they were intent on going as far as time allowed. However, on reaching 04°46′W the engine stopped. The engineers discovered a failed big-end bearing, potentially a very serious problem. *Norsel* limped slowly back to Maudheim.

I skied to the 'airstrip' just up the hill from Norselbukta to meet the aviators under the command of Captain Reinhold von Essen. Reinhold, 38 years old, was a fair-haired aristocrat who was too modest, or so we were told, to use his title of Baron. With Reinhold there were five Swedish airmen and one Norwegian. The Norwegian was Helge Skappel of Widerøes Flyveselskap.

The Swedes had brought two aircraft: a twin-engined Beechcraft-18R for aerial mapping photography and a single-engined Saab Safir (Sapphire) as back-up. The Beechcraft had served as a Swedish air ambulance since 1950. In 47 hours of flying the larger aircraft, they had photographed every mountain area between 16°W and 03°E and also the coastline from the Greenwich meridian to 21°W.

I was offered a flight in the Safir along the coast with 34-year-old Flight Sergeant O. Wijkman to see what changes had occurred since we had arrived at Maudheim in 1950. Icebergs with dimensions of

219

Maudheim as we left it in 1952. A wooden ventilator shaft and a chimney are the only things to indicate that people may be living below. A tabular iceberg drifts past (left). Pynten (right) marks the entrance to Norselbukta

kilometres, and many smaller ones, were drifting sedately westwards into the Weddell Sea but I could see no changes in the ice front. We cavorted among the summer clouds, circled, swooped and climbed to take in the view. Two years of sometimes hard work on the ground had not detracted from my sense of wonder at the landscape of unending ice around us. However, when the engine began to 'cough' over the sea, my wonder gave way to other emotions. As Reinhold mentioned in his report, ' . . . the cough did not inspire confidence'.[2]

The airmen had made one mistake. In order to render their runway (skiway) more conspicuous from the air, they had sprayed its edges with soot. This absorbed so much radiation that a deep ditch developed – it resembled a snow-bridged crevasse. At first glance I thought it *was* a crevasse. They had learned to taxi at right angles to the ditch as we had learned to cross crevasses.

220

Guttorm Jakobsen

I made a big mistake the same day. Trying to avoid the chaos below ground, I chose to develop my films from the seismic journey in the caboose. Its dark green colouring made the inside seem like an oven when I hung the films to dry. At night, however, the temperature dropped below freezing and caused mottling of the emulsion. The films are usable but prints made from them resemble antique photographs. Today, I suppose, they are genuine antiques.

After a couple of days I skied down to the quay to meet the newcomers in *Norsel*. There was Guttorm Jakobsen, bearded as in 1950 and beaming. When I asked why, he said that after reaching the Newfoundland sealing grounds last March, they had obtained 24,150 sealskins, the largest catch ever taken to Norway. This was certainly a remarkable achievement for a crew of only 30 men.

John Snarby was there, smiling and clean-shaven as before. Some faces were unfamiliar. Lieutenants David Blair and Robert Higgins of the Royal Navy had come on the voyage as observers. Halvdan Hydle, a tall, thin, middle-aged journalist from *Aftenposten,* had come to record the last chapter of our story.

During the last few days Ove consigned his mites to a refrigerator on board, and we packed and dragged down to the quay everything that was reusable and certainly all valuable instruments. However, the remaining year's food supply and much else was up for grabs.

221

Provided that we did the job ourselves without incurring shipping charges, we were free to go on a looting spree. I think each of us looted our bedding, and I took my bed as well. I also took a box containing 27 kilos of tinned butter.

Butter, I knew, was still rationed in England – the weekly ration was 2 ounces (57 grammes). This meant that my loot would keep me in double rations for the next nine years. The fact that the butter was rancid – which I had come to like – meant that I would never have to share it with even my best friends. It was a treasure.

Some of my colleagues helped themselves to equally bizarre items.[3] It was the first and last time in our lives that we could loot in full view of authority without fear of prosecution.

After the air unit had loaded their aircraft back on *Norsel*, she put to sea to give the engineers a chance to repair the engine. This they did, but there was an anxious moment while the engine was in pieces. The ship was on the point of drifting down on an iceberg, and only by launching a motor lifeboat did they manage to tow her clear before the collision.

One of the most traumatic events for all of us was when the moment arrived to shoot the dogs. They had become very dear to us and were part of our extended family. Sverdrup had decided that only four could be taken home. Two of these had recovered from the foot

Valter's last trip with his dogs. The Swedish aircraft are back on board and *Norsel* is ready for departure (8 January 1952)

222

disease that had taken such a heavy toll on *Thorshøvdi*, and it was hoped that veterinary pathologists might be able to identify the disease. It was a faint hope in that two years had passed, but worth a try. The grisly task of despatching most of the dogs fell to Valter, though Fred asked to shoot his own team.[4] When I saw them afterwards, they were clearly shaken. Any of us would have felt the same. Out of 56 dogs, only Bosun, King, Nafalik and Krane were spared.

When Rog's Maudheim Radio finally went off the air, its last telegram, like the first, was sent to King Haakon. Most of us carried our personal possessions aboard *Norsel* on 14 January. The following day we all returned to Maudheim for a farewell ceremony. On three hastily erected flagpoles flew our flags: Norway's in the middle, with the Union flag and the Swedish flag bracketing it. A case of champagne appeared and we doffed our hats as Giæver proposed a toast to each of the three kings, and then we drank to Maudheim, our home for the last two years. I was given the honour of lowering the Union flag – and made sure that the Norwegian government flag came down last of all.

It was a poignant moment for all of us. In the space of two years we had done what we came to do, we had spent many happy times together, we had lived through days of euphoria and moments of terror – and we would grieve forever for our lost comrades. We left the land as we found it – in the silence of eternity.

When everyone was on board, *Norsel* cast off and headed out to sea. The flag was dipped as Giæver threw wreaths over the side as a last tribute to Leslie Quar, Bertil Ekström and John Jelbart.

Thus ended a big chapter in our lives.

It took four days to clear the pack ice, during which Ove Wilson was still sucking our blood. Giæver quotes Riiser-Larsen: 'There are two moments of real pleasure during an expedition: seeing the first ice floe ahead – and leaving the last one behind.[5]

Our progress towards the Canary Islands, where we would leave the ship, was uneventful – with one exception. King George VI died on 6 February, the day *Norsel* crossed the equator. Giæver had planned to celebrate our return to the Northern Hemisphere but cancelled the party as a mark of respect.

On reaching Santa Cruz on Tenerife on 14 February, we disembarked from *Norsel* to allow the ship to pursue her calling – sealing off Newfoundland. Then, with our baggage, we joined the Norwegian liner *Venus* heading for England. The Swedish aircraft were unloaded at Las Palmas and prepared to fly to Sweden. At Grando airfield, Reinhold found a Spanish oil company worker on his Beechcraft busily feeding petrol into a funnel while puffing on a lighted cigarette. On seeing Reinhold's alarm, the man contemptuously doused the cigarette in the petrol. Thus did our airmen learn that not all airports adhere to the safe operating procedures of the Royal Swedish Air Force. They also learned what a casual refueller can – with luck – get away with.

All 14 wintering members of the expedition landed in Southampton on 18 February. The Royal Geographical Society held a reception for us on 20 February. On the 21st we were invited to dinner at the Norwegian Embassy. On the 22nd we were received by the Lord Mayor of London in the Mansion House, and later the same day we were entertained at the American Embassy.

Taking passage to Norway, we were invited by King Haakon into his palace in Oslo and presented, one by one, with a silver Kongens Fortjenstmedalje (the medal of merit). When my turn came, for one embarrassing moment I did not understand what the king said to me. I had spoken Norwegian and Swedish for two years and it had never crossed my mind that I would have any problem with the language in Oslo. My colleagues explained afterwards that Haakon had come to Norway in 1905 as a Danish prince; in 47 years on the throne he had never learned to speak good Norwegian.

Fortunately, I had no difficulty in understanding his people.

19

EPILOGUE

The scientific results of the expedition took time to appear in print because of the vast amount of data that we had brought home. It did not help that the expedition coffers were nearly empty, so that it was not possible to employ every member of the scientific staff full-time for long enough to complete the work. However, we did not give up. After taking jobs elsewhere, some of us sacrificed our spare time for years afterwards to finish what we had begun. So the results *did* appear.[*]

In this narrative I have not attempted to summarize them because nothing short of a major review paper could do justice to the scope of our discoveries. However, a comprehensive review of the main fields (glaciology, geology and meteorology) was published in 1953.[1] Our glaciological work led to the concept – later accepted – that world sea level is principally controlled by the state of the Antarctic ice sheet. The meteorological results led to an understanding of the importance of ice sheets in regulating world climate. The geological work recorded the nature of the rocks, though a generation was to pass before this led to the realization that Dronning Maud Land was once joined to southern Africa. Finally, Ove Wilson's research, which was not part of the expedition's programme but was undertaken on his own initiative, resulted in the publication of eight research papers in leading scientific journals.

I was lucky. There had been no prior agreement that I should play any part in analysing the results. However, Valter knew that if he took everything on himself, he might do little else for the next ten years. Our findings had so far exceeded what we had expected that he invited me to come to Stockholm University for a year. Once there, we shared all our records and decided which of us should be responsible for writing which sections.

I spent a very happy year in close collaboration not only with

---

[*] See *Bibliography* on pages 248 to 253

Valter but also with Gösta Liljequist, who was analysing his own data in the same office. Afterwards I returned to Oxford to use my part for a doctoral thesis. Few university theses ever get published *in extenso*, but mine was one of them.

Ultimately, six volumes of scientific results and many topographic maps were published by Norsk Polarinstitutt. In addition, there were dozens of shorter papers published in learned journals in several countries.

The scientific results of the expedition led to doctorates for Gösta Liljequist, Gordon Robin, Valter Schytt, Ove Wilson and me. Fred Roots already had a Ph.D.

Throughout the expedition, our activities had been followed by newspapers throughout the world.[2] Curiously by today's standards, one of the most faithful monitors of our fortunes had been *The Calcutta Statesman*.

Valter Schytt published his own assessment of the relative merits of national and international expeditions. He noted that, in our case, the tripartite management structure at home caused more problems than ever we had in the Antarctic. ' ... there were occasions when three organizing committees were two too many'.[3] Whereas we dealt with difficulties face to face, each of the national committees wanted to be involved in decisions but could only communicate by letter or telephone and – rarely – round the same table. National sensitivities had to be assuaged, whereas in the Antarctic these always took second place to relations between individuals.

On our return to England, John Giæver had said: 'I do not think there has ever been a polar expedition with so little friction between members'.[4] My own opinion is that, other things being equal, once away from home an international expedition encounters fewer difficulties than would a national expedition. At Maudheim, each one of us, to the best of our ability, leaned over backwards to suppress our national prejudices and preconceptions. That, surely, was the key to our success. We made allowance for the differences in cultural background; whereas on a national expedition it is all too easy to assume that men brought up in the same culture should think alike. Finding that this is not so can lead to conflict.

I do not recall a single occasion on which the senior man from each country – Giæver, Schytt or Robin – convened a meeting of his own countrymen to discuss a national policy. It probably helped that the meteorology programme involved a Norwegian and a Swede, the glaciology programme had Swedish, British and Australian participants, and the geology/survey programme had Canadian, British and Norwegian members. We knew that any alignment based on nationality would be disruptive, and that the success or failure of the expedition would be judged by its scientific results.

My colleagues and I were still writing up our results when the greatest international scientific enterprise of all time more or less took over research in Antarctica. The International Geophysical Year of 1957–58 (IGY) involved expeditions from 12 nations cooperating on agreed research programmes. While most were national expeditions, there were invited participants from other countries. Along with other erstwhile Maudheim staff, I was invited to become scientific leader of one of the American IGY stations.

All the scientists from our expedition were asked to supply advance copies of our work to guide those who were heading south – and we did so. The IGY was far more than a set of vaguely coordinated projects. Precise details of the timing of observations and of the instruments to be used were agreed at a series of international conferences that took place before 1957. In terms of scientific results, it was a success story without parallel.

It was also a political triumph. The IGY led to a treaty negotiated by all 12 participating states – the Antarctic Treaty of 1959. The treaty guarantees free access to any part of Antarctica for peaceful purposes, despite competing claims to sovereignty that before had dogged relations between some of the signatories.

Almost 50 years on, I believe that the success of our expedition helped to end the series of competing national expeditions that had characterized the first half of the twentieth century. Instead, it led to an era of international cooperation and collaboration that continues to this day.

Ten years after we left Maudheim, the Chief Scientist of the Office of Antarctic Programs of the US National Science Foundation put it this way:

> The era of expansive exploration now under way can be said to have had its beginning in the Norwegian-British-Swedish expedition of 1949–1952. This international enterprise conducted the first major traverses into the interior and laid a foundation for the Antarctic phase of the International Geophysical Year in 1957–1958.[5]

I can hardly imagine a more fitting epitaph – and epitaph it is for those who are no longer with us: Bertil Ekström,[6] John Giæver,[7] John Jelbart,[8] Gösta Liljequist,[9] Bjarne Lorentzen,[10] Leslie Quar,[11] Alan Reece,[12] Egil Rogstad,[13] Valter Schytt,[14] John Snarby,[15] and Ove Wilson.[16]

227

If I could be in touch with them beyond the grave, I believe that not one would regret having joined the expedition.

NOTES

Chapter 1

1. Alfred Ritscher, *Wissenschaftliche und fliegerische Ergebnisse der Deutschen Antarktischen Expedition 1938/39*, vol 1 (Leipzig, Koehler & Amelang, 1942)
2. Gunnar Hoppe and Valter Schytt, *Memorial to Hans W. Ahlmann* (Boulder, Colorado, Geological Society of America, 1974)
3. Donald Lindsay, *Friends for Life: A Portrait of Launcelot Fleming* (Seaford, Lindel Publishing Company, 1981); G. C. L. Bertram, 'Launcelot Fleming: An appreciation', *Polar Record*, 5:39, (1950), pp. 396–7
4. Charles Swithinbank, 'The origin of dirt cones on glaciers', *Journal of Glaciology*, 1:8 (1950), pp. 461–5
5. Charles Swithinbank, 'Mechanical transport of the Norwegian-British-Swedish Antarctic Expedition, 1949–52', *Polar Record*, 6:46 (1953), pp. 765–74
6. Roland Winfield, DFC, AFC (1910–70) was an applied physiologist with experience in the Arctic. *Polar Record*, 15:98 (1971), pp. 762–3
7. The leader's name was Giæver but it has been rendered as Giaever in some English language publications.
8. John Giaever, *The White Desert*, (London, Chatto and Windus, 1954), p. 27
9. These are gross registered tons of 100 cubic feet measured according to nautical conventions. *Norsel*'s net tonnage was 320, her length 45 metres and beam 9 metres. Contemporary usage is in one stage of a slow transition from imperial to metric units. In a scientific paper I would adhere uncompromisingly to the metric system. However, this narrative is not addressed to scientists, so consistency would be unhelpful. The speed of ships and aircraft would be reported in metres per second, whereas knots (nautical miles per hour) are hallowed by usage and enshrined in international conventions. So in this book I quote speeds in knots; while distances, heights and weights are in metric units.
10. *Times of Malta*, 22 November 1949
11. *Natal Mercury,* Durban, 6 December 1948

12. *Daily Herald*, London, 15 June 1949
13. *New York Herald Tribune*, Paris, 21 April 1949

Chapter 2

1. The anthropologist and explorer Vilhjalmur Stefansson considered that, for sledge dogs, wolves made the best cross. He 'had two dogs known to be half wolf and that in temperament and all other qualities they were about the finest he ever had'. Vilhjalmur Stefansson, *Arctic Manual* (New York, Macmillan, 1957), pp. 117–18
2. British food rations in October 1949 were (per person per week): meat 1s 6d; eggs 2; bacon or ham 113 g; cheese 57 g; butter 113 g; margarine 113 g; cooking fat 57 g; sugar 227 g; tea 57 g; chocolate or sweets 113 g. *ABC of Rationing in the United Kingdom* (London, Ministry of Food, 1951)
3. Flensing means stripping blubber, though the word is now used to cover the whole butchering process.
4. All times of day in this book are in hours and minutes according to naval usage; thus 0719 is 7.19 a.m., and 1905 is 7.05 p.m.

Chapter 3

1. Throughout the book, unattributed quotations are from my own diaries.
2. International Commission on Whaling, *First Report of the Commission* (London, International Commission on Whaling, 1950)

Chapter 4

1. I learned afterwards that the combined catch of all pelagic whalers in the Antarctic during the 1949–50 season was 29,017 whales, representing 16,062 blue whale units. Broken down, the catch was 6,168 blue, 18,061 fin, 2,117 humpback, 101 sei and 2,570 sperm whales. N. A. Mackintosh, *Polar Record*, 6:43 (1952), p. 403

Chapter 5

1. John Giaever, *The White Desert*, (London, Chatto and Windus, 1954), p. 61
2. Sir James Clark Ross, *A Voyage of Discovery and Research in the Southern and Antarctic regions during the years 1839–43*, 2 vols. (London, John Murray, 1847), vol. 1, p. 228
3. Hjalmar Riiser-Larsen, *Mot Ukjent Land* (Oslo, Gyldendal, 1930) p. 145. In 1953 I corresponded with Lars Christensen, who wrote to Riiser-Larsen on my behalf asking whether he had other aerial photographs from this area. He did not (letter of 5 August 1953 from Riiser-Larsen to Lars Christensen).
4. Sir James Clark Ross, op. cit., vol. 2, p. 365
5. Riiser-Larsen, op. cit., opp. p. 160
6. Wilhelm Filchner, *To the Sixth Continent. The second German South Polar Expedition (Zum sechsten Erdteil. Die zweite deutsche Sudpolar-Expedition)*, translated by William Barr (Huntingdon, UK, Bluntisham Books, 1994)
7. Sir Ernest Shackleton, *South, the Story of Shackleton's Last Expedition 1914–1917*, (London, William Heinemann, 1919)
8. John Giaever, op. cit., p. 69

Chapter 6

1. Otto Nordenskjöld, J. Gunnar Andersson, C. A. Larsen and C. Skottsberg, *Antarctic. Två År bland Sydpolens Isar*, 2 vols. (Stockholm, Albert Bonniers Forlag, 1904)
2. Sir Douglas Mawson, *The Home of the Blizzard*, 2 vols. (London, William Heinemann, 1915)
3. Alan Reece, 'The base of the Norwegian-British-Swedish Antarctic Expedition, 1949–52', *Polar Record*, 6:45 (1953), pp. 617–30
4. Roald Amundsen, *The South Pole. An account of the Norwegian Antarctic Expedition in the "Fram", 1910–1912*, 2 vols. (London, John Murray, 1912)
5. John Giaever, *The White Desert*, (London, Chatto and Windus, 1954), p. 75
6. G. B. Walford, 'Antarctica: An Airman's View', *Geographical Magazine*, 23:6 (1950), pp. 233–240 (p. 240)
7. Owing to the misplacement on the German map of the nunataks seen by Walford and Tudor, the Norwegians rejected the name Kraulberge and later named the group Vestfjella.

8. 'Evacuation flight to Halley Bay', *Antarctic Journal of the United States*, 3:1 (1968), pp. 14–15

Chapter 7

1. John Giaever, *The White Desert*, (London, Chatto and Windus, 1954), p. 92
2. E. F. Roots and C. W. M. Swithinbank, 'Snowdrifts around buildings and stores', *Polar Record*, 7:50 (1955), pp. 380–7
3. The wind-chill concept was developed by: Paul A. Siple and Charles F. Passel, 'Measurements of dry atmospheric cooling in subfreezing temperatures', *Proceedings of the American Philosophical Society*, 89:1, (1945), pp. 177–99. A more recent version of wind-chill is: W. G. Rees, 'A new wind-chill nomogram', *Polar Record*, 29:170 (1993), pp. 229–34
4. Fred Roots was born in Salmon Arm, British Columbia, on 5 July 1923.
5. Gösta Liljequist, 'Richard E Byrd's fyra Antarktiska Expeditioner 1928–47', *Ymer* (1948, 2), 104–20

Chapter 8

1. I use *inland ice* as an abbreviation of *inland ice sheet*, defined as: 'An ice sheet of considerable thickness...resting on rock'. The word *inland* in this definition can confuse, in that an ice sheet resting on rock may extend to the coast, as it does at Kapp Norvegia.
2. Alan Reece, 'Sledges of the Norwegian-British-Swedish Antarctic Expedition, 1949–52', *Polar Record*, 6:46 (1953), pp. 775–87
3. Auståsen (east hill). The *official* Norwegian place names only became available after most of our scientific results were published. It would be misleading in this narrative to use place names that did not exist in 1950–52. However, I have appended them in notes so that interested readers can follow our routes by referring to the Norwegian 1:250,000 map series, the first of which was published in 1961.
4. These cracks later became known as 'strand cracks'. Brian Roberts, E. F. Roots and Charles Swithinbank, 'Strand cracks', *Polar Record*, 8:52 (1956), p. 64
5. Søråsen (south hill)
6. Although we steered by compass, I have applied the magnetic

variation (declination) to convert all headings, bearings and directions to angles measured in degrees clockwise from true north.

Chapter 9

1. Theodore G. Lathrop, *Hypothermia: Killer of the Unprepared* (Portland, Oregon, Mazamas, 1975.)
2. J. Giæver and V. Schytt, 'General Report of the Expedition', *Norwegian-British-Swedish Antarctic Expedition 1949–52, Scientific Results*, 6:3 (Oslo, Norsk Polarinstitutt, 1963), p. 26
3. All ice thicknesses and many distances and surface elevations that I quote in this book are taken from: G. de Q. Robin, 'Seismic shooting and related investigations', *Norwegian-British-Swedish Antarctic Expedition, 1949–52, Scientific Results*, 5 (Oslo, Norsk Polarinstitutt, 1958). The preliminary results derived in field camps have been adjusted wherever possible to accord with the published data.

Chapter 10

1. John Giaever, *The White Desert* (London, Chatto and Windus, 1954) p. 115
2. John Giaever, op. cit., p. 117
3. Søråsen (south hill)
4. Thirty-six years were to elapse before we had some understanding of the German maps. It took a Ph.D. thesis to unravel the story. The solution was to use Nils Roer's maps and recent satellite images to resect the aircraft position from which each of the German photographs was taken. Karsten Brunk, *Kartographische Arbeiten und deutsche Namengebung in Neuschwabenland, Antartkis* (Frankfurt am Main, Verlag des Instituts für Angewandte Geodäsie, 1986)

Chapter 11

1. Ekströmisen (Ekström ice shelf)
2. Borgmassivet (fortress massif)
3. John Giaever, *The White Desert*, (London, Chatto and Windus, 1954), p. 162
4. E. F. Roots, in: Giæver, op. cit., p. 245

5. Twenty nine years later – in 1978 – I was using a solar-powered radio in Antarctica. Charles Swithinbank, *An Alien in Antarctica* (Blacksburg, McDonald and Woodward, 1997), p. 127
6. Halvfarryggen
7. Glasiologbukta (glaciologist bay)
8. Now Jelbartisen (Jelbart ice shelf)

Chapter 12

1. Giæverryggen (Giæver ridge)
2. V. E. Fuchs, 'Sledging rations of the Falkland Islands Dependencies Survey, 1948–50', *Polar Record*, 6:44 (1952), pp. 508–11
3. Vilhjalmur Stefansson, 'Pemmican', *The Military Surgeon*, 95:2 (1944), pp. 89–98
4. Per Dalenius and Ove Wilson, 'On the soil fauna of the Antarctic and of the Sub-Antarctic Islands. The Oribatidae (Acari)', *Arkiv för Zoologi*, 11:23 (1958), pp. 393–425
5. Schyttbreen (Schytt glacier)
6. Ahlmannryggen (Ahlmann ridge)
7. Giæverryggen (Giæver ridge)
8. Viddalen (broad valley)
9. Now Borga (the fortress), part of the mountain group Borgmassivet (fortress massif)
10. Halo-phenomena are described in Gösta Liljequist's 'Special Studies: Halo-phenomena and ice-crystals', *Norwegian-British-Swedish Antarctic Expedition 1949–52: Scientific Results*, 2:2 (1956). Edward Wilson's paintings (such as *SPRI 478* in the collection of the Scott Polar Research Institute, Cambridge) convey the beauty of a solar halo. Edward Wilson, *Diary of the Terra Nova Expedition to the Antarctic 1910–1912* (London, Blandford Press, 1972), opp. p. 241
11. Fasetfjellet (facet mountain)
12. Raudbergpasset (red mountain pass)
13. Raudbergdalen (red mountain valley)
14. Raudberget (red mountain) and Högsætet (high seat)
15. Point 2039
16. The glacier now bears the name Charlesbreen (Charles glacier).
17. Point 1935

Chapter 13

1. This was Blåisen. For 37 years I lived with the idea of lai.
   transport aircraft on naturally occurring blue ice in Antarctic.
   We finally did it. (Charles Swithinbank, *Forty Years on Ice*
   (Lewes, The Book Guild, 1998), pp. 174–87
2. The rate of ablation was very slow indeed. Some of these stakes
   were found still standing 34 years later. Changes in the exposed
   length had averaged 1 or 2 centimetres per year. Karsten Brunk
   and Rudolf Staiger, 'Nachmessungen an Pegeln auf einem Blaueisfeld im Borgmassiv, Neuschwabenland, Antarktis', *Polarforschung*,
   56:1/2 (1986), pp. 23–32
3. Nashornet (rhinoceros) and Nashornkalvane (the rhino's calves)
4. Jutulstraumen (the giant's stream)
5. Roald Amundsen, *Sydpolen. Den Norske Sydpolfærd med Fram
   1910–1912*, 2 vols. (Kristiania, Jacob Dybwads Forlag, 1912)
6. Jutulröra (the giant's pipe) in H.U. Sverdrupfjella
7. Forty-six years later, an ice depth of 2,800 metres was measured
   not far from where we had crossed this ice stream. Jens-Ove
   Näslund, 'Airborne radar soundings of ice depth, gps measurements of ice velocity and studies of landform evolution in central
   Dronning Maud Land, East Antarctica', *Norsk Polarinstitutt
   Meddelelser*, 148 (1997), pp. 125–36
8. Strong feelings between dog drivers are not unprecedented. On
   their epic journey over the Arctic Ocean pack ice in 1895, Hjalmar
   Johansen wrote of his leader Fridtjof Nansen: 'He is angry with
   me, as if it is my fault that he has beaten his dogs too much'.
   Quoted in: Roland Huntford, *Nansen: The Explorer as Hero*,
   (London, Duckworth, 1997), p. 278

Chapter 14

1. *Irish Times*, Belfast, 14 November 1950
2. Telegram from Giæver to Sverdrup, 26 February 1951 (translation).
3. John Giaever, *The White Desert*, (London, Chatto and Windus,
   1954) p. 181
4. Richard E. Byrd, *Alone*, (London, Putnam, 1938) pp. 214–15
5. Brian Roberts, 'Journal kept during the Antarctic voyage of
   Norsel 1950–51; Norwegian-British-Swedish Antarctic Expedition,
   1949–52', 6 January 1951, p. 41, unpublished (Scott Polar
   Research Institute MS 1308/7)

Chapter 15

1. However, an ordinary pedal cycle had been used: R. F. Scott, *Scott's Last Expedition*, 2 vols. (London, Smith, Elder & Co., 1913), vol. 1, p. 424
2. Charles Swithinbank, 'Mechanical transport of the Norwegian-British-Swedish Antarctic Expedition, 1949–52', *Polar Record*, 6:46 (1953), pp. 765–74
3. Quoted in: Roland Huntford, *Nansen. The Explorer as Hero* (London, Duckworth, 1997), p. 195
4. John Giaever, *The White Desert*, (London, Chatto and Windus, 1954), p. 194
5. John Giaever, op. cit., pp. 194–5
6. John Giaever, op. cit., p. 110.
7. Charles Swithinbank, 'The movement of the ice shelf at Maudheim', *Norwegian-British-Swedish Antarctic Expedition 1949–52, Scientific Results*, 3C, pp. 77–96, (Oslo, Norsk Polarinstitutt, 1957), p. 95.
8. Valter Schytt, 'The inner structure of the ice shelf at Maudheim as shown by core drilling', *Norwegian-British-Swedish Antarctic Expedition 1949–52, Scientific Results*, 4:C, pp. 113–51 (Oslo, Norsk Polarinstitutt, 1957)
9. John Giaever, op. cit., p. 204

Chapter 16

1. On reading a draft of this paragraph after an interval of 47 years, Fred Roots confessed that his dogs loved to use my survey stakes for slalom practice. Now at last I have an explanation for some small discrepancies in my angle measurements.
2. In reporting such things here, I am leaping ahead of the facts; because although we understood the general picture at the time, it was not until Gordon Robin spent years analysing the results in detail after our return to England that the subglacial landscape could be described.
3. Raudbergpasset (red mountain pass)
4. In addition to the Norwegian map that now covers Borgmassivet at a scale of 1:250,000, an independent map at a scale of 1:50,000 with a 25-metre contour interval was published in 1989. Karsten Brunk, 'Geomorphologische-glaziologische Detailkartierung des arid-hochpolaren Borgmassivet, Antarktika', *Berichte zur Polarforschung*, 66, (1989)

236

5. Raudbergdalen (red mountain valley)
6. Breidskaret (broad pass)
7. Frostlendet (frost land)
8. Möteplassen (meeting place) and Stridbukken (hardhead)
9. Pencksökket (Penck trough)

Chapter 17

1. Swithinbankhallet (Swithinbank slope)
2. Now Kirwanveggen (Kirwan wall)
3. Charlesrabbane (Charles nunataks)
4. Neumayerskarvet (Neumayer plateau)
5. Later mapping suggested that heading due south would have gained altitude faster, but we had no way of knowing this.
6. In July 1952 I arranged for this flag to be presented to King Haakon, who sent a very warm letter of thanks.
7. Robinsökket (Robin trough)
8. Mellebynuten (Melleby peak)
9. Peterbreen (Peter glacier)
10. Breidskaret (broad gap) between Högfonna (high snowfield) and Jökulgavlen (glacier gable)
11. Geologists from the Soviet Antarctic Expedition found our boxes in December 1960 – V. I. Bardin, 'U pokinutoy bazy', *Sovetskaya Antarkticheskaya Ekspeditsiya. Informatsionnyy Byulleten*, 32 (1962), pp. 52–3. A South African party added to the store of supplies in 1965. They thawed some of our bread and found that 'it was quite tasty' – E. de Ridder, 'Sanae to Söyla', *Antarktiese Bulletin*, 20/21, (1967), pp. 8–10. A joint Belgian and South African party in 1967 noted that the food was still edible. A later South African party inspected the depot on 16 December 1975 and reported the contents in good condition (personal communication from Richard Otto, 1998).

Chapter 18

1. Ten years later, while working on Byrd Glacier on the other side of the continent, I found parts of it moving at the rate of 840 metres per year – Charles Swithinbank, 'Ice movement of valley glaciers flowing into the Ross Ice Shelf, Antarctica', *Science*, 141:3580, (1963), pp. 523–4
2. Reinhold von Essen, 'Air operations of the Norwegian-British-

237

Swedish Antarctic Expedition in 1952', *Polar Record*, 8:54 (1956), pp. 230–6

3. Gordon Robin took the masthead light that had so often guided us home in the dark. Years later he presented it to Polarmuséet in Tromsø, where now it occupies a place of honour.

4. In a letter of 11 September 1998, Fred Roots wrote: 'I loved and respected my team, and felt that I would be betraying their trust, after all we had been through together, if I was not with them at the end. . . Rachel came last of all, and I held her head in my hands for a long time. Undemonstrative but close as ever, she simply pressed against me, a true friend.'

5. John Giæver, *Maudheim. To år i Antarktis* (Oslo, Gyldendal Norsk Forlag, 1952), p. 367 (translation)

Chapter 19

1. E. F. Roots, 'The Norwegian-British-Swedish Antarctic Expedition 1949–52', in: A. W. Haslett, (ed.), *Science News*, 26 (1953), pp. 9–32 (London, Penguin)

2. In addition to the Norwegian and Swedish press, English language reports appeared in: *Aberdeen Evening Express, Adelaide Advertiser, Adelaide Mail, Aeroplane, Anglo-Swedish Review, Auckland Star, Auckland Weekly News, Belfast Newsletter, Belfast Telegraph, Birmingham Gazette, Birmingham Mail, British Guiana Chronicle, Buenos Aires Herald, Building Digest, Bulawayo Chronicle, Bulawayo Sunday News, Calcutta Statesman, Cambridge Daily News, Cape Argus, Cape Times, Carrefour, Christchurch Press, Christian Science Monitor, City Press, Civil & Military Gazette, Continental Daily Mail, Coventry Evening Telegraph, Croydon Advertiser, Cumberland Evening News, Daily Graphic, Daily Herald, Daily News, Daily Record, Daily Telegraph, Diamond Fields Advertiser, Discovery, Dominion, Dublin Evening Herald, Dundee Courier and Advertiser, Dundee Evening Telegraph, Dunedin Evening Star, East Anglian Daily Times, East London Dispatch, Edinburgh Evening Dispatch, Edinburgh Evening News, Egyptian Gazette, Electrician, Engineer, Evening Chronicle, Evening Express, Evening News, Evening Standard, Fairplay, Farmer & Settler, Farmer's Weekly, Fighting Forces, Flight, Food Manufacture, Friend, Geographical Journal, Glasgow Evening Times, Glasgow Herald, Greenock Telegraph, Grimsby Telegraph, Guardian, Halifax Courier & Guardian, Hobart Mercury, Hong Kong Telegraph, Huddersfield Examiner, Iraq Times, Irish Daily*

Telegraph, Irish News, Irish Press, Jersey Evening Post, Johannesburg Star, Journal of Commerce, Lancashire Daily Post, Leicester Mercury, Liverpool Echo, Liverpool Evening Express, Lloyds List, Madras Mail, Manchester Daily Telegraph, Manchester Evening News, Manchester Guardian, Melbourne Age, Melbourne Sun, Montreal Daily Star, Montreal Gazette, Montreal Standard, Morning Advertiser, Natal Daily News, Natal Mercury, Natal Witness, Nature, Newcastle Evening Chronicle, News Review, New York Herald Tribune, New York Times, New Zealand Herald, Northampton Evening Telegram, Northern Daily Mail, Northern Daily Telegraph, Northern Dispatch, Northern Echo, Nottingham Evening Post, Nottingham Guardian, Nottingham Journal, Otago Daily Times, Ottawa Citizen, Ottawa Journal, Overseas Daily Mail, Oxford Mail, Perth Daily News, Petroleum, Port of London Authority Monthly, Portsmouth Evening News, Rand Daily Mail, Reading Standard, Recorder, Rhodesia Herald, St Johns Evening Telegram, Saturday Night, Scarborough Evening News, Scotsman, Sheffield Weekly Telegraph, Shields Evening News, South China Morning Post, Southern Daily Echo, Southland Daily News, South Wales Echo, Star, Sunday Mail, Sunday Sun, Sunday Times, Sunday Tribune, Sunderland Echo, Sussex Daily News, Sydney Daily Telegraph, Sydney Morning Herald, Sydney Sun, Syren, The Times, Times of India, Times of Malta, Toronto Globe, Trident, Washington Post, Wellington Evening Post, West Australian, Western Daily Press, Western Evening Herald, Western Mail, Western Morning News, Yorkshire Evening Post, Yorkshire Observer, and *Yorkshire Post*

3. J. Giæver and V. Schytt, 'General Report of the Expedition', *Norwegian-British-Swedish Antarctic Expedition 1949–52, Scientific Results*, 6:3 (Oslo, Norsk Polarinstitutt, 1963), p. 34
4. *The Times*, London, 19 February 1952
5. A. P. Crary, 'The Antarctic', *Scientific American* 207:3, (1962), pp. 60–73.
6. Bertil Ekström was born in Svenstorp, Sweden, in 1919 and died near Maudheim on 24 February 1951.
7. Nils Jørgen Schumacher, Obituary: John Schjelderup Giæver, *Norsk Polarinstitutt Årbok* 1970, pp. 237–9, (Oslo, Norsk Polarinstitutt, 1972). John Giæver was born in Tromsø on 1 January 1901 and died in Oslo on 11 November 1970.
8. John Ellis Jelbart was born in Ballarat, Australia, in December 1926 and died near Maudheim on 24 February 1951.
9. Charles Swithinbank, Obituary: Gösta Hjalmar Liljequist, *Polar Record*, 31:178 (1995), pp.360–1. Liljequist was born in

Norrköping, Sweden, on 20 April 1914 and died near Stockholm on 18 February 1995.

10. Bjarne Lorentzen was born on 10 April 1900 and died in Lødingen, Norway.

11. Leslie Quar was born in Croydon, England, on 27 March 1923 and died near Maudheim on 24 February 1951.

12. G. de Q. Robin, Obituary: Alan Reece, *Polar Record*, 10:67 (1961), pp. 443–4. Alan Reece was born in London on 31 May 1921 and died near Resolute, Canada, on 28 May 1960.

13. Nils Jørgen Schumacher, Obituary: Egil Rogstad 1908–1987, *Aftenposten*, 19 May 1987. Egil Rogstad was born in Opset, Norway, on 23 January 1908 and died in Kongsvinger 10 May 1987.

14. Gordon Robin and Charles Swithinbank, Obituary: Professor Valter Schytt, *Polar Record*, 22:141, 1985, pp. 724–6. Valter Schytt was born in Stockholm on 17 October 1919 and died in Lapland on 30 March 1985.

15. John Snarby was born in Tromsø on 12 May 1922 and died there on 22 April 1991.

16. Charles Swithinbank, Obituary: Dr Ove Wilson, *Polar Record*, 20:129, 1981, p. 582. Ove Wilson was born in Berlin on 26 April 1921 and died in Lund, Sweden, on 14 March 1981.

GLOSSARY

Ablation	All processes by which snow, ice or water in any form is lost from a glacier.
Altimeter	Aneroid barometer used to measure altitude of aircraft.
Barrier	Obsolete term for ice front and/or ice shelf.
Berg	An abbreviation of iceberg.
Baleen	Commonly known as whalebone, occurs as a series of flexible, horny plates in the palate on the roof of the mouth of baleen (filter feeding) whales. It is used to separate krill from sea water.
Blizzard	A storm of drifting snow.
Brennevin	Distilled grain spirits.
Caboose	A shelter mounted on a sledge towed behind a vehicle.
Calving	The breaking away of a mass of ice from a floating ice shelf, glacier, or iceberg.
Cornice	An eave or shelf of snow overhanging a precipice.
Crevasse	A fissure formed in a glacier, ice sheet, or ice shelf. Crevasses are often hidden by snow bridges.
Depot	Supplies left in the field for later use.
Diorite	A granular crystalline igneous rock.
Dunnage	Short planks used to separate layers of cargo in a ship's hold.
Fast ice	Sea ice attached to the shore or to an ice shelf. An abbreviation of land-fast ice.
Flensing	Butchering a whale or seal.
Floe	A piece of floating ice other than fast ice or glacier ice.
Galley	Ship's term for kitchen. In practice used to include dining room.
Grounding line	The junction between a floating ice shelf and an ice sheet resting on rock.
Hinge line	Alternative name for grounding line where, because of tidal rise and fall, an ice shelf bends.
Hypothermia	Cooling of the body to danger level as a result of heat loss from exposure.

Iceberg	Large mass of floating or stranded ice which has broken away from a glacier or ice shelf.
Ice blink	White glare on the underside of clouds, indicating the presence of pack ice or an ice sheet which may be beyond the range of vision.
Ice drill	A coring device for obtaining ice samples. May be hand- or motor-powered.
Icefall	A heavily crevassed area in a glacier at a region of steep descent.
Ice front	The vertical cliff forming the seaward face of an ice shelf or other floating glacier, varying in height from 2 to 50 metres above sea level.
Ice sheet	A mass of ice and snow of considerable thickness and large area. Ice sheets may be resting on rock (inland ice sheet) or floating (ice shelf). Ice sheets of less than 50,000 square kilometres in area are called ice caps.
Ice shelf	A floating ice sheet of considerable thickness attached to a coast. Ice shelves are usually of great horizontal extent and have a level or gently undulating surface. They are nourished by the accumulation of snow and often by the seaward extension of land glaciers. Limited areas may be aground.
Ice stream	Part of an ice sheet in which the ice flows more rapidly and not necessarily in the same direction as the surrounding ice. The margins are sometimes clearly marked by a change in direction of the surface slope, but may be indistinct.
Inland ice sheet	An ice sheet of considerable thickness and more than about 50,000 square kilometres in area, resting on rock. Inland ice sheets near sea level may merge into ice shelves.
Katabatic	Air cooled at a higher level flowing downhill under the influence of gravity.
Knot	A unit of speed equal to one nautical mile per hour.
Krill	A small crustacean, *Euphausia superba*.
Lead	A navigable passage through floating ice.
Microtome	An instrument for cutting extremely thin sections for microscope work.
Mirage	Optical phenomenon in which distant objects appear uplifted above the horizon. Caused by abnormal refraction with a surface temperature

242

	inversion in which air temperature increases with height.
Moraine	Ridges or deposits of rock debris transported by a glacier. Common forms are: lateral moraine, along the sides; medial moraine, down the centre.
Nunatak	A rocky crag or small mountain projecting from and surrounded by a glacier or ice sheet.
Pack ice	An area of sea ice other than fast ice, no matter what form it takes or how it is disposed.
Radiosonde	Meteorological sensors attached to a balloon. Instrument readings are transmitted to the ground by radio.
Rawin	Radio theodolite used to track radiosonde balloons.
Refraction	Deflection of light rays from a straight path.
Resection	Determining an observer's position by measuring angles to points whose coordinates are known. The converse of intersection.
Sastrugi	Sharp, irregular ridges formed on a snow surface by wind erosion and deposition. The ridges are parallel with the direction of the prevailing wind.
Sea ice	Any form of ice found at sea which originated from the freezing of sea water.
Seismograph	An instrument for automatic recording of earthquakes or artificial explosions.
Seismometer	An instrument for measuring the intensity of earthquakes or artificial explosions.
Sill	A tabular body of igneous rock injected while molten between other rocks.
Snow bridge	An arch formed by snow which has drifted across a crevasse, forming first a cornice, and ultimately a covering which may obscure the opening.
Snowdrift	An accumulation of wind-blown snow deposited in the lee of obstructions or heaped by wind eddies.
Sublimation	The direct conversion of ice to vapour without going through the liquid phase.
Tabular	The most common type of iceberg in Antarctic waters, flat-topped and generally calved from an ice shelf.
Theodolite	A precise angle-measuring instrument consisting of a telescopic sight mounted on graduated horizontal and vertical circles.
Weasel	Amphibious tracked snow vehicle.
Whiteout	A condition in which daylight is diffused by

multiple reflection between a snow surface and overcast sky. Contrasts vanish and the observer is unable to distinguish snow surface features.

Water sky   Dark streaks on the underside of clouds, indicating the presence of open water or broad leads in pack ice.

REFERENCES

Amundsen, Roald, *The South Pole. An account of the Norwegian Antarctic Expedition in the "Fram", 1910–1912*, 2 vols., London, John Murray, 1912

Amundsen, Roald, *Sydpolen. Den Norske Sydpolfærd med Fram 1910–1912*, 2 vols., Kristiania, Jacob Dybwads Forlag, 1912

Antarctic Journal, 'Evacuation flight to Halley Bay', *Antarctic Journal of the United States*, 3:1, 1968 (pp. 14–15)

Bardin, V. I., U pokinutoy bazy, *Sovetskaya Antarkticheskaya Ekspeditsiya. Informatsionnyy Byulleten'*, 32, 1962 (pp. 52–3)

Bertram, G. C. L., 'Launcelot Fleming: An appreciation', *Polar Record*, 5:39, 1950 (pp. 396–7)

Brunk, Karsten, *Kartographische Arbeiten und deutsche Namengebung in Neuschwabenland, Antartkis*, Frankfurt am Main, Verlag des Instituts für Angewandte Geodäsie, 1986

Brunk, Karsten and Rudolf Staiger, 'Nachmessungen an Pegeln auf einem Blaueisfeld im Borgmassiv, Neuschwabenland, Antarktis', *Polarforschung*, 56:1–2, 1986 (pp. 23–32)

Brunk, Karsten, 'Geomorphologische-glaziologische Detailkartierung des arid-hochpolaren Borgmassivet, Antarktika', *Berichte zur Polarforschung*, 66, 1989

Byrd, Richard E, *Alone*, London, Putnam, 1938

Crary, A P, 'The Antarctic', *Scientific American*, 207:3, 1962 (pp. 60–73)

Daily Herald, London, 15 June 1949

Dalenius, Per, and Ove Wilson, 'On the soil fauna of the Antarctic and of the Sub-Antarctic Islands. The Oribatidae (Acari)', *Arkiv för Zoologi*, 11:23, 1958 (pp. 393–425)

Essen, Reinhold von, 'Air operations of the Norwegian-British-Swedish Antarctic Expedition in 1952', *Polar Record*, 8:54, 1956 (pp. 230–6)

Filchner, Wilhelm, *To the Sixth Continent. The second German South Polar Expedition (Zum sechsten Erdteil. Die zweite deutsche Sudpolar-Expedition)* translated by William Barr, Huntingdon, Bluntisham Books, 1994

Fuchs, V. E., 'Sledging rations of the Falkland Islands Dependencies Survey, 1948–50', *Polar Record*, 6:44, 1952, (pp. 508–11)

Giæver, John, *Maudheim. To år i Antarktis. Den norsk-britisk-svenske vitenskapelige ekspedisjon til Antarktis 1949–1952*, Oslo, Gyldendal Norsk Forlag, 1952 (pp. 367, translation)

Giaever, John, *The White Desert. The official account of the Norwegian-British-Swedish Antarctic Expedition*, London, Chatto and Windus, 1954

Giæver, John and V. Schytt, 'General Report of the Expedition', *Norwegian-British-Swedish Antarctic Expedition 1949–52, Scientific Results*, 6:3, Oslo, Norsk Polarinstitutt, 1963

Hoppe, Gunnar, and Valter Schytt, *Memorial to Hans W. Ahlmann*, Boulder, Colorado, Geological Society of America, 1974

245

Huntford, Roland, *Nansen. The Explorer as Hero*, London, Duckworth, 1997

International Commission on Whaling, *First Report of the Commission*, London, 1950

Irish Times, Belfast, 14 November 1950

Lathrop, Theodore G, *Hypothermia: Killer of the Unprepared*, Portland, Oregon, Mazamas, 1975.

Liljequist, Gösta, 'Richard E Byrd's fyra Antarktiska Expeditioner 1928–47', *Ymer*, 1948, 2, (pp.104–20)

Liljequist, Gösta, 'Special Studies. Halo-phenomena and ice-crystals', *Norwegian-British-Swedish Antarctic Expedition 1949–52: Scientific Results*, 2:2, Oslo, Norsk Polarinstitutt, 1956

Lindsay, Donald, *Friends for Life: A Portrait of Launcelot Fleming*, Seaford, Lindel Publishing Company, 1981

Mackintosh, N. A., 'The Antarctic whaling seasons of 1948–49, 1949–50, and 1950–51', *Polar Record*, 6:43, 1952 (pp. 403–4)

Mawson, Sir Douglas, *The Home of the Blizzard*, 2 vols., London, William Heinemann, 1915

Ministry of Food, *ABC of Rationing in the United Kingdom*, London, 1951

Natal Mercury, Durban, 6 December 1948

Näslund, Jens-Ove, 'Airborne radar soundings of ice depth, gps measurements of ice velocity and studies of landform evolution in central Dronning Maud Land East Antarctica', *Norsk Polarinstitutt Meddelelser* 148, 1997 (pp. 125–36)

New York Herald Tribune, Paris, 21 April 1949

Nordenskjöld, Otto, J. Gunnar Andersson, C. A. Larsen and C. Skottsberg, *Antarctic. Två År bland Sydpolens Isar*, 2 vols., Stockholm, Albert Bonniers Forlag, 1904

Polar Record, Obituary: Roland Henry Winfield, 15:98, 1971 (pp.762–3)

Reece, Alan, 'The base of the Norwegian-British-Swedish Antarctic Expedition, 1949–52', *Polar Record*, 6:45, 1953, pp. 617–30

Reece, Alan, 'Sledges of the Norwegian-British-Swedish Antarctic Expedition, 1949–52', *Polar Record*, 6:46, 1953 (pp. 775–87)

Rees, W. G., 'A new wind-chill nomogram', *Polar Record*, 29:170, 1993 (pp. 229–34)

Ridder, E. de, 'Sanae to Söyla', *Antarktiese Bulletin*, 20/21, 1967 (pp. 8–10)

Riiser-Larsen, Hjalmar, *Mot Ukjent Land*, Oslo, Gyldendal, 1930 (p. 145)

Ritscher, Alfred, *Wissenschaftliche und fliegerische Ergebnisse der Deutschen Antarktischen Expedition 1938/39*, vol. 1, Leipzig, Koehler & Amelang, 1942

Roberts, Brian Birley, 'Journal kept during the Antarctic voyage of *Norsel* 1950–51; Norwegian-British-Swedish Antarctic Expedition, 1949–52', unpublished, Scott Polar Research Institute MS 1308/7 (p. 41)

Roots, E. F., 'The Norwegian-British-Swedish Antarctic Expedition 1949–52', in: Haslett, A. W. (ed.), *Science News*, 26, 1953, London, Penguin (pp. 9–32)

Roberts, B. B., E. F. Roots and Charles Swithinbank, 'Strand cracks', *Polar Record*, 8:52, 1956 (p. 64)

Robin, G. de Q., 'Seismic shooting and related investigations', *Norwegian-British-Swedish Antarctic Expedition 1949–52, Scientific Results*, 5, Oslo, Norsk Polarinstitutt, 1958

Robin, G. de Q., Obituary: Alan Reece, *Polar Record*, 10:67, 1961 (pp. 443–4)

Robin, Gordon, and Charles Swithinbank, Obituary: Professor Valter Schytt (1919–85), *Polar Record*, 22:141, 1985, pp. 724–6

Roots, E. F., *in*: Giaever, John, *The White Desert. The official account of the Norwegian-British-Swedish Antarctic Expedition*, London, Chatto and Windus, 1954 (p. 245)

Roots, E. F., and C. W. M. Swithinbank, 'Snowdrifts around buildings and stores', *Polar Record*, 7:50, 1955 (pp. 380–7)

Ross, Captain Sir James Clark, *A voyage of Discovery and Research in the Southern and Antarctic Regions During the Years 1839–43*, 2 vols., London, John Murray, 1847 (vol. 1, p. 228)

Schumacher, Nils Jørgen, Obituary: John Schjelderup Giæver, *Norsk Polarinstitutt Årbok 1970*, Oslo, Norsk Polarinstitutt, 1972, (p. 237–9)

Schumacher, Nils Jørgen, Obituary: Egil Rogstad, *Aftenposten*, 19 May 1987

Schytt, Valter, 'The inner structure of the ice shelf at Maudheim as shown by core drilling'. *Norwegian-British-Swedish Antarctic Expedition 1949–52, Scientific Results*, 4C, Oslo, Norsk Polarinstitutt, 1957, (pp. 113–51)

Scott, R. F., *Scott's Last Expedition*, 2 vols., London, Smith, Elder & Co., 1913 (vol. 1, p. 424)

Shackleton, Sir Ernest, *South. The story of Shackleton's Last Expedition 1914–1917*, London, William Heinemann, 1919

Siple, Paul A., and Charles F. Passel, 'Measurements of dry atmospheric cooling in subfreezing temperatures', *Proceedings of the American Philosophical Society*, 89:1, 1945 (pp. 177–99)

Stefansson, Vilhjalmur, 'Pemmican', *The Military Surgeon*, 95:2, 1944 (pp. 89–98)

Stefansson, Vilhjalmur, *Arctic Manual*, New York, Macmillan, 1957 (pp. 117–8)

Swithinbank, Charles, 'The origin of dirt cones on glaciers', *Journal of Glaciology*, 1:8, 1950 (pp. 461–5)

Swithinbank, Charles, 'Mechanical transport of the Norwegian-British-Swedish Antarctic Expedition, 1949–52', *Polar Record*, 6:46, 1953 (pp. 765–74)

Swithinbank, Charles, 'The movement of the ice shelf at Maudheim', *Norwegian-British-Swedish Antarctic Expedition 1949–52, Scientific Results*, 3C, Oslo, Norsk Polarinstitutt, 1957 (p. 95).

Swithinbank, Charles, 'Ice movement of valley glaciers flowing into the Ross Ice Shelf, Antarctica', *Science*, 141:3580, 1963 (pp. 523–4)

Swithinbank, Charles, Obituary: Dr Ove Wilson, *Polar Record*, 20:129, 1981 (p. 582)

Swithinbank, Charles, Obituary: Gösta Hjalmar Liljequist, *Polar Record*, 31:178, 1995 (pp.360–1)

Swithinbank, Charles, *An Alien in Antarctica*, Blacksburg, McDonald and Woodward, 1997 (p. 127)

Swithinbank, Charles, *Forty Years on Ice*, Lewes, The Book Guild, 1998 (pp. 174–87)

The Times, London, 19 February 1952

Times of Malta, 22 November 1949

Walford, G. B., 'Antarctica: An Airman's View'. *Geographical Magazine*, 23:6, 1950 (p. 240)

Wilson, Edward, *Diary of the Terra Nova Expedition to the Antarctic 1910–1912*, London, Blandford Press, 1972 (opp. p. 241)

BIBLIOGRAPHY

Apart from newspaper reports and articles by journalists (of which there were over 600), more than 140 papers were published. A fully annotated bibliography of the scientific results of the expedition can be obtained from the Scott Polar Research Institute, University of Cambridge, Lensfield Road, Cambridge CB2 1ER. What follows is a selected bibliography from which I have excluded preliminary reports where their content was later incorporated in the principal *Scientific Results* volumes. I have excluded general narratives that were superceded by John Giæver's *The White Desert*. Out of ten editions of the book, I have listed only the Norwegian, British, and Swedish versions.

Dalenius, Per, and Ove Wilson, 'On the soil fauna of the Antarctic and of the Sub-Antarctic Islands. The Oribatidae (Acari)', *Arkiv för Zoologi*, 11:23, 1958 (pp. 393–425)

Essen, Reinhold von, 'Erfarenheter från den svenska Antarktisflyggruppen 1951–1952', *Teknisk Tidskrift*, Stockholm, 82:40, 1952 (pp. 917–24)

Essen, Reinhold von, 'Air operations of the Norwegian-British-Swedish Antarctic Expedition in 1952', *Polar Record*, 8:54, 1956 (pp. 230–6)

Giæver, John, *Maudheim. To år i Antarktis. Den norsk-britisk-svenske vitenskapelige ekspedisjion til Antarktis 1949–1952*, Oslo, Gyldendal Norsk Forlag, 1952

Giaever, John, *The White Desert. The official account of the Norwegian-British-Swedish Antarctic Expedition*, London, Chatto and Windus, 1954

Giæver, John, and Valter Schytt, *Antarktisboken. Med Norsel till Maudheim och Antarktis. Den norsk-brittisk-svenska vetenskapliga expeditionen till Antarktis 1949–1952*, Uddevalla, Forum, 1952

Giæver, John and V. Schytt, 'General Report of the Expedition', *Norwegian-British-Swedish Antarctic Expedition 1949–52, Scientific Results*, 6:3, Oslo, Norsk Polarinstitutt, 1963 (pp. 1–41)

Hagen, K., 'Aerology. The surface inversion', *Norwegian-British-*

Swedish Antarctic Expedition 1949–52, Scientific Results, 1:1C, , Oslo, Norsk Polarinstitutt, 1958 (pp. 125–40)

Higgins, R G, 'A radar survey of the ice barrier', *Journal of the Institute of Navigation*, 5:2, 1952 (pp. 195–7)

Hisdal, Vidar, 'Surface observations. Wind', *Norwegian-British-Swedish Antarctic Expedition 1949–52, Scientific Results*, 1:2B, Oslo, Norsk Polarinstitutt, 1958 (pp. 67–121)

Hisdal, Vidar, 'Surface observations. Temperature', *Norwegian-British-Swedish Antarctic Expedition 1949–52, Scientific Results*, 1:2C, Oslo, Norsk Polarinstitutt, 1960 (pp. 125–82)

Hisdal, Vidar, 'Surface observations. Visibility, cloudiness, humidity and precipitation', *Norwegian-British-Swedish Antarctic Expedition 1949–52, Scientific Results*, 1:2D, Oslo, Norsk Polarinstitutt, 1963 (pp. 185–223)

Hisdal, V., O. Amble, and N. J. Schumacher, 'Surface observations. Air pressure', *Norwegian-British-Swedish Antarctic Expedition 1949–52, Scientific Results*, 1:2A, Oslo, Norsk Polarinstitutt, 1956 (pp. 5–64)

Liljequist, Gösta, 'Energy exchange of an Antarctic snowfield. Short-wave radiation', *Norwegian-British-Swedish Antarctic Expedition 1949–52: Scientific Results*, 2:1A, Oslo, Norsk Polarinstitutt, 1956 (pp. 11–109)

Liljequist, Gösta, 'Energy exchange of an Antarctic snowfield. Long-wave radiation and radiation balance', *Norwegian-British-Swedish Antarctic Expedition 1949–52: Scientific Results*, 2:1B, Oslo, Norsk Polarinstitutt, 1957 (pp. 113–84)

Liljequist, Gösta, 'Energy exchange of an Antarctic snowfield. Wind structure in the lower layer', *Norwegian-British-Swedish Antarctic Expedition 1949–52: Scientific Results*, 2:1C, Oslo, Norsk Polarinstitutt, 1957 (pp. 187–234)

Liljequist, Gösta, 'Energy exchange of an Antarctic snowfield. Surface inversions and turbulent heat transfer', *Norwegian-British-Swedish Antarctic Expedition 1949–52: Scientific Results*, 2:1D, Oslo, Norsk Polarinstitutt, 1957 (pp. 235–98)

Liljequist, Gösta, 'Special Studies. Halo-phenomena and ice-crystals', *Norwegian-British-Swedish Antarctic Expedition 1949–52: Scientific Results*, 2:2A, Oslo, Norsk Polarinstitutt, 1956 (pp. 5–85)

Liljequist, Gösta, 'Special Studies. Refraction-phenomena in the polar atmosphere', *Norwegian-British-Swedish Antarctic Expedition 1949–52: Scientific Results*, 2:2B, Oslo, Norsk Polarinstitutt, 1964 (pp. 89–120)

Liljequist, Gösta, 'Long-wave radiation and turbulent heat transfer in the Antarctic winter and the development of surface inversions'. *Polar Atmosphere Symposium, Proceedings, July 2–8, 1956,* London, Pergamon Press, 1957 (pp. 167–81)

Nybelin, Orvar, 'Fishes collected during the Norwegian-British-Swedish Antarctic Expedition 1949–52', *Göteborgs kungliga Vetenskaps-och Vitterhets-Samhälles Handlingar*, B6:7, 1952 (pp. 1–13)

Reece, Alan, 'The base of the Norwegian-British-Swedish Antarctic Expedition, 1949–52', *Polar Record*, 6:45, 1953 (pp. 617–30)

Reece, Alan, 'Trail markers used by the Norwegian-British-Swedish Antarctic Expedition, 1949–52', *Polar Record*, 6:45, 1953 (p. 690)

Reece, Alan, 'Sledges of the Norwegian-British-Swedish Antarctic Expedition, 1949–52', *Polar Record*, 6:46, 1953 (pp. 775–87)

Reece, Alan, 'Sledge dogs of the Norwegian-British-Swedish Antarctic Expedition, 1949–52', *Polar Record*, 7:47, 1954 (pp.32–7)

Roberts, B. B., E. F. Roots and Charles Swithinbank, 'Strand cracks', *Polar Record*, 8:52, 1956 (p. 64)

Robin, G. de Q.,'Seismic shooting and related investigations', *Norwegian-British-Swedish Antarctic Expedition 1949–52, Scientific Results*, 5, Oslo, Norsk Polarinstitutt, 1958

Robin, G. de Q., and Vidar Hisdal, 'Aerology. Upper wind', *Norwegian-British-Swedish Antarctic Expedition 1949–52, Scientific Results*, 1:1D, Oslo, Norsk Polarinstitutt, 1971 (pp. 141–73)

Roer, Nils, 'Antarktis: Klatretur med lang anmarsj', *Norsk Fjellsport 1958*, Oslo, Grøndahl, 1958 (pp. 156–67).

Roots, E. F., 'Preliminary note on the geology of western Dronning Maud Land', *Norsk Geologisk Tidsskrift*, 32:1, 1953 (pp. 18–33)

Roots, E. F., 'The Norwegian-British-Swedish Antarctic Expedition 1949–52', In: Haslett, A W (ed.), *Science News*, 26, 1953, London, Penguin (pp. 9–32)

Roots, E. F., 'Geologic maps of Antarctica: geology of western Queen Maud Land', *Antarctic Map Folio Series*, Folio 12, Sheet 6, New York, American Geographical Society, 1969

Roots, E. F., and C. W. M. Swithinbank, 'Snowdrifts around buildings and stores', *Polar Record*, 7:50, 1955 (pp. 380–7)

Schumacher, N. J., 'Some problems of meteorological observing in polar regions', *Polar Atmosphere Symposium, Proceedings, July 2–8, 1956,* (pp. 167–81) London, Pergamon Press, 1957

Schumacher, N. J., 'Aerology. Temperature, height and humidity', *Norwegian-British-Swedish Antarctic Expedition 1949–52, Scientific Results*, 1:1A, Oslo, Norsk Polarinstitutt, 1958 (pp. 1–95)

Schumacher, N. J., 'Aerology. The tropopause', *Norwegian-British-Swedish Antarctic Expedition 1949–52, Scientific Results*, 1:1B, Oslo, Norsk Polarinstitutt, 1962 (pp. 97–123)

Schytt, Valter, 'Snow studies at Maudheim', *Norwegian-British-Swedish Antarctic Expedition 1949–52, Scientific Results*, 4A, Oslo, Norsk Polarinstitutt, 1958 (pp. 1–64)

Schytt, Valter, 'Snow studies inland', *Norwegian-British-Swedish Antarctic Expedition 1949–52, Scientific Results*, 4B, Oslo, Norsk Polarinstitutt, 1958 (pp. 65–112)

Schytt, Valter, 'The inner structure of the ice shelf at Maudheim as shown by core drilling', *Norwegian-British-Swedish Antarctic Expedition 1949–52, Scientific Results*, 4C, Oslo, Norsk Polarinstitutt, 1958 (pp. 113–51)

Schytt, Valter, 'Snow and ice temperatures in Dronning Maud Land', *Norwegian-British-Swedish Antarctic Expedition 1949–52, Scientific Results*, 4D, Oslo, Norsk Polarinstitutt, 1960 (pp. 153–79)

Schytt, Valter, 'Blue ice-fields, moraine features and glacier fluctuations', *Norwegian-British-Swedish Antarctic Expedition 1949–52, Scientific Results*, 4E, Oslo, Norsk Polarinstitutt, 1961 (pp. 181–204)

Sverdrup, H. U., 'The currents off the coast of Queen Maud Land', *Norsk Geografisk Tidsskrift*, 14:1-4, 1953, pp.239–49

Swithinbank, Charles, 'Mechanical transport of the Norwegian-British-Swedish Antarctic Expedition, 1949–52', *Polar Record*, 6:46, 1953, (pp. 765–74)

Swithinbank, Charles, 'The morphology of the ice shelves of western Dronning Maud Land', *Norwegian-British-Swedish Antarctic Expedition 1949–52, Scientific Results*, 3A, Oslo, Norsk Polarinstitutt, 1957 (pp. 3–37)

Swithinbank, Charles, 'The regime of the ice shelf at Maudheim as shown by stake measurements', *Norwegian-British-Swedish Antarctic Expedition 1949–52, Scientific Results*, 3B, Oslo, Norsk Polarinstitutt, 1957 (pp. 41–75)

Swithinbank, Charles, 'The movement of the ice shelf at Maudheim', *Norwegian-British-Swedish Antarctic Expedition 1949–52, Scientific Results*, 3C, Oslo, Norsk Polarinstitutt, 1957 (pp. 77–96)

Swithinbank, Charles, 'The morphology of the inland ice sheet and nunatak areas of western Dronning Maud Land', *Norwegian-British-Swedish Antarctic Expedition 1949–52, Scientific Results*, 3D, Oslo, Norsk Polarinstitutt, 1958 (pp. 99–117)

Swithinbank, Charles, 'The regime of the ice sheet of western Dronning Maud Land as shown by stake measurements', *Norwegian-British-Swedish Antarctic Expedition 1949–52, Scientific Results*, 3E, Oslo, Norsk Polarinstitutt, 1958 (pp. 121–44)

Swithinbank, Charles, 'Ice movement inland', *Norwegian-British-Swedish Antarctic Expedition 1949–52, Scientific Results*, 3F, Oslo, Norsk Polarinstitutt, 1958 (pp. 145–58)

Swithinbank, Charles, 'Maudheim revisited: the morphology and regime of the ice shelf, 1950–60', *Årbok 1960*, Oslo, Norsk Polarinstitutt, 1962 (pp. 28–31)

Walford, G. B., *RAF Report. Norwegian-British-Swedish Antarctic Expedition 1949–50*, Unpublished,

Walford, G. B., 'Antarctica: An Airman's View', *Geographical Magazine*, 23:6, 1950 (pp. 233–40)

Walford, G. B., 'The Royal Air Force part in the Antarctic expedition', *Journal of the Royal United Service Institute*, 96, 1951 (pp. 74–80)

Wilson, Ove, 'Physiological changes in blood in the Antarctic: a preliminary report', *British Medical Journal*, 4851, 1953 (pp. 1425–8)

Wilson, Ove, 'Basal metabolic rate in the Antarctic', *Metabolism*, 5:5 1956 (pp. 543–54)

Wilson, Ove, 'Changes in body-weight of men in the Antarctic', *British Journal of Nutrition*, 14, 1960 (pp. 391–401)

Wilson, Ove, 'Basal metabolic rate of "tropical" man in a polar climate', in: Tromp, S. W. (ed.), *Biometeorology. Proceedings of the Second International Bioclimatological Congress, London 1960* New York, Macmillan, 1962 (pp. 411–26)

Wilson, Ove, 'Cooling effect of an Antarctic climate on man with some observations on the occurrence of frostbite', *Norsk Polarinstitutt Skrifter* 128, 1963 (pp. 1–32)

Wilson, Ove, 'Human adaptation to life in Antarctica', In: Van Oye, P., and J. Van Mieghem (eds.), Biogeography and Ecology in Antarctica, *Monographiae Biologicae*, 15, 1965 (pp. 690–752)

Wilson, Ove, 'Field studies on the effect of cold on man with special reference to metabolic rate', *Acta Universitatis Lundensis*, 2:21, 1966 (pp. 1–27)

INDEX

258

259